The two greatest commandments of God speak about love — love of God and love for our neighbors. But love that is not demonstrated is no love at all. "For God so loved the world … that He acted … He did something … He sent His Son, Jesus, to be our salvation. And Jesus has now sent us to love the same world that He died for. Read this book and feel the pain in our world — then do something, because that's what *Zealous Love* is all about.

Richard Stearns, President, World Vision U.S., and author of *The Hole in Our Gospel*

Every Christian in America needs to read *Zealous Love*. It's just what we need to open our eyes to the hurting people around the world that are crying out for our attention. I have people ask me all the time for practical ways to get involved in caring for "the least of these." This book will not only be a powerful resource in their hands; it will lead us all back to the heartbeat of God.

Francis Chan, author of *Crazy Love*

This is a book about love … not the sentimental love of fair   id romance novels. This is a book about the love that keeps us up at night -   .th poverty, groaning with a wounded creation, raging over the madness   t is an invitation to feel, and ache, and cry over the broken world that G   . and it is an invitation to reimagine it.

Shane Claiborne, author, activist, and rec

Timely. Accessible. Comprehensive. *Zealous Love*   es the world's most challenging issues and calls us to a radical biblical pursuit of love and justice in accordance with God's will.

Ken Wytsma, Lead Pastor of Antioch Church in Bend, Oregon, and Co-Creator of the World Relief NEXT project

A winsome book about injustice? That is what Mike and Danae Yankoski have managed to do with *Zealous Love*. It disarms and captivates the reader with great stories about and by people on the front lines, solid data and information about the struggle, and scores of helpful things we can all do right now to side with the poor — God's favorite people group.

Ben Patterson, Campus Pastor, Westmont College, S

Zealous Love engages our imaginations and practices with stories of people who know the breadth and depth of God's love for the world and the odd blessing of being misfits in the world for the sake of faithfulness to the way of Jesus Christ. It invites us to the full life of discipleship to Jesus Christ that joyfully grows beyond a concern for my own salvation and peace of mind to embrace God's redeeming work throughout creation. Read it. Live it. Know the abundant joy of God's zealous love for the world.

Jonathan R. Wilson, Pioneer McDonald Professor of Theology, Carey Theological College

While terms like "prophetic" and "social justice" are too often paired with edgy, angry individuals guilt-tripping others to share their ideology, Mike and Danae offer us helpful information alongside invitational and riveting stories. In so doing, they are able to provide true hope, genuine inspiration, and a concrete path for action.

Dr. Rod Wilson, President, Regent College, Vancouver, British Columbia

As the voices of the next generation of North American evangelical Christianity, Mike and Danae Yankoski are impressive in both their passion and their pragmatism. They combine clarity of thought and excellent organization of material with personal candor and passion in this book which will not merely *stir* the reader, but *move* her to act — and to that end, give her some basic information and first steps. As one of the contributors to this volume puts it, "We must overcome the noise of our affluence" in order to hear and respond to Christ's call in the cries of our neighbours. In *Zealous Love*, Mike and Danae present the church with a "hearing aid" to help us with that process.

Maxine Hancock, PhD, author and speaker; Professor of Interdisciplinary Studies and Spiritual Theology, Regent College

This compelling book invites readers into an honest and timely conversation that retrieves the ancient meaning of that word — to *walk with*. The stories gathered here invite us not only to hear and reflect on the lives of those who suffer, but to participate, in entirely possible and practical ways, in the great work of healing. No one will emerge from these readings unchanged or unchallenged, or uncertain about what to do. Many hands are extended here to clasp ours and lead us to those whose needs may teach us how to walk humbly, in love.

Marilyn McEntyre, professor and author

A Practical Guide to Social Justice

ZEALOUS

LOVE

Mike and Danae Yankoski

Executive Editors

Foreword by Eugene Peterson

ZONDERVAN®

ZONDERVAN.com/
AUTHORTRACKER
follow your favorite authors

ZONDERVAN

Zealous Love
Copyright © 2009 by Mike and Danae Yankoski

This title is also available as a Zondervan ebook. Visit www.zondervan.com/ebooks.

This title is also available in a Zondervan audio edition. Visit www.zondervan.fm.

Requests for information should be addressed to:

Zondervan, *Grand Rapids, Michigan 49530*

Library of Congress Cataloging-in-Publication Data

Yankoski, Michael.
    Zealous love : a practical guide to social justice / Mike and Danae Yankoski.
        p.   cm.
    ISBN 978-0-310-29076-6 (softcover)
    1. Social justice — Religious aspects — Christianity. 2. Christianity and justice. 3. Church and social problems. I. Yankoski, Danae. II. Title.
    BT738.Y37   2009
    261.8 — dc22   2009020793

Published in association with the literary agency of D.C. Jacobson & Associates LLC, an Author Management Company. www.dcjacobson.com

Please note that some names in this book (marked with an asterisk) have been changed in order to protect individuals' privacy.

Interior design by Beth Shagene

Printed in China

09 10 11 12 13 14 15 16 • 25 24 23 22 21 20 19 18 17 16 15 14 13 12 11 10 9 8 7 6 5 4 3 2 1

*To every person in this world who is suffering from injustice
and to every person who is working to alleviate that suffering.*

Keep on.

Contents

REFUGEES | 77

HUNGER | 105

LACK OF EDUCATION | 129

A Prayer
for Zealous Love

Lord, thank you for being a God of love, who selflessly surrendered to death by crucifixion for the sake of sinful men and women like us. Thank you, Maker of Life, that you were not bound by death but that you rose again on the third day. Thank you that you have made us your children, heirs to the promise of new life, and that our lives here on this earth can bring you glory. Please use the following pages in a transforming, worldview-shifting way. As we explore eight areas of need affecting billions in our world, move in our hearts and minds, planting seeds of love that will grow into a strong harvest. Direct us away from selfish indifference and toward selfless action. Only you can change hearts; only you can draw us closer to your heart. Do that, we ask, through these stories. Cause us to move and live and give and act as you direct your Body. May thousands, millions, tens of millions — dare we pray — billions of lives be impacted as your people discover more of the role we have to play in our world. Come quickly, Lord. But until you do, teach us to live lives worthy of the calling you have given us.

Amen.

Foreword
by Eugene Peterson

Many lament the loss of a truly prophetic voice in our affluent, self-satisfied, and sin-ravaged land. "Where is Amos when we need him?" "How much longer do we have to wait for Isaiah to raise his voice?" "Is there an Elijah in the house?"

The book you at this moment are holding in your hands is the answer to your questions. They are all over the place. Some of them are in your neighborhood. Their voices are bold, courageous, insistent, and compelling. The voice of the biblical prophets is alive and passionate and robust in our land: *Zealous Love* gives voice to local prophets — home-grown, *American*-grown prophets — who have sat at the feet of Moses and Jeremiah and Micah and John the Baptist and Jesus. These are men and women who have sat listening until the fire burned, and then got to *their* feet — for "our God is a consuming fire." They are at this very moment out in the streets and byways, beginning in America and now dispersed throughout the world.

I, along with you, have read about the high-profile prophets, I'm sure, with admiration: Mother Teresa caring for the dying in Calcutta; William Wilberforce dismantling the slave trade; Martin Luther King, Jr. of Birmingham marching for racial equality; Dorothy Day giving hospitality to the poor in New York City's Bowery; Rachel Carsen patiently and insistently arousing an awareness of the widespread poisoning of our planet; Father Damien living among and serving the lepers on Moloka'i. But admiration doesn't often translate into participation — how many golfers improve their game by admiring Tiger Woods? How many swimmers get faster in the water by watching videos of Michael Phelps?

I admire and set my sail by the celebrity prophets. They inspire and motivate me. But they also intimidate me — I know that I am not made of such stuff. But I absolutely love the neighborhood prophets — they provide a foothold, or handhold, for helping me out of the ruts of my self-preoccupation and getting me into the action. The prophets who give their witness in this book are our neighbors, or could be. None has yet won a Nobel Prize. Still, they are not obscure. Or they won't be once you have read this book.

This is a skillfully organized and written book that brings a biblically prophetic life into participating reach of any and every Christian willing to spend the time to listen and believingly imagine himself, herself, into an obedient response to Jesus' presence among people for whom Christ died. Mike and Danae Yankoski give us a focused understanding of eight areas of social injustice. And then they tell the stories of forty prophets who right now are doing prophetic work in these areas, speaking and enacting the compassion of Jesus among the suffering children of God, our brothers and sisters. The understanding and the storytelling invite us to participate in a way of life that brings us into a deeper humanity, a mature holiness.

The term *prophet* is cheapened when it is reduced to denouncing those who seduce us into sin and perpetrate evil. Being against sin and evil is not social justice. And feeling sorry for the victims of injustice is not a prophetic act. We live in a culture that has replaced compassion with sentiment. Sentiment is mere feeling, disconnected from relationship. Sentiment is *spilled* compassion. It looks like concern; it could develop into compassion, but it seldom does. Sentiment is the tears that flow while watching a sad movie — tears that never get connected with visiting your dying friend. We feel sorry for people; we mourn the pain and suffering in the world. But having felt the internal motions of pity, wept a few requisite tears of sorrow, and sent off ten dollars to a charitable appeal, we've exhausted our capacity for care. In this callous, dog-eat-dog world, how insensitive we are! We return to our homes and jobs without knowing the names of the people we shed tears over, without visiting a single prisoner whose fate we lament, without writing one letter to the lonely over whom our hearts break. And of course, we let no strangers into our double-locked homes.

This is more than anything a book of hope: there *is* something to be done about the evil and injustice, the illness and hunger, the war and hate that ravage the world. The something to be done is not denunciation. Denunciation is not gospel. "Christianity has taught us to care. Caring is the greatest thing — caring matters most" (von Hugel). Gospel comes to life when we share the suffering, follow Jesus and his disciples, and enter the place of suffering with a "zealous love."

Eugene H. Peterson
Professor Emeritus of Spiritual Theology
Regent College, Vancouver, B.C.

Zealous Love:
An Introduction

Are you passionate about working for social justice and living a more just lifestyle? Perhaps you *want* to care about social justice, but don't know where to start when there are so many needs in our world. All of us — regardless of our religious or political convictions — want to live life well. When Danae and I talk about what it means to live well, our conversations often circle round to the idea of social justice. And speaking with friends and strangers alike, we know we're not alone.

Recently I was invited to speak at a fund-raiser for a Christian ministry in New Jersey. During dinner, I sat next to a seventy-five-year-old woman named Lucy. She was decked out for the gala, wearing a shiny gold dress and earrings that danced when she spoke. I'm always curious to hear from people who've experienced more life than me, so I asked Lucy to tell me more about herself. She paused, put down her fork, closed her eyes, and began remembering aloud.

When Lucy was fifteen, she had become a prostitute, using the money she earned to feed her growing drug addiction. Soon she was living with several other prostitutes in a rundown apartment owned by a cruel pimp. One day, after Lucy had spent ten years as a prostitute, an older Christian woman moved into the apartment next door.

Under normal circumstances, these very different women would have remained strangers, but the older Christian woman was determined to bridge the distance. Immediately she began talking with Lucy and her prostitute friends whenever she could about Christ, forgiveness, salvation, and hope for a different life.

"We used to laugh right in her face, cuss her out, call her every foul name we could think of, tell her we didn't need her or Jesus," Lucy told me, a look of regret dimming the gleam in her brown eyes. But the older woman had responded to the prostitutes' mockery and derision with nothing but ongoing love. She continued telling them about Christ and trying to communicate God's love with her actions, demonstrating to Lucy and the other prostitutes what unconditional love looks and feels like.

One particularly dreadful evening, Lucy stumbled back to her apartment complex having been badly beaten. A rib or two was broken, her arms and legs were bruised, and she was bleeding profusely from a shattered nose. Her eyes were nearly swollen shut. The Christian woman next door could hear Lucy's pained sobs as she crawled her way up the stairs.

Instead of turning a deaf ear or smugly reminding herself of "all she had tried to do for those stone-hearted prostitutes," the woman rushed into the stairwell to help. Gently she brought Lucy into her own apartment, cleaned her, doctored her wounds as best she could, and allowed her to stay the evening in relative safety and comfort. This was the final act in a series of persistent, loving actions that ultimately broke through Lucy's defenses. Lucy became a Christian and began the long, slow journey toward a new life.

"It was a long road," Lucy said with a sigh and a chuckle, closing her eyes again and reliving the memory. The older woman helped Lucy find another job and gave her enough money for a deposit on a new apartment, far away from the dismal streets where Lucy had worked as a prostitute. A few years later, Lucy married a wonderful, caring man named Howard. Soon after the wedding, Lucy got word that the Christian woman who had reached out to her had died.

Now here is the part that really got me. Lucy and Howard chose to move into the Christian woman's old apartment, on the same street where Lucy used to prostitute herself. Lucy and Howard wanted to love others in the same way Lucy herself had been loved.

There's a name for this kind of love: agape. Agape is unconditional and selfless — the kind of love that gives us new breath and heals even the oldest wounds. Agape can never remain just an idea; it always enters our world with action.

So for the past forty-five years, Lucy and Howard have lived in the same apartment. Their door is always open, offering a safe haven amidst the unimaginable pain found in her inner-city neighborhood. Prostitutes, drug addicts, the homeless, and anyone else in a hard spot knows that if they need help, they can come to "Lucy's."

Fiddling with the edge of her napkin, Lucy said to me softly, "We don't have much. There have been some days when I've looked in the pantry, and there wasn't even a can of beans amidst the dust." Then she chuckled softly, her eyes misting a little. "But you know what, Mike? God has always provided a way for us to meet the needs of the people that he brings across our path. The only question is whether we are willing to help."

Then Lucy turned to face me, her wizened hand gripping my arm. "We've never had much. We never will. But I'll tell you this: the more I give, the more God fills me up. It's like he just keeps on giving me more than I can give away! What is the point of this life if not to love him and then love others? When I've held onto things — that's when I've lost them. But when I give them to God for him to use as he sees fit, well, that's when I come alive!" As Lucy spoke, tears rolled down her wrinkled cheeks — evidence that she'd lived decades long and hard enough to prove the truth of her words.

Listening to Lucy's story, I kept hearing Jesus' words ring in my ears: "For whoever wants to save his life will lose it, but whoever loses his life for me will find it" (Matt. 16:25). The question is, do I live to save my life, or do I live to lose my life for God? Or, put another way, do I live only for myself, or for God and for others too?

Danae and I want more than anything to live like Lucy has. We want to use everything God has given us to serve him. At the end of our lives, we want to hear him say, "Well done, good and faithful servants."

Part of me would like to believe that going to church on Sunday and reading my Bible every once in a while is enough to dupe Jesus into mumbling those words in my general direction when I enter heaven. But another part of me isn't satisfied with that — the part of me that remembers what Christ has done for us. He died, was buried, and then *got up again* so that we might have Life. Not lower-case, live-for-our-own-pleasures life, but live-to-change-the-world Life with a capital *L*. This Life doesn't require checking things off my "Christian to-do list" but rather giving everything to Christ, because he gave up everything for us (Phil. 2:6 – 7). It means living like Lucy, who spent the last forty-five years of her life discovering the way of agape.

But how? How are we to live that way when so much of what we read, see, and listen to each day commends selfishness? Two particular passages of Scripture (among many) address this question. First, let's look at the Old Testament prophet Ezekiel. His book contains one of the Bible's most unsettling statements about money and poverty: "Now this was the sin of your sister Sodom: She and her daughters were arrogant, overfed and unconcerned; they did not help the poor and needy" (Ezek. 16:49).

This is an astounding passage if we remember the history behind Ezekiel's words. Remember Sodom from Genesis 19? God utterly destroyed the city with fire and brimstone. Whatever other factors may have resulted in God's judgment on Sodom, Ezekiel's words should cut us to our core: God destroyed them in part because, in spite of all their wealth, they did not care for those in need.

God does not deal kindly with those who are wealthy and yet ignore the poor.

Conversely, consider how Jesus speaks about even the tiniest gesture of love. Addressing those who cared for the needy, he said, "Whatever you did for one of the least of these brothers of mine, you did for me" (Matt. 25:40). Jesus isn't talking about heroic, earth-shattering accomplishments, but rather simple — and even obvious — responses to need: food for the hungry, water for the thirsty, acceptance for the outsider, clothes for the naked, comfort for the sick, relationship for the lonely. If a child scrapes her knee, you comfort her and get her a bandage. It's not rocket science. Jesus is talking about obvious responses to real needs. Despite their simplicity, God counts these actions as services rendered directly to him.

The first time I really had to struggle through what my response to poverty ought to be in light of the Scriptures was a number of years ago in high school. I had traveled to the Dominican Republic for my first summer mission trip. One afternoon I saw a few boys, maybe three or four years old, running along the dirt road, laughing as only kids do. One of them — the smallest of the group — wore only a torn, filthy pair of shorts. He was pulling a bottle cap tied to a string. I was shocked — this piece of trash was his only toy. Yet his smile was a mile wide as he looked back at the bouncing bottle cap. The other boys were just as enthralled with the smallest boy's contraption. Then it hit me — the boy's friends didn't *have* their own bottle cap tied to a piece of string. No one thought to reach into the gutter for a piece of trash and fashion a toy for them.

> If you spend yourselves on behalf of the hungry
> and satisfy the needs of the oppressed,
> then your light will rise in the darkness,
> and your night will become like the noonday.
> **Isaiah 58:10**

I didn't know it then, but that sight was preparing me to understand what Lucy would tell me over ten years later. During my time in the Dominican Republic, I felt crushed by guilt. Why had I been born in America — with more than enough toys, food, clothes, money, etc. — while these young boys had been born into poverty? I returned home to the United States and felt flat-out awful about the food I ate, the bed I slept in, and the roof over my head. I wasn't thankful for these things — just feeling guilty that I had them while others didn't.

Let's be clear: this book is not about guilt.

Even though some guilt may initially help to change our hearts, minds, and actions, we mustn't continue to operate out of guilt. Like a college student surviving on too much caffeine and not enough sleep, a guilty Christian will eventually crash. Instead, we're after something healthier and more sustainable — something we can *live*.

Zealous Love is about an active, renewable love. It's about understanding that we can't help but love others, because we ourselves are already loved perfectly (1 John 4:19). This is the foundation of agape: we are inexplicably, undeservedly, and unfathomably loved. Since we are loved so absolutely, we are free to love others in the same way. Fear often makes us hesitate, but perfect love casts out fear. This love is more than a duty; it is a natural impulse, like a tree growing toward the sun or the well-loved child clinging to her father's fingers.

Make no mistake: our broken world is desperate for agape. Despite the widespread abhorrence of slavery in the developed world, nearly 12.3 million people are still enslaved today.[1] In the developing world, 1.1 billion people do not have access to safe drinking water, causing nearly five thousand deaths each day.[2] Every six seconds a child dies in the developing world because of hunger-related issues — over fourteen thousand per day.[3] In 2000, there were 862 million illiterate adults (not to mention children) worldwide.[4] It is estimated that 33 million people worldwide are living with HIV, the vast majority of them in developing countries.[5] Last year 2.6 billion people, or roughly 40 percent of the world's population, survived on less than two dollars a day.[6] The chasm between rich and poor — between the haves and the have-nots — is widening at an ever-increasing rate. Our world is a broken place — there is no way around this fact.

Chances are that if you're reading this book you're a high school graduate — maybe even have some college under your belt. You have enough disposable income to buy a book (even if it was in the bargain pile), so you probably have a job and aren't wondering if you'll be forced to join the sex trade to make ends meet. You're not wondering whether the water you just drank will kill you. True, gas prices are a bit high, but at least your home hasn't been burned down or your child murdered by a rebel army. Nor are you worried that you might not eat dinner tonight. If you do have HIV or any other serious disease, most likely you're getting the best care modern science can offer. You may not have the most exciting job, but you certainly aren't trying to survive on less than two dollars a day.

In short, most of us reading this book are unimaginably rich. I'm not suggesting our lives are easy. Life can be tough in many ways — for all of us. But the reality is that by every conceivable measure, those of us in the developed world — whether we're sitting in a coffee shop or riding the subway to work — are wealthy beyond belief. Caring about social justice is difficult when most of the evils that might cause us to yearn for a more just society are kept a safe distance away from our privileged lives.

Unsatisfied with our present level of wealth, our culture continually craves more. Modesty and simplicity are demeaned, while excess and decadence are celebrated as human rights. Yet the God who doesn't deal kindly with the indifferent rich calls us to another way of living. As Paul writes to the church at Corinth, "At the present time your plenty will supply what they need, so that in turn their plenty will supply what you need. Then there will be equality … You will be made rich in every way so that you can be generous on every occasion, and through us your generosity will result in thanksgiving to God" (2 Cor. 8:14; 9:11).

God's idea of equality and justice completely upends the standards most of us live by. But how do we *live* like that is true? How do we establish habits of thought and consumption that take other people's needs into consideration in light of the Great Commandment to love God and love others? How do we fight against injustice and work for justice? How, in short, do we live like Lucy?

Our hope is that *Zealous Love* will help you answer these questions. We've divided the book into connected sections that engage contemporary issues of social justice: human trafficking, unclean water, refugees, hunger, lack of education, creation degradation, HIV and AIDS, and economic inequality. Each section begins with a Briefing, providing relevant background to the issue before a series of Field Notes, which share personal stories of those who are giving their blood, sweat, and tears to remedy that particular injustice. Such stories can inspire us to imagine what's possible when agape is let loose, through us, in our world. Finally, each section concludes with several questions and reflections that seek to help you personalize each injustice and think about how you might become part of the solution. Ideas for action and contact information for several organizations will enable you to begin working for justice in whatever way God calls you.

The fact is, we're all different. We've each been given different gifts, different experiences, and different opportunities. But our prayer is that God will work through this book to help you discover how he wants *you* to live, to use every gift he's entrusted *you* with — time, abilities, education, skills, connections, wealth, and so on — for his glory.

This isn't about information so much as inspiration. We hope these stories will give you a glimpse of the miraculous, redemptive work that is taking place all over the world *right now*. Allow yourself to listen to God's whisper inside you. Listen to his movement in your heart and mind as he directs you to the good works he has purposed for you since before there was time (Eph. 2:10). Maybe you and your family will decide to change your eating habits. Perhaps your small group will begin to study social justice together. Maybe you'll tutor an illiterate adult in your community. Or begin sending part of your monthly paycheck to an organization working for social justice.

Zealous Love is not the only guide to social justice, nor is it the definitive word on the subject. We hope that what you learn in these pages inspires you to dig deeper — to invest even more of your passion, time, and skill in whatever issue God calls you to. Who knows? Maybe you'll quit your job, move to Africa, and build a medical station. Maybe you'll downsize your house and sell your car. Maybe you'll eat only rice for breakfast, lunch, and dinner one day to see a little of what it feels like to be malnourished. God calls each of us to something different.

Yet God calls each of us to the same thing too. Like Lucy, we are all called to love others as we have been loved; we are called to agape. So ask God. Even now, ask him what actions these stories, statistics, and photographs are calling you to. Ask God to reveal his purpose for you. And praise him for his promise to finish the good work that has already begun in you.

May we all be led toward lives of informed action flowing from God's great love for us. Keep on.

Mike and Danae Yankoski

Note to the Reader:

In our research for *Zealous Love* we've made use of many different types of sources, including reputable websites and published reports available online. Because of the nature of the Internet as well as frequent organizational updates of new statistical data, the Internet links and statistical data provided in *Zealous Love* will not be accurate forever.

Please use your Internet search tool to locate the cited documents if you are having trouble following the provided links, or to discover newly released reports.

No, O people, the LORD has told
   you what is good,
and this is what he requires of you:
to do what is right, to love mercy,
and to walk humbly with your God.

Micah 6:8 NLT

HUMAN TRAFFICKING

Each leg of a three-legged stool is essential for balance and function. Similarly, we must not separate justice from mercy or humility. One danger in pursuing social justice wholeheartedly is that we may become self-righteous and prideful, feeling that only *we* are really doing as Christ commands his Body. Humility is often the trait we have the greatest difficulty sustaining when we begin acting justly and loving mercy. Let us then keep Micah's admonition in our hearts and minds as we consider the question: What does it look like for us to live lives of justice and mercy *with* humility before our God?

BRIEFING

As I looked through the "Trafficking in Persons Report" published annually by the U.S. government, the pictures, facts, and stories tore me apart. Over and over I turned my laptop to show Mike the images of small boys working at a brick factory, a skinny, terrified girl being sold to a huge white man, a group of protesters holding up a sign that read, "We are oppressed." I was reminded again of our hopes for a response from readers like you and, more importantly, for change in the lives of victims like those in the pictures I saw.

Modern-day slavery includes, among other things, sex trafficking and involuntary servitude. Sex trafficking happens when "a commercial sex act is induced by force, fraud, or coercion, or in which the person induced to perform such an act has not attained 18 years of age."[1] Involuntary servitude is the "recruitment, harboring, transportation, provision, or obtaining of a person for labor or services, through the use of force, fraud, or coercion for the purpose of subjection to involuntary servitude, peonage, debt bondage, or slavery."[2]

When I first learned that human trafficking occurred in our world every day, I had a hard time believing it. But the facts are hard to deny. Around 1.2 million children are trafficked *each year*, many of them for purposes of sexual exploitation.[3] All told, there are between 12.3 million and 27 million children, women, and men in slavery today.[4] (Such a large disparity exists between the numbers given by reliable sources because it's impossible to account for all that goes on in the dark corners of our world. After all, brothel owners don't exactly turn in annual reports to the UN.) The fact is, either number means that more people are enslaved today than during the whole of the trans-Atlantic African slave trade.[5] The fact is, this illicit trade creates profits of at least 32 billion dollars a year for those involved in illegally trafficking human beings.[6] This is more than the individual gross domestic product (GDP)[7] of more than half of the countries (127) in our world.[8] These numbers are staggering. But perhaps even more horrifying than the sheer number of people who are trafficked is the easily forgotten reality that each one of the untold millions is an individual human being, made in God's image.

When I learned about this issue in college, I got involved in our campus chapter of International Justice Mission (IJM), an organization working against human trafficking. I read books. I wrote letters. Every week I printed information about trafficking cases around the world so that I could pray for both the victims *and* the traffickers. I did my best, as a college student with limited time and money, to make a difference.

Mike and I have since moved from our college town to a different state. I've learned about a lot of other problems and atrocities in our world. To be honest, some of my passion for the human trafficking issue began to wane, almost without me noticing.

Then recently, a group of friends began talking about the issue. All were in their mid-to-late twenties, and everyone had a basic understanding about the presence of human trafficking in our world. One of the women spoke through gritted teeth about what was happening to people around the world. As she spoke, tears of pain and brokenness seeped out. The horror of the world's second largest illegal industry (after arms/drug dealing) was real to her.[9] Later, I asked her why she was so passionate about the issue. This was her response:

> Part of my experience with human trafficking came when I was in Thailand and Cambodia. It was heartbreaking for me to see the vast numbers of young girls lined up on the streets with dresses on and numbers pinned to their chests. These were places (entire cities, actually) that the travel guides said to avoid unless you wanted a sex show or a prostitute for the night. And the worst part was that when the sun went down and darkness came, I would walk out of my hostel down the streets and see numerous middle-aged, white men with these beautiful, young, innocent girls by their sides, each with a look of death and fear in her eyes.

As my friend spoke through her tears, I found myself wanting to re-engage with the effort against human trafficking — when had I forgotten?

Human trafficking takes many shapes. The following stories deal mostly with sex trafficking, but other forms include labor trafficking, bonded labor, involuntary servitude, debt bondage, involuntary servitude among guest workers, involuntary domestic servitude, forced child labor, child soldiers, children exploited for commercial sex, and child sex tourism.[10] Human trafficking is a multifaceted, multinational evil. However, it is important to remind ourselves of the steps being taken and the successes that have been realized.

It's easy to overlook our own responsibility by assuming that human trafficking exists only in developing countries. Yet according to the Polaris Project, "an estimated 17,500 foreign nationals are trafficked annually in the United States alone."[11] These numbers do not include U.S. citizens trafficked within the country, which is an even higher number. An estimated 200,000 *American* children are at a high risk of being trafficked into the sex trade each year.[12] So, even if we were to focus only on addressing this injustice in one developed world country, we would still have a lot of work to do.

However, as citizens of God's kingdom, it would be myopic to be concerned only for those who hold the same kind of passport as we do. Throughout the Scriptures we read of God's care and concern for those who are oppressed. We see it clearly in Psalm 10, which reads, "You hear, O Lord, the desire of the afflicted; you encourage them, and you listen to their cry, defending the fatherless and the oppressed, in order that man, who is of the earth, may terrify no more" (vv.17 – 18). For me, this is an incredibly hopeful passage — so often I get discouraged when I learn about the evil loose in our world. For a majority of people living right now, the world is not a kind or hopeful place. Verses like these offer a piece of genuine hope to those who are oppressed, trafficked, and desperate. Especially as we allow God to work through us to defend the fatherless and the oppressed.

Something Bigger Than Me

Sean Litton

In 2002, I received a call from Gary Haugen, president and CEO of International Justice Mission (IJM). Gary asked me to lead IJM's counter-sex-trafficking project in Thailand, an office that had recently experienced a great deal of turmoil. My family and I were approaching the end of our second year with IJM in the Philippines, and we were planning to return home to the United States after another year in Manila. Things were going well, and we thought we were in the home stretch.

I knew the situation in the Thailand office was bad, so I was reluctant to accept. As my wife, Shannon, and I discussed the move, she said, "Well, girls are being forced into prostitution. There's a real need, and you're the only one in IJM who's available to go. I don't see how we can say no." Shortly after that conversation, I accepted the assignment and we moved with our one-year-old son, Jasper, to Thailand. Thus began the most difficult year of my life.

Nearly all of the problems in the Thailand office began with a pervasive lack of trust. The community had grown distrustful of IJM, and relationships that were once productive had been broken. Every day I went to work, and every day I seemed to fail.

The first case we began working on involved a young woman named Elisabeth,* whom our investigators had located in a brothel in Chiang Mai, in northern Thailand. Elisabeth told the investigators that she had been tricked into coming to Thailand — lured by the promise of a good job and then forced to work in the brothel with several other girls. I referred the case to an organization responsible for coordinating counter-trafficking efforts in Chiang Mai, but they declined to take action. There was no trust.

After two months of urging them to act, I finally suggested that we at least offer Elisabeth safe passage home. Most likely, this would compromise our investigation, but at least it would ensure that Elisabeth got home safely. I also hoped it would give us an opportunity to debrief with Elisabeth and confirm the information in our report.

Elisabeth, once held in forced prostitution, has recently graduated with a university degree.

Eventually, one of the investigators paid the brothel owner for the opportunity to take Elisabeth out of the brothel for the night. He took her to dinner and offered to help her get home. After telling him her story and her real name, she accepted the offer of assistance. Elisabeth also asked the investigator to help the other girls who were trapped in the brothel.

Elisabeth's confirmation of IJM's initial report was enough to convince local law enforcement officials to act. Thai authorities raided the brothel and rescued more than twenty trafficked women, seven of whom were minors.

Shortly after the operation, I was sitting at my desk when one of my staff members showed me a picture of a wall inside the tiny room where Elisabeth had been locked up at the brothel. There was something written on the wall in tiny letters, and I asked a coworker to translate it for me. It was Psalm 27:1 – 3 NLT:

> The LORD is my light and my salvation — so why should I be afraid?
> The LORD is my fortress, protecting me from danger, so why should I tremble?
> When evil people come to devour me, when my enemies and foes attack me,
>   they will stumble and fall.
> Though a mighty army surrounds me, my heart will not be afraid.
> Even if I am attacked, I will remain confident.

Elisabeth had written these words on the wall of her room, a visible reminder of her daily prayer for God to rescue her from the brothel.

Sitting at my desk, thinking about the evil that had been perpetrated in that tiny room, the power of the Psalmist's words flooded over me, and I broke down and wept. Of all the girls trafficked into Thailand, we had rescued one who was praying for deliverance. Despite our obvious failings and our sometimes difficult relationship with the local officials, God guided us to Elisabeth. With the information she provided, we were able to facilitate the rescue of many more of God's beloved daughters.

This was only one of many successful IJM operations in Southeast Asia, but it remains a watershed moment in my life. Never have I been reminded more powerfully that the work of social justice is God's work, and we are simply his tools to get it done. Though we face mighty armies, our hearts will know no fear.

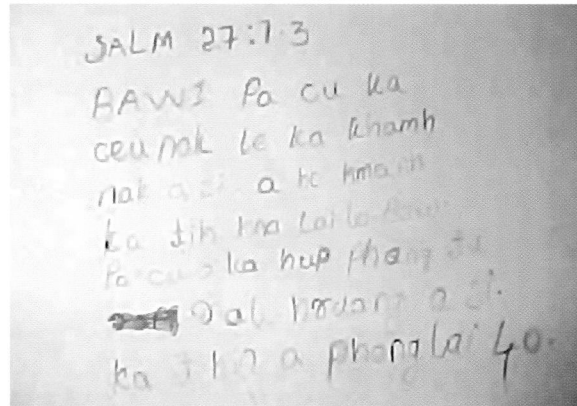

Held against her will in a brothel, Elisabeth wrote Psalm 27 on the wall of the room where she was kept, praying every day that God would send rescue to her.

BIO

Sean Litton serves International Justice Mission as the Vice President of Field Operations. Mr. Litton joined IJM in September 2000, after previous positions at Young Life, Christ Church in Roswell, New Mexico, and the law firm of Kirkland and Ellis in Washington, DC. Mr. Litton received a B.S. in Business Administration from Miami University and a J.D. from the University of Notre Dame Law School. Prior to his current role at IJM, Mr. Litton served as the director of operations for Southeast Asia and director of the IJM office in Manila, Philippines. Presently, he directs IJM's casework operations in Latin America, Africa, South Asia, and Southeast Asia.

Why I Do What I Do

Bob Goff

Curled beneath the covers was an angry girl. Barely twelve years old, she was thin and pretty, her hair caught up in a disheveled ponytail. The girl already knew what the older woman had come to tell her — that there was another customer waiting to rape her, and she had better get up and cooperate. The words that passed between the two were inaudible on the video footage, but their gestures required no interpretation. The girl protested violently and turned her face to the wall in defiance. Then she threw the covers over her head in a heart-wrenching, childlike display of helplessness mixed with rage.

The video was taken during an undercover investigation I helped conduct in India, and the experience caused a fundamental change in my life. Now I work alongside a group of dedicated professionals who, like me, have day jobs but feel called to do something more. We are Restore International, and we are a varied crew — members of my law firm, an attorney and former career FBI agent, a number of college students, a fireman, CEOs, and many others. We all felt we couldn't just sit by and *think* about young people being sold like products. We wanted to get to the "do" part of our faith. Sometimes that means showing up in the red-light district of a city halfway around the world, and sometimes it means holding a prayer meeting at the local church or a fund-raising banquet for an anti-trafficking organization. Sometimes you show up and bring as many people with you as you can, so they can see the need too.

I am blessed with a compassionate wife, two courageous sons, Richard and Adam, and a daughter, all of whom have traveled around the world with me, working for justice. The reflections of my teenage daughter, Lindsey, came to mind one day while thinking of the tragedy of child trafficking. The reality that every trafficked girl is someone's daughter pierced me like a knife as I rode in a car with Lindsey through one of Mumbai's red-light districts. She agreed to share a bit of her journal from that trip here:

The weariness settled over me, weighing me down both physically and emotionally. We had been awake and traveling from Chennai since six a.m., a long sixteen hours ago. In a small rented van we drove through the red-light area, and the reason my dad does the work he does became obvious.

Outside the car window, the street was packed with bright-yellow rickshaws, motorcycles, and a crush of people moving by. Men ambled along, crowding into each other, and women holding babies wrapped in rags knocked on car windows, begging for food or money.

The thick air, smelling of sweat, curry, exhaust, and dust, seeped in through the closed window. "There's a brothel up there," our friend said, pointing to one of the dark buildings next to us. "A lot of times you will see a group of girls gathered around a storefront, and there will be a dark staircase next to them that leads up to the brothel," he explained as we passed a few more buildings.

"Those girls over there — are they prostitutes?" I asked.

About twenty girls were crowded around a dark stairwell next to the entrance to a shady looking store. I felt an immediate ache inside, realizing those girls were my age.

Then the horror of it hit me: In this city, on the other side of the world from my comfortable, safe home in the United States, almost every girl outside my window was a prostitute, and nearly every man was either a pimp or a potential customer. I choked on tears and went numb. This reality was beyond anything I had ever imagined.

Some of the brothels were arranged like stalls, with rooms open to the street and a sheet hanging over the entryway. I spotted a girl only a few yards away, standing in front of a dimly-lit green room. She was wearing a dark-blue sari draped over thin shoulders. If you traded the sari for jeans and a T-shirt — the grimy building for the freshly painted ones back home, and the shadows of Mumbai for the San Diego sunshine — this girl could have been one of my friends.

Lindsey understood that each of the girls trafficked into brothels could easily have been her friend; I realized that each could have been my own daughter. This is why I do what I do. Every person is a human being made in God's own image. Every person has hopes and dreams, likes and dislikes. What differentiates us are circumstances — the situations into which we are born.

Whether it's a boy who is abducted and given a gun with which to kill his family or a girl who is swept into a brothel in the city nearby, each of these trafficked children are crying out for help. Kids should spend their childhoods playing with other kids, not suffocating in the filth of human depravity. We must overcome the noise of our own affluence and listen closely for the opportunity to become active participants — not simply passive observers — in the reality of God's coming kingdom. May God give us the courage to listen and act.

BIO

Bob Goff is the Founder and Chief Executive Officer of Restore International. He has a passion and vision for meeting the needs of people throughout the world in tangible ways. He loves finding audacious ways to restore justice to children and the poorest of the poor. Bob is the founding partner of a law firm in Washington: Goff and DeWalt, LLP. In addition to his law practice and career as an adjunct professor at Point Loma Nazarene University, Bob serves as Honorary Consult for the Republic of Uganda. He has worked actively with the Ugandan judiciary and the Restore team to facilitate the trial of many cases in Northern Uganda.

The Prophet James

Rachel Goble

A year and a half ago, a prophet named James spoke to me in the back of a surf shop in Santa Monica by quoting from the biblical book that bears his name: "Religion that God our Father accepts as pure and faultless is this: to look after orphans and widows in their distress and to keep oneself from being polluted by the world" (James 1:27). My calling, James told me, was to look after the women and children that are most vulnerable. A year later I traveled to India and South Africa to learn more about human trafficking — not only to ask what can be done to end it, but also to identify the root causes.

India Red Light

It was like a war zone. In the narrow hallways, bits of ceiling hung from twisted wires, and piles of rocks littered the floor. We made our way past rooms full of girls just finishing breakfast and getting ready for another night's work in the red light district of Mumbai. I was led into a small waiting room where we spoke with the boss of the brothel (a young girl in her twenties) and one of the prostitutes, who looked about nineteen. The prostitute spoke bluntly, telling me that she did not choose this life, but that she had no other choice. "I am not like you. I have no other chance, no other opportunity. This is it for me. I have nowhere else to go." She was desperate to make a living, and she believed this was the only possible way. Even so, her longing for a different life — free from sex slavery — was unmistakable.

Many of the women found in the brothels of Mumbai come from neighboring countries or other cities within India. Many are trafficked against their will. Most are driven by poverty. The needs of each woman — whether it's the need for food, proper medicine, or clothing — force them into an otherwise unimaginable life.

Hillbrow, South Africa

Two months later I was walking through the alleyways of inner-city Johannesburg. The air was thick with alcohol fumes and smoke. On the street, men drank the local brew out of cartons, while cigarettes hung from the corners of their mouths. We left the street to climb a narrow flight of stairs to a bar, our presence causing quite a stir. I was with a group of nine ex-prostitutes who were visiting the place where they had once sold their bodies. Thankfully, each had escaped that life in search of something different.

Upon arrival in the upstairs brothel, the women broke into song: "Put your condoms on, put your condoms on. Don't forget the condom, put your condoms on." I didn't know whether to laugh out loud, turn red, or weep at the seriousness with which they sang these lyrics. So I continued to watch as they sang to a dozen drunk men, suddenly very attentive.

The women were Peer Educators from the New Life Centre. After leaving a life of prostitution, they spend their days visiting the red light districts of Johannesburg in the hopes of helping other women and girls like them. They visit brothels, encouraging girls to seek out new lives — and to make sure no one working there is the victim of trafficking. Other days are spent in bars educating the men about AIDS and the importance of practicing safe sex. (Editor's Note: Obviously, the Peer Educator's decision to educate about safe sex is controversial. However, given the harsh reality of the environment in which they work, these women had prayerfully determined that safe sex education was an important component of working to help the prostitutes. It was an "imperfect world / imperfect solution" situation.) The women are animated, passionate, and humble as they seek to bring light to the inner-city darkness, one encounter at a time.

Now What?

Human trafficking is a complicated industry. Most victims' stories are tales of poverty, need, want, or dissatisfaction with the way life is — and a desire to discover what might be. Both economic and spiritual poverty drive people into situations of vulnerability. When a person is in survival mode, he or she is not concerned with moral or social status. Driven by the need to survive, the poor are the perfect prey for traffickers promising good jobs in nearby cities.

Those of us who want to help must be aware. Human trafficking has become a multi-billion dollar industry largely because the average person has ignored it. The public isn't aware of the extent of human trafficking and therefore does little to stop it. By bringing stories of human trafficking to light, however, more and more citizens are playing an active part in the eradication of this modern-day slavery.

We must also address the root causes of trafficking: economic inequality, inadequate health care, economic and social hardships imposed by governments, political unrest, improper food distribution, unemployment, the absence of citizenship or travel documents, and a host of other factors — not to mention people's seemingly insatiable demand for illicit sex. Where there is demand you are sure to find supply.

Human trafficking is a tangled mess, to be sure, and the size of the problem can make us feel helpless. Yet people caught in the sticky, malicious web of human trafficking are being freed, one by one, through hard work and fervent prayer.

I began my journey with a simple prayer, the prayer Bob Pierce, the founder of World Vision had prayed: "God, let the things that break your heart break mine." I still pray that prayer, but I've coupled it with a quote from International Justice Mission. "Let these things break your heart, let them make you cry — and then get over it and do something." Let your heart break for the injustices of this world, and let that motivate you to act. We are called to love others as we have been loved. So how will you love those who suffer injustice this very day?

BIO

Rachel Goble grew up in the San Francisco Bay Area and has always had a heart for social justice issues. In 2007 she started her own trafficking awareness organization, The Elpis Project, in response to the overwhelming problem of human trafficking in the United States, specifically in California. In 2008 she crossed paths with The SOLD Project, a grassroots movement dedicated to using film to expose the truth behind sexual exploitation of children in Thailand and the U.S. Rachel now acts as executive director and has merged The ELPIS Project into The SOLD Project, combining forces to help put an end to sexual slavery.

Investing in Our Actions

CJ Adams

The first time I met Kate,* my reaction was anything but compassionate. I remember thinking that her hair looked terrible. Half brown and half bleached blonde, it was a disheveled mess with a pink rubber band hanging loosely out of it. She sat quietly on an office couch, staring disinterestedly at her cell phone. Her face was plain and unassuming — like the person from high school whose name you've since forgotten. She looked about twenty, but not a youthful twenty. We met in the headquarters of Polaris Project, a leading anti-trafficking NGO, where I had begun an internship a few weeks earlier. Staff walked down the hall briskly, taking calls and shuffling papers, but nearly everyone paused to say hello to Kate. With each "good morning" or "hey there," Kate grew a bit more comfortable in her skin, giving a nod or an answer and sitting more confidently.

The couch where she sat was just a few feet from my desk. I had never seen her before, and to be honest, I thought it was a little rude that she had not introduced herself. She'd walked in a few moments earlier and flopped down with a huff as if I weren't there. As the new kid in the office, I wasn't about to introduce myself, but I couldn't figure out why she wouldn't. Clearly this woman knew Polaris, so couldn't she take a little bit of time to greet an eager intern? And why was the busy staff making such a point to greet her, anyway? I wondered if she might be a past intern visiting the office, or maybe someone's sister.

All day Kate went in and out of what appeared to be important meetings. When she wasn't in the conference room she was back on the same couch, waiting, still just four feet from my desk. Yet she never introduced herself. I couldn't figure it out, so I just ignored her and concentrated on researching sex trafficking operations at U.S. truck stops.

By the end of the day the sofa was clearly her domain, and it was starting to get on my nerves. She was listening to loud hip-hop on her cell phone, chewing gum, and making a point to compliment or criticize the outfits of anyone she knew as they walked by. Finally, in exasperation I let out a noticeable sigh. Kate snapped her head in my direction. *Can I* help *you?* she demanded without words. There was a surprising amount of attitude behind those dark, intense eyes, and it threw me off — literally. Her look sent me bumbling backwards into my chair like a fool. I grabbed the arm rests and shifted my eyes uncomfortably between the desk and her stare. Dark bags hung under her eyes, and a bruise was fading from purple to yellow on the left ridge of her chin. "Um, good morning," I blurted. It was 4:30 p.m. "Humph." She dismissed me with a lift of the brow, but she wasn't about to say hello in return. So I kept my head down and stayed quiet. She held the phone in front of her, sunk down into the couch, and skipped to the next song.

A few days later, while meeting with my supervisor, I mustered up the courage to ask casually, "Who is Kate?"

My supervisor smiled. It was clear I was clueless.

"Kate is a client." Everything came together. "She came in from a STAT three months back." STAT (Sex Trafficking Assessment Team) is the name of the group Polaris sends out to provide services whenever law enforcement thinks they have a victim of trafficking on their hands (usually after a raid on a trafficking operation). "She was recruited by a pimp in Nashville, groomed in a couple other cities, and sold to a pimp in Washington, DC a couple months after she got here." I felt like an absolute idiot as I painfully played back my initial reaction to Kate. "She was controlled for four years. She hasn't even turned eighteen yet."

"It looks like she might be part of a solid case against this sex trafficker; we've always known this pimp has had minors but haven't been able to pin it on him yet."

I was dumbfounded.

Kate had been forced into commercial sex when she was thirteen. She had been trafficked on the streets of five U.S. cities for more than four years. If it hadn't been for a Washington, DC police officer who had been trained on human trafficking and called Polaris, Kate would probably still be prostituted, forced to earn a quota of $300 to $500 per night for her pimp. Kate's story is identical to thousands of other women in our country. And though the details vary with different trafficking networks (brothels, massage parlors, domestic servitude, forced agricultural labor, cantina bars, forced begging, and peddling rings), all of their victims experience similar paths of exploitation and abuse, leading them into modern-day slavery. They were all vulnerable when they were first trafficked, and since then, their traffickers — through force, fraud, and coercion — have perfected a scheme to turn exploitation into profit.

When I first began studying human trafficking six years ago, I expected to read about crimes in distant, developing countries. The truth, however, is that this evil exists everywhere, and some of the most overlooked victims of trafficking are exploited in towns and cities throughout the United States. Their plight is obscured in large part by a profound lack of awareness. A few years before my awkward interaction with Kate, I sat in front of a computer screen, having just finished my first research paper on trafficking, staring at horrific case studies and mind-numbing statistics. It dawned on me — the abolition of slavery in the United States is a fight yet to be won.

I joined the Polaris Project in college, starting as an intern and then, years later, returned to join their staff. As I write these words, I am covering a phone shift for Polaris' 24/7 National Human Trafficking Hotline. It is late — two in the morning — and there are very few calls at the moment. When they do come in, however, they often involve information on a new trafficking case or an urgent request — an officer needing an immediate

referral for a victim, a man with a tip on a forced labor operation, or a girl reporting on a residential brothel where her friend is being held. Such calls bring home the complexity of the problem — and its solution.

Today, slavery is multifaceted and decentralized — ranging from a single-family maid being held in domestic servitude to large-scale networks of brothels. Most forms of trafficking are incredibly profitable and shamefully low-risk operations. Anti-trafficking efforts must take a holistic approach that turns the tables, increasing the risk and lowering the potential profit for any trafficker. At the same time, they must make a priority of rescuing and actively supporting the women, children, and men who are currently victimized by the sex trade.

It *can* be done. Polaris Project has helped rescue and stabilize hundreds of victims of human trafficking and has increased pressure on traffickers. Thanks to the efforts of all the anti-trafficking organizations in the Washington, DC area, for example, today it is much more difficult to exploit and sell women and children in this city than it was just six years ago. Still, an enormous amount of work remains. Slavery still exists. It's there in the ads for forced brothels on the bottom of the sports section of major U.S. newspapers; in the supply chains that bring us diamonds, tire rubber, shrimp, coffee, and produce; in our country's pimp-controlled streets, cities, and truck stops. It exists, but many of us choose not to see it.

Ending slavery ought to be the concern of every person. We need to continue working — here in DC, throughout the United States, and around the world — to serve victims, punish traffickers, and change the consumer demand that enables the trade.

No lasting change will take root, however, unless we invest ourselves in the lives of the people affected by trafficking. By focusing our involvement on and measuring success in terms of the lives of real people — both current and potential victims of trafficking — we ensure that the work we do has a meaningful impact. If we skip this step, we will simply spin our wheels, rushing around in a busy effort to build campaigns, start programs, and talk about the issue while victims and traffickers remain untouched.

Take Kate, for example. I was sitting directly across from her in the office of one of the leading anti-trafficking organizations in the country. Even then I was ready to ignore her just because she was different. I didn't notice her bruise, didn't think about why she might have been so closed, and had no idea that she was someone who had been forced into commercial sex since she was thirteen. All I saw was a loud, rude woman whom I didn't understand — and I moved on.

Compared to others who have already given decades to this cause, my contributions have been minuscule. But I have seen enough of this problem to commit myself to the issue and to sharing the reality of modern-day slavery with others.

I have watched brothels and pimp-controlled tracks firsthand, taught roomfuls of Johns (prostitutes' "customers") the truth about what they are doing to women and children, and worked for legislation delivering harsh consequences to anyone taking part in this crime. While these experiences have left me with powerful memories, by far the most disheartening thing I've seen was not the sight of a pimp beating a woman on the street corner, but the sight of the others walking by on the sidewalk as it happened. In my first interaction with Kate, I felt the same kind of blind apathy. It was almost comical — an oblivious intern being, well, oblivious — but it is also a dangerous reality in the wider world. It is in this environment of apathy that the second largest criminal industry in the world has continued to grow and exploit innocent victims. Our indifference to the vulnerable is real — in fact, it is often what makes them vulnerable to begin with. And the traffickers count on it.

BIO

CJ Adams was raised in rural Oregon and has worked with Polaris Project since 2006. He holds a bachelor's degree in philosophy from Brown University. In 2006, CJ was awarded the Watson Institute's Marla Ruzicka Fellowship for Human Rights Activism. He currently lives in Washington, DC.

Destroying Shadows

Dave Batstone

The slave trade operates in the shadows. Clients who engage in commercial transactions with traffickers — the ordinary man who visits a sleazy massage parlor or even a retailer who sells dresses made in a slave-labor garment factory — find comfort in covert conditions. Silence is a catalyst for evil. Once the slave operation is subjected to widespread public scrutiny, people will become less likely to engage in slave-based commerce.

Understanding these mechanisms helps us to form effective strategies to fight the slave trade. Imagine the impact if trafficking investigation centers sprung up all over the world to identify and monitor trafficking activity in every region. A growing number of schools in the United States already require students to participate in "service learning" as part of their degree program. Students, working in collaboration with their professors, could use their service hours to conduct community-based research on human trafficking. It would not be overly difficult to conduct interviews with community residents, local police, social workers, probation officers, migrant workers, and a host of others to collect local intelligence on trafficking. These local trafficking investigation centers could partner with local media to expose traffickers and trafficking sites.

Students at the University of San Francisco piloted just such a project during the 2006 – 2007 academic year. They came up with startling results about the prevalence of slavery in northern California. In response to the students' research and the attention it received, law enforcement agencies across northern California designed new enforcement strategies to intervene in trafficking cases.

Not For Sale, the organization I work with, built on these successes at the University of San Francisco and designed two wikis (websites for public collaboration) to inspire action against slavery. One enables researchers to document the results of investigations anywhere on the globe where slavery has been discovered, while another offers an open platform for research on how companies use labor in their production processes.

Like any other commercial market, the forces of supply and demand are what drive the slave trade. Criminal agents make handsome profits from unpaid labor — slaves make goods cheaper to produce. Due to these financial advantages, slaveholders compete successfully in most any market. Their profit margins rise as high as the demand will bear.

We may not realize how each one of us drives the demand for slavery every day. Slave labor may have produced the sugar we put in our coffee, the carpets we stand on, or the shirts on our backs. Equipping passionate people with the right information will help to make these links between our everyday lives and the reality of modern day slavery more transparent and eventually fuel a consumer movement to buy "slave free" products. Knowledge can literally liberate.

Freedom advocates can get involved in more than ethical purchasing. Some volunteer in shelters or build local coalitions to support recently emancipated slaves. In that vein, the Not For Sale Campaign has produced "demand reduction materials" — drink coasters for bars and nightclubs, sleeves for coffee cups, and get-help cards for high-risk labor sites — that individuals and clubs distribute in their own communities. These materials are printed with information about where people can turn if they have information but don't know who to trust. I've been amazed to see reluctant witnesses and frightened victims come forward when they realize there are safe places to tell their stories.

> We hear a Christian assure someone that he will "pray over" his problem, knowing full well that he intends to use prayer as a substitute for service. It is much easier to pray that a poor friend's needs may be supplied than to supply them.
>
> **A.W. Tozer**

Even organizing school sporting events can be an effective way to generate more awareness and raise support for abolitionist efforts. Our Free to Play activities help athletes and fans alike realize that playing a game can be a celebration of freedom. After all, millions of kids in the world are not free to play. Imagine the power of making a pledge to tie athletic results — the number of touchdowns scored or baskets made — to financial support for a school for former child soldiers in Africa or newly emancipated sex slaves in Thailand.

Somewhere between 12.3 and 27 million individuals live as slaves at this moment.[13] Regardless of which number is right, that anyone is enslaved is wrong. And unfortunately,

the balance of power is on the side of the oppressor. But a wave of abolitionist activism is swelling, and our movement gains power every time a new individual commits to fight for justice and human equality.

BIO

David Batstone is an international anti-slavery advocate, award-winning journalist, professor, and social entrepreneur. Co-founder and president of the Not For Sale Campaign, Batstone teaches ethics at the University of San Francisco and was a founding editor of Business 2.0 magazine. He is co-owner of Earthware Enterprises, which supplies recyclable agricultural supplies to enable sustainable agriculture. His most recent books are Not For Sale and Saving the Corporate Soul.

NOW WHAT?

We live in a world that claims to have abolished slavery, yet more men, women, and children are enslaved today than at the height of the trans-Atlantic slave trade. Modern slavery exists in the shadows, yet each of us may be linked to it without even knowing. Perhaps there is a brothel in your city, or perhaps a multinational corporation used slave labor to manufacture the jeans you're wearing.

The evil of human trafficking takes many forms. Will you join the fight against slavery?

Reflect

1. *What do you think?* What emotions has this chapter stirred in you? Frustration? Confusion? Anger? Doubt? Why do you think it evoked these feelings? Take some time to journal about your experience. Include things you may have learned and new ideas you might have — and don't be afraid to ask yourself hard questions.

2. *Open your eyes.* Assuming that human trafficking would never happen where you live is exactly what allows it to continue undetected. Let your eyes be opened. Be aware. Think back through some of your experiences: does anything strike you as out of place now that you are better educated? The point is not to imagine human traffickers where there are none but to view what is happening in our communities with steady, sober eyes. Even in the relatively affluent community of less than 100,000 people where Mike and I live, several instances of trafficking have been uncovered. Think about how you would respond if you came across something that seemed suspicious. What would your first steps be? Who would you contact for help?

3. *Imagine it was your child.* Imagine that your son or daughter (or brother or sister) was trafficked into one of the wretched situations described in this section. How would you feel? How would you respond? What do you hope someone would do for you and your family if you were in that situation? Are you willing to "love your neighbor as yourself" and respond the way that you hope someone would respond if it were your family member?

Pray

Spend time praying about human trafficking and its effect on people around the globe. Try writing out your prayer. List a few countries that are affected by modern slavery and then pray specifically for those countries — for mercy and freedom, but also for long-term solutions that dismantle oppression and glorify God.

Respond

1. *Open your eyes to today's slave trade.* What was your response when you learned that there are more slaves today than ever before? Did you have trouble believing it? Did you wonder what in the world you could do? We look at historical atrocities like the Holocaust and wonder how people could have allowed them to happen. Then again, the Rwandan genocide occurred in 1994, despite the supposed lessons of history and the benefit of 24-hour global news. It's easy to judge the past — but sometimes not so easy to respond to something that's happening now. Take some time to consider how you can work to avoid being blind to the atrocities taking place today. How will you open your eyes to the needs of others?

2. *Get involved.* CJ Adams told us: "When I receive the next hotline call from a potential trafficking victim, my ability to help that woman or child — and ultimately our ability to help shut down a trafficker's operation — is directly tied to the strength of the anti-trafficking movement in the local area." Learn about trafficking, teach others, and work to organize an anti-trafficking movement in your city, if one doesn't already exist. Get involved with the organizations on the "front lines." Make a donation or raise money on their behalf. Become a volunteer at an anti-trafficking organization. Write letters to your local paper or give talks to community organizations and charities. The possibilities are endless.

Additional Resources

www.castla.org

www.hagarinternational.org

www.humantraffickingsearch.net

www.nightlightbangkok.com

www.slaverymap.org

Visit *www.zealouslove.org/trafficking* for more information and organizations.

3. *Advocate for political change.* Politics govern the land, and politicians do listen to persistent constituents. Write your elected officials and ask them to pass legislation against trafficking and to allocate resources to stop modern-day slavery. Support federal and state anti-trafficking legislation when it comes up. Effective political action requires

you to spend time researching what is going on and how you can be a part of it, but it can be well worth it. Get as many people as you can to join with you in advocating, writing, and supporting legislation — begin to bring change.

4. *Make a career of it.* If your heart is especially stirred by this issue, consider a career in the anti-trafficking movement. Search for the relevant training and experience and then join an organization engaged in the movement, such as a law enforcement agency, an NGO (non-governmental organization), research institution, or a law firm specializing in human rights.

5. *Make the little things count.* There are several small things almost anyone can do. Commit yourself to doing at least one. It may require some effort on your part, but isn't it worth it to know that you are not standing by and doing nothing in the face of this modern-day atrocity?

- Research supply chains and buy slavery-free products.
- Promote slavery-free products to your friends and family (see the Freedom Store at *www.notforsalecampaign.org*).
- Buy survivor-made products to empower survivors (see *www.madebysurvivors.com* and *www.saribari.com* and *www.ransomwear.org*).
- Buy products made by at-risk individuals through alternative channels to help decrease their vulnerability to trafficking.
- Spend less so you can give more to support the work against human trafficking.

6. *Keep learning.* If you're a student or educator, enroll in or create a course on human trafficking. Contact one of the trafficking organizations listed here; request materials to educate yourself and others. Take every opportunity to share your knowledge about human trafficking with friends, family, peers, and colleagues.

7. *Report it.* If you suspect a case of human trafficking in your community, don't let it continue any longer. Report potential cases by calling the NHTRC (1-888-3737-888).

Spread the Word

Individually, it can be daunting to confront such a growing, worldwide evil. But tremendous change happens when we work together. Consider spreading the word about human trafficking, the lives that are affected, and the organizations doing something about it. Now that you've read this chapter, it isn't "someone else's responsibility" — it's yours. Change begins with individuals deciding they are going to live differently. What role can you play? Maybe it's inviting some friends to coffee, starting an action group at your church, or getting your youth group to hold a rally. Help change lives. Spread the word. To help you do so, we've created a simple and effective tool at *www.zealouslove.org/spread*.

Share Your Ideas

Have a great idea about something other people can do to engage the issue of human trafficking? Do you want to connect with others who are getting involved? Join in the conversation at *www.zealouslove.org/share*.

Discover More

In this section you've heard from several contributors about the harsh realities of human trafficking. You've also read about the incredible work being done to address the issue, both on a personal and corporate scale. Remember, there is no "one-size-fits-all" solution. If you feel led to get involved, check out the following organizations. You can also visit *www.zealouslove.org/trafficking*.

Polaris Project

Vision: Polaris Project's vision is for a world without slavery.

Method: Created in 2002, Polaris Project uses a comprehensive approach to combat human trafficking and modern-day slavery. Polaris Project is one of the few organizations working to serve both U.S. citizen and foreign national victims of human trafficking through activities that include operating local and national crisis hotlines, conducting direct outreach and victim identification, providing social services and housing to victims, advocating for stronger state and national anti-trafficking legislation, and engaging community members in local and national grassroots efforts.

Contact:
Polaris Project
PO Box 77892
Washington, DC 20013
Phone: (202) 745-1001
www.polarisproject.org

International Justice Mission (IJM)

Vision: IJM is a human rights agency that secures justice for victims of slavery, sexual exploitation, and other forms of violent oppression.

Method: IJM's multinational staff work in twelve countries throughout Asia, Africa, and Latin America to ensure that the global poor are protected by their countries' own laws. IJM's lawyers, investigators, and social workers partner with local officials to respond to violent oppression by ensuring immediate victim relief, pursuing perpetrator prosecution, and providing aftercare for victims. IJM staff seek to determine the specific source of corruption, lack of resources, or lack of goodwill responsible for denying victims the protection of their legal systems. In collaboration with local authorities, IJM addresses these specific points of brokenness to meet the urgent needs of victims of injustice.

Contact:
International Justice Mission
PO Box 58147
Washington, DC 20037
Phone: (703) 465-5495
www.ijm.org

Restore International

Vision: Restore International seeks to break cycles of violence and oppression and help raise a new generation of leaders.

Method: The organization rescues and restores children who are victims of human trafficking and prosecutes the perpetrators. Through investigations, raids, and legal action, Restore International has helped rescue victims of forced prostitution. Through the construction of two new high schools in war-torn Northern Uganda, Restore International has helped to educate and develop young leaders in order to promote love, peace, justice, servant leadership, and human dignity.

Contact:
Restore International
3226 Rosedale Street NW
Suite 100
Gig Harbor, WA 98335
Phone: (253) 853-3162
www.restoreinternational.org

Not For Sale Campaign

Vision: Not for Sale is a campaign of students, entrepreneurs, artists, people of faith, athletes, law enforcement officers, politicians, social workers, skilled professionals, and justice seekers united to fight the global slave trade.

Method: Not for Sale aims to educate and mobilize an international abolitionist movement through the innovation and implementation of open-source activism. Inside the United States, the campaign identifies trafficking rings and collaborates with local law enforcement and community groups to shut them down and provide support for the victims. Internationally, the campaign partners with poorly resourced abolitionist groups to enhance their capacity.

Contact:
www.notforsalecampaign.org

The SOLD Project

Vision: The SOLD Project is a grassroots movement dedicated to exposing the reality of child prostitution in our world through film and the collaborative response of individuals seeking to create change.

Method: In 2007, a team of twenty-somethings traveled to Thailand to report on child sexual exploitation and create effective ways to fight it. In August 2008, The SOLD Project began their national tour, bringing these stories to universities, churches, civic groups, and other venues. Our hope is to bridge the gap between people and the issue through awareness and action as we continue to advocate for the freedom and innocence of children.

Contact:
The SOLD Project
3037-T Hopyard Road
Pleasanton, CA 94588
Phone: (925) 786-8286
www.thesoldproject.com

UNCLEAN WATER

But let justice roll on like a river,
righteousness like a never-failing stream!

Amos 5:24

Imagine a powerful river rushing down from snow-covered mountains. Boulders, trees, and even the foothills of the mountains cannot block its path for long. The river is persistent and dauntless. Given enough time, water will overcome any obstacle and continue its endless journey.

The prophet Amos exhorts us to let justice be like that, to never let it fail, never grow weary, never fade. Justice, in simple terms, is "rightness." Part of letting justice "roll on like a river" means working against that which is wrong — against injustice. This is a delicate balance; we can't do it on our own strength, nor can we simply turn a blind eye and get on with our lives. Ask the Lord to show you ways that your actions might reflect the loving justice that rolls on like a river, overcoming any obstacles along the way.

BRIEFING

Water is everywhere. More than 70 percent of the earth's surface area is covered by water. Depending on your age, gender, and health, between 50 and 60 percent of your body's weight is water. Having grown up in developed countries, access to safe water has never been a big problem for most of us. Sure, water from an older drinking fountain may taste a bit strange, and perhaps there are some "floaters" in our glass after a gulp at mealtime, but most of us never have to wonder whether the water in our faucets could be lethal.

Just over a billion people aren't so lucky.[1] They were born in developing countries, and at this point, they don't have reliable access to safe drinking water. One of these 1.1 billion people is a child named Manuel from the Dominican Republic. Manuel and his four siblings each have experienced horrible bouts of diarrhea and vomiting because the closest water source is contaminated with human feces. Another person without safe drinking water is thirteen-year-old Brenda in Uganda. She can't go to school because her never-ending chore is to use a jerry can to fetch water — five miles from where she lives. At the other end of her trek is a filthy pool where local livestock also come to drink and cool off. But it's her family's only option. One trip per day in the hot African sun carrying thirty-five pounds of light brown water leaves Brenda utterly exhausted — not to mention vulnerable to attack every step of the journey and susceptible to water-borne disease.

Water is life. After air, it's the most essential bodily requirement. All of our bodies' mechanisms — the digestive system, the urinary tract, the skin, the eyes — depend on water. The average human can survive only about three days without water. And dehydration is a brutal way to die. When the body is deprived of water, brain function deteriorates quickly. The tongue swells and cracks. The eyes deflate as the volume of fluid decreases. Seizures follow, accompanied soon by delirium. Drinking contaminated water can be almost as awful. Vomiting and diarrhea rapidly dehydrate the body, often leading to death if medical attention isn't readily available. Water-borne worms make their new home in children's stomachs, robbing their bodies of essential nutrients and initiating a long, slow wasting.

Most of us flush our toilets several times a day without stopping to consider that between two and three gallons of clean water just went down the drain. That's more than some people in developing countries may have for an *entire day's* cooking, cleaning, and hygiene. Never flushing our toilets isn't the answer, but the privilege of so much clean, cheap water ought to make us pause. Our brothers and sisters in other countries are dying because they lack clean water while we wealthy folks in developed countries have so much clean water to spare that we defecate in it and then flush it away.

Simply having access to safe water isn't the end of the story, though. There are 2.6 billion people who lack adequate sanitation and hygiene.[2] Remember how your mother used to scold you when you didn't wash your hands with soap and hot water before dinner? What if you didn't have any soap? What if you didn't even know you needed to wash your hands? Or, what if the only water you had to wash with was contaminated with dangerous microorganisms or harmful chemicals? What if there wasn't any place for you to go to the bathroom, and every day you had to squat on the ground? These aren't hypothetical questions but rather a dangerous reality for billions of people around the world. Even if someone has access to a source of clean water, lack of adequate sanitation and training in hygiene can cause that person to spread disease and sickness to their own family and even their entire community.

> Not to love is, psychically, spiritually, to die. To live for yourself alone, hoarding your life for your own sake, is in almost every sense that matters to reduce your life to a life hardly worth the living, and thus to lose it.
>
> **Frederick Buechner**

These three injustices — unclean water, lack of sanitation, and inadequate hygiene — have unimaginably broad repercussions. Every day nearly five thousand children die from water-related illnesses — that means one child dies approximately every twenty seconds.[3] Six million people are visually impaired because of trachoma, a disease commonly contracted by washing with contaminated water.[4] Even if the Millennium Development Goals are achieved, there will still be over 800 million people without access to clean water and over 1.8 billion people without basic sanitation in 2015.[5] The United Nations' Human Development Report 2006 states it perfectly: "Water insecurity violates some of the most basic principles of social justice."[6]

Beyond the deaths caused by water-related diseases, a lack of safe water, basic sanitation, and hygiene prevents billions of people from living productive lives. Think about the last time you had the stomach flu. Did you feel like doing anything besides staying in bed and hoping you'd soon get better? Were you able to concentrate on school or work? Every year, more than 443 million school days are lost globally because of water related diseases, and untold billions are lost from the world economy.[7]

As people suffer the effects of unsafe water and inadequate sanitation, the *last* thing they want to do is walk for hours hauling heavy water containers. But they don't have the luxury of recuperating in bed — they *must* walk and fetch water, even if it is contaminated and will make them even sicker.

Recently, Danae and I spent time in Ecuador and Uganda, becoming more familiar with the issues of water, sanitation, and hygiene — and some of the people who are affected by them. Serving in those countries greatly informed our theological perspective on water. We now notice water more often in the Scriptures — it's everywhere. From Moses hitting the rock and God giving the Israelites water in the wilderness to Jesus washing the disciples' feet, water plays a central role in the biblical narrative, flowing through both Testaments.

The New International Version (NIV) contains more than 620 references to water. [8] In the Old Testament God is referred to as "living water" (Jer. 2:13; 17:13). In the New Testament Jesus says that he can give streams of "living water" (John 4:10) to those who are thirsty. We like to talk about the significance of the metaphor, but somehow the image of the Holy Spirit as a stream of living water must be harder to appreciate when the only water source available to you is a contaminated, stagnant pool.

Water does fall from the sky, but it is nonetheless a limited resource. Many countries in our world are embroiled in disputes over water. Sudan, Ethiopia, and Egypt threaten each other over access to the Nile's waters, while Turkey, Iraq, and Syria argue about the Tigris and Euphrates Rivers. Disputes regarding lakes, rivers, reservoirs, and underground aquifers will only intensify as potable water becomes scarcer. Some go so far as to say that World War III will be fought over water rights, and population projections seem to lend some credibility to this suggestion. While charting population growth is a highly speculative business due to unknowns surrounding mortality and fertility rates, the most sobering projections suggest that by the year 2100 there will be more than 14 billion people on the planet — more than two times the current population. [9] Such numbers indicate that the scarcity of clean water could worsen significantly.

There is hope, however. Increasing awareness of water issues is generating helpful responses. Many organizations have developed sustainable practices for addressing the three key areas of safe water, basic sanitation, and improved hygiene. Some of their stories are told on the following pages. Let the words of Christ echo in your heart as you read this section: "I was thirsty and you gave me drink … As you did it to one of the least of these my brothers, you did it to me" (Matt. 25:35, 40 ESV).

Trees of Hopelessness

Jena Nardella

Recently, I was studying the lives of Abraham and Sarah. In Genesis 21, Sarah has just sent Hagar and her son, Ishmael, to wander in the desert with little hope of survival. They go on their way, having absolutely no direction whatsoever. In the intense heat, Ishmael becomes so frail from dehydration that death is imminent. Hagar places him under a tree to die and stays close enough for Ishmael to know she is there, but far enough to hide her pain-wracked face from him.

God hears Ishmael's cries. The angel of God speaks to Hagar and tells her to not be afraid, that Ishmael will be cared for. Not only will he survive, he will become a nation. And the sweetest surprise of this story is that God opens Hagar's tearful eyes and gives her a well. A well! He just plops one down in the middle of the desert because he's God and he loves his children. Can you imagine the relief Hagar must have felt after preparing to watch her only child die?

Until recently, I had never noticed that Ishmael almost died of thirst. I know so many children who, like Ishmael, have been on the brink of death because they lacked water. I have heard the cries of mothers who hide their faces in shame and heart-wrenching pain because they simply cannot do anything for the ones they would do anything for.

Utamuriza is an eight-year-old Rwandan girl I know. Her family does not have access to clean water. As a result, her perpetual thirst causes dangerous dehydration. Utamuriza misses school to walk several miles to the nearest water source, a contaminated spring. She and her brothers and sisters regularly suffer from stomach aches and skin rashes as a result of the dirty water. There are no good options for Utamuriza — she is the victim of a cruel injustice.

Thousands of years ago, God brought cool, clean water to those who thirsted. I love that God heard their cries. I love that he promised to be with Ishmael for the rest of his life. I love that life pushed imminent death out of the picture — all through water. And today, he continues to do the same thing. The amazing thing is that he has given us — broken and unworthy as we are — the privilege of being his hands to carry water to a thirsty world.

Through Blood:Water Mission, over 250,000 people's cries have been heard and answered. Ordinary people like you and me have raised the funds necessary to provide African communities with clean water. Sometimes a small donation seems insignificant, but a single dollar provides a year's water for someone like Utamuriza in Africa. The funds also support community building, village leadership, sanitation, and hygiene training to help ensure that communities have a chance to thrive for years to come.

Because young Americans are finding creative, compassionate ways to raise awareness in their churches, schools, and families, thousands of mothers and fathers in Africa no longer have to lay their sick children under trees of hopelessness. It certainly doesn't erase all the problems that our dear friends face, but it is fertile ground in which to plant seeds of hope and new beginnings. After Hagar and Ishmael drank their fill at God's providential well, the hardships of life still awaited them. But God provided for their most immediate need as an indication of his concern for them — as a sign of promise for the future.

"Then God opened her eyes and she saw a well of water. So she went and filled the skin with water and gave the boy a drink" (Gen. 21:19).

BIO

Jena Nardella is the Executive Director for Blood:Water Mission. She graduated from Whitworth College with a Political Studies degree. During her college years, she focused on issues of poverty, social stratification, global health, and the psychology of prejudice. At the age of twenty-two, Jena was hired as the Executive Director to establish, execute, and maintain the vision of Blood:Water Mission. In its first three years, she has led the organization to provide assistance for over 250,000 Africans while engaging thousands of Americans in worldview development and action. Jena is a contributing writer for *Relevant* magazine and author of *Hope in the Dark* (Relevant Books, 2006).

How to Conquer the World

Paul Rawlins

Our church had been working with the Sabiny tribe of Eastern Uganda for several years before we understood their reasons for settling on the steep hillside of Mount Elgon. "Why not live on the plain?" we naively wondered. Life on the hillside was tough. Moving their cattle down to the plains in the morning and then back to the mountain hideaways in the evening was laborious. Torrential rain eroded the mountain's soil, making farming more difficult. Harnessing usable water wasn't easy because the many volcanic fissures swallowed much of the surface water.

Decades earlier, the Sabiny tribe flourished on the fertile plains below Mount Elgon, but they simply can't live there anymore. Many of the Karamojong, a neighboring tribe, had plagued the Sabiny tribe for several years, giving the Karamojong a reputation of being raiders and thieves.[10] Thus, the Sabiny tribe has fled to the mountains to seek refuge from raids that often involve machine guns and machetes. The events of the past few decades have decimated the Sabinys. There are too many stories of men, women, and even children being killed while trying to save their family's only cow. Families often flee to neighboring villages, leaving burning homes behind — and that's only if they survive the initial raid.

We sat in stunned disbelief as families recounted one horrific story after another. Mouths dry and hearts racing, we all felt we needed to do more than just sympathize — we needed to act. Godwin, a young pastor in the area, spoke up with a pointed question: "What would Christ do?" After much deliberation, a plan was formed: with the support of our church, this pastor's own church would partner with another ministry to freely give the Karamojong a much-needed gift — water.

There was only one problem. Not many people would dare *approach* a Karamojong village, let alone expect to be allowed inside. And once inside, there would be no guarantee of leaving alive. Once again, Pastor Godwin offered a solution. Peter*, an American on our team, was going to pretend to be a long-lost Karamojong tribesman who had returned after traveling abroad. If the Karamojong responded well, then he and Pastor Godwin would reveal the true purpose of their visit. Who knew? Maybe it would work.

There was only one small problem. Peter is white.

A day later, Godwin stepped out of a truck and approached the gate of the Karamojong village, calling out to the guards. They didn't seem very welcoming as they trained their guns on him. Godwin spoke with great excitement. "I've brought a son of yours who wishes to return to his tribe!" Pointing to Peter, he continued, "This man has traveled the world. The time away has turned his skin white." This generated some curiosity, possibly even a few smiles. Godwin continued, "See how he carries the traditional wooden stool" (a tribal custom for a traveling warrior). "He even has the meat of a tribesman." Peter held up the wooden stool and some beef jerky for emphasis. The guards laughed. This was a good sign.

Godwin pressed on, "May we come in and talk with your leaders?" After some deliberation, the gate opened and Peter and Godwin were ushered in. The leaders came to meet them. With a final portion of courage, Godwin explained the real reason they were there: to offer the gift of water from their decades-long enemies, the Sabiny tribe.

Skepticism flooded the conversation, threatening to upend the whole situation. But Godwin kept trying to explain while Peter prayed silently. Finally, the leaders agreed. A drilling rig was allowed to pass through the gate and work began. A week later, Godwin and Peter returned to find many people gathered. Curiosity and wonder had spread among the tribe, and all the leaders were there as Godwin and Peter preached about the living water of Jesus Christ that heals all wounds and forgives all debts. The hearts of those listening were pierced. At the end of the sermon, Godwin began pumping the hand well, and clean, cool water poured onto the lifeless ground. Deafening cries of joy erupted from the men, women, and children gathered there.

"What would Christ do?" Godwin asked. "If [your enemy] is thirsty, give him something to drink" (Rom. 12:20). That's exactly what the Sabiny did for those who had been raiding them for decades. Fredrick Buechner says it well: "And then there is the love for the enemy — love for the one who does not love you but mocks, threatens, and inflicts pain. The tortured's love for the torturer. This is God's love. It conquers the world."[11]

BIO

Paul Rawlins is the Pastor of Outward Ministries at Sisters Community Church in Sisters, Oregon. Before becoming a pastor, Paul spent many years working for the Indonesian national school system, helping to create the first system in which westerners were allowed to teach students English. Paul's passion is to help build God's kingdom through the local church and to see the church become relevant to the next generation of leaders.

"Pi en Kwo" (Water Is Life)

Mike and Danae Yankoski

Kids love playing in sprinklers. What's better than spending an entire summer afternoon laughing and screaming with your friends as jets of cold water soak you from head to toe? As children, we don't examine our actions very much, but as adults we're called to consider the impact our decisions have on other people around the world. Water, the unlimited source of so much fun for us as kids, is a scarce resource for much of the world — and obtaining it is almost never as simple as turning on the tap.

Danae and I developed a new passion for the water issue after spending time in Ecuador and Uganda, focusing on the need for clean water, improved sanitation, and hygiene education. In Uganda we partnered with several organizations drilling wells and providing sanitation and hygiene training in dusty villages. For the first time we glimpsed the desperate need for water, sanitation, and hygiene faced by billions of people around the world.

In Uganda we camped in two rural villages for about a month. They were well beyond the reach of electric grids or city water supplies. During that month, local village chiefs led us on more than 125 miles of dusty, single-track paths to show us their water sources. Some were shockingly contaminated; we saw opaque water, algae, tadpoles and frogs, and cow feces. The effects were undeniable. One afternoon, as we walked past a family's hut, we noticed ten graves. One was adult-size; nine were the size of children. Suddenly, the statistics were all too real — how could one family have lost so many members from something as preventable as unsafe drinking water?

A week later, we were walking toward a neighboring village. We rounded a bend in the footpath, and suddenly the hot afternoon silence was pierced by cries of joy, whooping, and singing. From a cluster of nearby huts, several women came running toward us, their voices rising and falling as they stomped their feet in time with the song they were singing. We had no idea what was going on as we stood there, dazed and more than a little confused. The women came closer, their voices growing louder as they neared. Soon we found ourselves encircled by the women, who were now singing at the top of their lungs in their native Luo language. Great smiles stretched across their faces. Infants stared wide-eyed, comfortably attached to their mothers with brightly colored, cloth sarongs.

Our mouths hung open at this unexpected welcome. We had been in Uganda for nearly a month, but we hadn't experienced anything quite like this before. I turned to Leonard, our good friend and translator, and asked, "What are they singing? Why are they so happy?"

"They are singing, 'Praise God, for clean water has come!'" As he answered he mimicked the women's chorus, substituting English for Luo and dancing in similar rhythm. "You see, Mike and Danae, they are so very happy. An organization drilled a well here, in their

village, some months ago. They are singing because they are so happy. They are no longer sick. Their children no longer die from diarrhea. They no longer have typhoid. *Pi en Kwo.* Water is Life. Wouldn't you sing and dance too if this had happened to you?"

It is astonishing to see what people are willing to do for access to water. In Uganda we saw a nine-year-old girl named Annette carrying more than twenty pounds of water from a newly installed well — it was her third trip of the day, and the well was two miles from her home.

The point is not that we should keep kids from playing in the water on a hot summer day. After all, clean, refreshing water causes celebration wherever it is found! But maybe we could fill a plastic pool once instead of running the sprinklers every afternoon. Perhaps as we begin to appreciate the great gift that water truly is, we'll be inspired to fund water projects in developing countries.

If I've learned anything on our recent travels, it is this: allowing people to die because they lack clean, safe water compromises our testimony that Jesus is the Living Water. Water is life, and in the truest sense, the opportunity to help bring life-giving water to those in need is a vital extension of Jesus' command to love one another.

BIO

Mike and Danae Yankoski met at Westmont College where Mike studied Computer Science and Religious Studies and Danae studied English. Mike is a nationally known speaker who spent five months living as a homeless man on the streets of six American cities — an experience that led him to write *Under the Overpass* (Multnomah, 2005). Danae recently coauthored *Crazy Love* (Cook, 2008) and *The Forgotten God* (Cook, 2009) with Francis Chan. Mike and Danae are passionate about understanding social justice issues and communicating ways that ordinary Christians can work to bring God's love to the victims of injustice. They currently live in Vancouver, BC, where they are pursuing their graduate degrees at Regent College.

A Community Transformed

Bruce and Cherith Rydbeck

Cesar, a simple carpenter, lives in Rancho Alto, a barrio perched precariously on a volcanic mountainside above Quito, Ecuador. Rancho Alto is home to about a hundred families living in modest dwellings built with their own hands. They serve in the city as guards, maids, and workers, earning just enough to get by. Ninety-five percent of the children in Rancho Alto are born at home.

In the past, the health of Rancho Alto's citizens was imperiled because of the muddy irrigation-ditch water on which they depended. Rancho Alto is situated too high above Quito to receive water from the city water system. To make matters worse, rich hacienda owners above them on the mountain would frequently cut off the water supply.

Cesar built a home for his family in this barrio despite death threats from neighbors who despised his commitment to follow Jesus. Cesar even held worship services in his home for the few families who dared to attend. Over the years his evident faith would have a profound impact on the surrounding community. As the community's water situation grew more desperate, Cesar's trustworthiness led the community to elect him as the leader in a new effort to bring clean, reliable water to the barrio — despite their objections to his faith in God.

Before this, Rancho Alto had never successfully completed a community project. Other leaders had either cheated the community out of their meager resources or simply quit because of the difficulty. However, Cesar worked tirelessly for the people in his community. One day he came to me at the Vozandes Community Development office where I worked, asking for help. Tears rolled down his face as he explained his barrio's need for water. Design work began, and soon we found that gravity could deliver spring water from a spring source just over three miles away.

With our help, the one hundred families of Rancho Alto accepted the challenge to build their own water system. Since they were unable to leave their low-paying jobs in the

city, they decided to work on the project during weekends. The few Christians in the community provided leadership. They prayed for the Lord to direct their efforts and to supply the funds for the necessary pipe and building materials.

Construction began in August 2002, when volunteers from a U.S. church came for a week to help dig the pipe trenches. In the afternoons, they held Bible classes with almost a hundred children from the community. Over the next few months, God provided the finances needed to protect the community's spring source, build two fifty-cubic-meter reservoirs, and bury nine kilometers of pipe that would bring clean water to every home. Each family provided manual labor and sacrificed to cover some of the costs for building the water system. Now every home has a spigot providing a constant supply of safe water.

God astounded the residents of Rancho Alto, helping them overcome difficult challenges with the neighboring hacienda owners and providing uniquely for their needs. Their understanding of God grew mightily through this experience. Now, many dysfunctional families damaged by abuse, neglect, alcohol, and infidelity are praying and seeking restoration under Cesar's pastoral care. Providing clean water is not an opportunity for "do-gooding" by wealthy people — it's about working and praying together to create sustainable, life-giving solutions that testify to the Living Water.

"The poor and homeless are desperate for water, their tongues parched and no water to be found. But I'm there to be found, I'm there for them, and I, God of Israel, will not leave them thirsty. I'll open up rivers for them on the barren hills, spout fountains in the valleys. I'll turn the baked-clay badlands into a cool pond, the waterless waste into splashing creeks … Everyone will see this. No one can miss it — unavoidable, indisputable evidence that I, God, personally did this. It's created and signed by The Holy of Israel" (Isa. 41:17 – 20 MSG).

BIO

Bruce Rydbeck serves as a civil engineer on community development water and sanitation projects in Ecuador, South America. He directs a fifteen-member community development team. Hundreds of rural communities have been helped to improve health and receive clean water. Bruce and his wife, Cherith, have served as missionary volunteers on a wide variety of development projects in Ecuador, Colombia, and Kenya since 1980. They live in Quito, Ecuador, and have two married sons, a daughter, and one granddaughter — all living in the USA. As a graduate of Clarkson University and Northeastern University, Bruce holds engineering credentials in the U.S. and Ecuador. He enjoys mountain biking and has climbed several of Ecuador's Andean peaks, including Cotopaxi at 19,350 feet.

Akwia-Woro

Daniel Stevens

My eyes burned and my throat ached as I entered the hot, dusty village of Akwia-Woro in northern Uganda. Several elderly villagers greeted my companions, leaders of Divine Waters (Lifewater International's Ugandan partner) and me. Together we gathered for a brief community meeting under a tree. As I sat down, I noticed a cluster of young men and boys standing at a safe distance, unwilling to engage with us.

Afterward, the elders led us to the community's only source of water: a muddy, unprotected spring. I watched as women scooped the chocolate-colored water into buckets for their families' use. Other women did laundry, washing soap and dirt into the cloudy pool. Muddy hoof prints ringed the water hole, evidence of the livestock that came to drink here. "Please," said the village elders, "help us get water. Without you, we have no hope."

"Lord, remember your promises," I prayed as I thought of Jeremiah 29:11. " 'For I know the plans I have for you,' declares the Lord, 'plans to prosper you and not to harm you, plans to give you hope and a future.' "

For nearly twenty years, a violent conflict had raged across northern Uganda between government forces and the rebel group known as the Lord's Resistance Army (LRA). To escape the bloodshed, the people of Akwia-Woro, like thousands of others, had abandoned their village and crowded into camps for displaced persons. Sadly, the camps were not safe havens. Rape, murder, and disease were commonplace. Now, with violence finally diminishing, the citizens of Akwia-Woro were returning home. The village was filled with people once again. It takes a lot to rebuild the life of an entire village. Though the long conflict had robbed many in Akwia-Woro of dignity and hope, they were asking us to come alongside them and help them take steps forward.

A few months later, I returned to Akwia-Woro. Since my last visit, Lifewater's partner organization had installed a well and begun hygiene and sanitation education. As we sat down under a familiar tree, I noticed the young men and boys standing just beyond the meeting's perimeter. Arms folded, they were observant but showed little interest. During the meeting, the elders shared how much they appreciated the new well. "Yet," they said, "we need your help with many other things."

The third time I visited Akwia-Woro, the atmosphere had changed. A current of energy and excitement rippled through the community meeting as young men crowded in with their elders to share what was happening in Akwia-Woro. "Look!" they said. "Now, along with a well, we have latrines that we built ourselves." They pointed to a thatched structure with the comical but fitting words "Divine Toilet" etched into its cement side.

Why this remarkable change? The answer came in the form of a soccer ball. Some

months earlier, Lifewater's partner organized a community health and soccer league as a way of reaching out to the young people of Akwia-Woro and other area villages. In order to join the league, each team had to complete a survey of its village's current hygiene and sanitation practices. Once the team members turned it in, they received a soccer ball and became part of the league.

Soccer games happened as usual, with one notable exception. At halftime, teams shared ways they were helping improve their villages' health practices. For each improvement, such as installing hand washing devices or buckets for cleaning water, teams received additional points. Also during the halftime break, league organizers shared the gospel — the message of hope and a future available through Christ's love.

Soccer games on a dusty field. The privacy and dignity of a latrine. Safe, clear water pouring from a new well. For the people of Akwia-Woro, these simple things became a road map toward hope. They point to the ultimate source of hope: a loving God. Through his mercy, this community is working together daily to embrace a better, healthier future.

BIO

Before becoming the Executive Director of Lifewater International in 2002, Dan Stevens served as the Senior Pastor at Eastminster Presbyterian Church in Ventura, California, for twenty-six years. During that time, Dan helped found IMPACT, a short-term missions training program affiliated with the Santa Barbara Presbytery, and was instrumental in bringing Young Life to Ventura County. In 2002, he was the first recipient of the Dan Stevens Shalom award created in his honor in Ventura County. Through extensive travel and involvement with cross-cultural ministry, he has gained a wealth of knowledge and personal experience in forming transnational partnerships and working with the poor. Dan holds a Master of Divinity from Princeton Seminary and a Bachelor of Science from Pepperdine University. He is married and has two grown children and one grandchild.

NOW WHAT?

Most of us didn't thank God the last time we took a drink of water. Clean, safe water is considered a given in most developed countries. Yet over a billion around our world have to live (and die) without it. Billions more are hindered by a lack of sanitation and hygiene. Allow this section to help you engage a bit more with this global reality, and perhaps discover how you can become part of the solution.

Reflect

1. *What do you think?* Which article on clean water had the greatest impact on you? Maybe a photograph or a story sticks in your mind — why? What impressed you the most — the people, the need, the difficulty, God's provision, or a person's selfless service? Spend some time describing your own thoughts, feelings, and reactions.

2. *Put yourself in another's shoes.* Flip back through the Field Notes and pick one entry — maybe the one that had the greatest impact on you. Imagine that you are part of the story for a day, that you've been transported to a new life with no recollection of your previous existence. Think about what your day looks like — how do you spend your time? What do you think about? What makes you smile? What are you most concerned about? Compare these reflections to your actual life.

3. *Examine your rhythms.* What are some patterns in your life that you might need to reconsider after reading this section? What are some habits you might want to include in your life? It can be anything from replacing your shower head with a less wasteful one to supporting an NGO doing water-based work abroad. Spend some time examining your lifestyle and thinking about how God may be asking you to consider something new, or something old in a new way.

Pray

Spend time praying about unclean water and its effect on people around the globe. Write out the words of your prayer as they come to mind. List a few countries that are affected by a lack of clean water, sanitation, and hygiene — then pray specifically for the people in those countries. Pray not only for this day's needs, but also for long-term solutions that provide sustainable water and glorify God.

Respond

1. *Cultivate thankfulness.* As with other issues we're exploring in *Zealous Love*, perhaps you're feeling that unclean water is something far too big and complicated for you to do anything about. The first step may well be an internal one. Practice being thankful for the things you have in your life. Begin by trying to cultivate a habit of being thankful for the clean water, improved sanitation, and hygiene you enjoy, and by being careful not to waste.

2. *Take a three-gallon challenge.* Try to experience what it's like not having accessible, clean water. Most Europeans and Americans use between 50 and 150 gallons of water per day.[12] Most people in developing nations use around 2½ gallons of water per day. That's for everything: cooking, cleaning, drinking, hygiene, flushing the toilet (assuming you're lucky enough to use a toilet), and so on. This weekend, get three gallons of water from a local store and limit yourself to those three gallons for an entire day. That's all you can use for washing your clothes, cooking, cleaning your body, brushing your teeth, etc. To find out what it's really like, consider the fact that millions of children have to carry their family's water from distant sources. So if you want a real challenge, walk three to five miles outside your home carrying those three gallons of water. No backpacks allowed! Try to imagine what it would be like to do this every day, never having reliable access to clean water in your town, much less in your home. Remember, this is reality for 1.1 billion people around the world.

Additional Resources

www.thinkoutsidethebottle.org

www.thirstrelief.org

www.water.cc

www.worldwater.org

Visit *www.zealouslove.org/ water* for more information and organizations.

3. *Organize a bottled water drive.* Start a bottled water drive to raise money in support of organizations doing water-based development. Encourage people in your community to fill empty water bottles with dollars and coins. Then pool all of the money together and send it to one of the organizations listed at the end of this section. This is a great way to get whole groups involved and informed about the lack of clean water, sanitation, and hygiene around the world.

Spread the Word

Individually, it feels daunting to confront such a global problem. But tremendous change can happen when we work together. Would you consider spreading the word about the water crisis, the people whose lives are affected, and the organizations that are doing something to make a difference? Now that you've read this section, it isn't "someone else's responsibility" — it's yours. Change begins with individuals deciding that they are going to live differently. What role can you play? Maybe it's inviting some friends to coffee, start-

ing an action group at your church, or getting your youth group to hold a rally. Help change lives. Spread the word. To help you do so, we've built a simple and effective tool: *www.zealouslove.org/spread*.

Share Your Ideas

Have a great idea about something other people can do to engage the need for safe water? Do you want to connect with others who are getting involved? Join in the conversation at *www.zealouslove.org/share*.

Discover More

In the Field Notes, you've heard from several contributors about the devastating consequences caused by a lack of clean water, sanitation, and hygiene. You've also heard some
about the incredible work that's being done to help meet those needs. Remember, there
is no one-size-fits-all solution. It requires different organizations and different people working together. If you want to get involved and change lives in this area, check out the following organizations or visit *www.zealouslove.org/water.*

Lifewater International

Vision: Lifewater International is a Christian
training organization that focuses on helping
communities gain health and dignity through
safe water, adequate sanitation, effective hygiene, and the knowledge of God's love.

Method: Lifewater accomplishes this by
equipping Christian national partner organizations in Africa, Asia, and Latin America in
shallow well drilling, hand pump repair, bio-
sand filtration, sanitation promotion, latrine
construction, and community health through
hygiene. National partners use these skills to
empower communities to meet their basic
water and sanitation needs and gain confidence in their own ability to promote the
health and well-being of their people.

Contact:
Lifewater International
PO Box 3131
San Luis Obispo, CA 93403
Phone: (888) 543-3426
www.lifewater.org

Blood:Water Mission

Vision: Blood:Water Mission exists to tangibly
reduce the impact of the African HIV/AIDS
pandemic, to promote clean blood and clean
water in Africa, and to build equitable, sustainable, and personal community links.

Method: Blood:Water Mission is partnering
with groups and individuals to empower Africans to build healthier communities through
sustainable clean blood and clean water solutions while developing social responsibility in
the U.S. through initiatives that provoke personal engagement and ownership. The 1000
Wells Project is building 1000 wells and clean
water projects in 1000 African communities.
Businesses, churches, schools, artists, and
individuals are collecting funds so they can
sponsor the construction of wells in Africa. In
the process, they are learning about how HIV/
AIDS affects African communities and what it
means to partner humbly with communities
to pursue transformation.

Contact:
Blood:Water Mission
PO Box 60381
Nashville, TN 37206
Phone: (615) 550-4296
www.bloodwatermission.com

Community Development Vozandes

Vision: Community Development Vozandes, a part of HCJB Global, is an organization committed to improving the health of rural Ecuadorian communities through clean water and preventive health care.

Method: Community Development Vozandes began serving the health needs of rural and urban Ecuadorian communities in 1980. In addition to the water and sanitation ministry, the ministry includes low-cost family practice clinics, a medical caravan ministry, and rural health teaching. Community Development Vozandes is a part of HCJB Global, an interdenominational missionary organization with worldwide communications, health care, and leadership development ministries. HCJB began Christian radio broadcasting in 1931 from Quito, Ecuador. A medical work began in 1949, which now includes two hospitals in Ecuador, and community development work.

Contact:

HCJB Global — Clean Water Projects
Casilla 17 – 17 – 691
Quito, Ecuador
Phone: (593) 2227-6389 ext. 3670
http://water.hcjb.org

Living Water International

Vision: Living Water International exists to demonstrate the love of God by helping communities acquire desperately needed clean water, and to experience "living water"—the gospel of Jesus Christ—which alone satisfies the deepest thirst.

Method: At Living Water International, our approach — to train, equip, and consult nationals — ensures that the energy and resources contributed by volunteers and donors result in sustainable, participatory water systems that meet the long-term needs of communities.

We train community development volunteers and professionals how to implement integrated water solutions. Many of our trainees have gone on to work with a wide variety of social sector organizations. Participants are prepared to train others, with the goal of seeing national teams meeting the needs of their own people.

We provide trained national teams with all the components needed to implement community water solutions. This includes supplying capital outlay and logistic support while the national teams grow to become self-sustaining. We hire local people and buy local materials whenever possible, creating jobs and income to further benefit the community at large.

We make our expertise and data available wherever water is needed most. Consultation is a natural outgrowth of training and equipping—and is a practical way that we can walk alongside people who want to include a water component to their work. We're watching the work multiply as we act as a consultant to other organizations that also provide safe, clean water.

Contact:

Living Water International—Headquarters
PO Box 35496
Houston, TX 77235–5496
USA
Phone: (877) 594-4426
www.water.cc

World Vision

Vision: World Vision is a Christian humanitarian organization dedicated to working with children, families, and their communities worldwide to reach their full potential by tackling the causes of poverty and injustice.

Method: Access to clean water and sanitation is foundational to all aspects of development, and often the first work World Vision does in a community. Through wells, water-storage containers, water-piping systems, protection of natural springs, water purification systems, latrine constructions, and laundry pad construction, World Vision has provided access to clean water and improved sanitation for more than 10 million people worldwide.

Contact:

World Vision
PO Box 9716, Dept. W
Federal Way, WA 98063-9716
Phone: (888) 511-6548
www.worldvision.org

REFUGEES

So you, too, must show love to foreigners,
for you yourselves were once foreigners in the land of Egypt.

Deuteronomy 10:19 NLT

Deuteronomy is known as the "Book of the Covenant," in which God defines the relationship between himself and his chosen people. It's filled with instructions and laws meant to guide both individual and communal life for God's people. As Christians we are no longer under the law (Rom. 6:14) and yet Jesus himself did not come to abolish the law but to fulfill it (Matt. 5:17). At a minimum, the laws God gave to his people in Deuteronomy should help us modern-day Christians as we consider what it means to love our neighbors.

In this passage from Deuteronomy God instructs his people to care for foreigners. The NIV renders the word for foreigners as "aliens," while the ESV uses "sojourners." The idea is someone who is displaced, away from their home, land, customs, language, etc., away from what is familiar. The point is that God's people are to care for those in that situation. We are to show love.

As you read this section on refugees, consider what it might look like for you to show love for the "foreigners," "aliens," and "sojourners" in our world.

BRIEFING

What comes to mind when you hear the word "refugee"? Until I became friends with a political refugee from Zimbabwe, the word meant very little to me. For a long time I had associated the word with people in rags who were desperate for food and without homes. If asked, I probably would have said that people become refugees when war breaks out in their country.

A paraphrase of the United Nations' 1951 Convention defines a refugee this way:

> A refugee is someone with a well-founded fear of persecution on the basis of his (or her) race, religion, nationality, membership in a particular social group or political opinion, who is outside of his or her country of nationality and unable or unwilling to return to it.[1]

I had the basics right, but there is nothing basic about being a refugee. Refugees are often poor and hungry, having been stripped of just about everything except what they can carry. They are driven from their former homes, often because of war, genocide, or some other horrid conflict in their country. Perhaps a better question is "*Who* do you think of when you hear the word refugee?" Do you know anyone who is or was a refugee? By connecting with *people* who are refugees, we equip ourselves with the personal resources to begin making a difference.

When I first met Rachel, my Zimbabwean friend, I was charmed by her accent and graceful way of interacting with people. It wasn't until several months later when we sat down to a cup of tea in her college dorm room that I heard her story. She shared that she and her family had been forced to flee Zimbabwe several years earlier, because of unrest and violence there. She looked at me and said simply, "I am a political refugee." I hardly knew how to respond — so I listened and learned as Rachel recounted stories of her childhood in Zimbabwe. She spoke fondly, wearing a quiet smile of remembrance.

As Rachel traveled further into her memories, a deep sadness crept in where the fond smiles had been previously. She told me that she missed her home. She was proud to be Zimbabwean, and she prays often for those who still live there, including some of her extended family. Then she said something I will never forget: "Danae, someday I may go back to Zimbabwe. I may visit or perhaps even move there, if the situation stabilizes. But I will never go back to the Zimbabwe I knew as a child. That place — my home, the country I knew — no longer exists. And even if peace comes, it will never be the same."

In some ways, my friend Rachel is fortunate. She didn't have to flee her home in the middle of the night with nothing but the clothes on her back. She and her family now live in the relative safety and comfort of America. They do not have to stand in line to receive emergency food rations like so many other refugees living in displaced people's camps around the world. Rachel and her family have a house and clothes and enough food to eat, while many refugees lack these basic necessities. However, that does not lessen my friend's pain in losing her home and knowing that she can never go back to the way things were.

The refugee crisis is a global issue, with most countries affected in some way. The 1948 Universal Declaration of Human Rights asserts that everyone has the right "to seek and to enjoy in other countries asylum from persecution."[2] This means that people who have suffered human rights abuses should be able to flee their country and find safety in another. This is a controversial issue, as many governments see an influx of refugees as a logistical burden to be discouraged or even refused. In the past fifty years, many nations have reneged on their commitments to offer refugees asylum.[3]

In particular, Australia and many countries in Europe and North America — who led the way in protecting refugees after World War II — have begun passing restrictive laws, making life difficult for refugees. Governments have begun to arrest and detain refugees, close borders, and discriminate against refugees displaced within their own borders. Some of the more common migratory patterns of refugees are from North Africa to Spain or France, from Haiti and Cuba to the southern United States, and from Eastern Europe to Western Europe. At times, governments violate the most basic principle of international refugee law, "non-refoulement," which means they deny entrance and force refugees to return to the country they are fleeing.[4] For example, in 2007 the United States forced more than fifteen hundred Haitian refugees to return to their home country, a move sharply criticized by the U.S. Committee for Refugees and Immigrants.[5]

> You can find Calcutta anywhere in the world. You only need two eyes to see. Everywhere in the world there are people that are not loved, people that are not wanted nor desired, people that no one will help, people that are pushed away or forgotten. And this is the greatest poverty.
>
> **Mother Teresa**

The transient, unstable situation of refugees makes estimating their worldwide number difficult, if not impossible. However, most organizations that work with refugees estimate that the total number — which does not include those who have been resettled and granted official asylum or people displaced within their own countries — is approaching (or exceeds) fifteen million.[6] The Office of the UN High Commissioner for Refugees (UNHCR) considers well over twenty million people to be "people of concern," which includes refugees, asylum seekers, returnees, stateless people, and some of the world's internally displaced persons (IDPs).[7] And these are the conservative numbers — other sources estimate the number is over thirty million.[8]

These numbers are shocking. Over twenty million people have been displaced from their homes in some capacity or another — twenty million people who have stories like my friend Rachel. Stories of lost property, stolen childhoods, destroyed homelands, torn families, diminished hope, and robbed livelihoods. Stories of losing everything, and sometimes everyone, that matters. The story of even a single refugee can conjure angry tears and questions, yet there are millions more we will never know.

Speaking with Rachel, I found myself hoping that, at the very least, we as a country would stand up for refugee rights. The truth is, while rich countries like the United States, Australia, and those of Western Europe do accept some asylum seekers, there is much more they could do — especially when we consider what far less prosperous countries are doing. Countries with a per capita GDP[9] of less than $2000 host roughly 65 percent of the world's refugees, while those with per capita GDPs over $10,000 host approximately 5 percent of the refugee population. To illustrate the difference, 1 in every 2,032 persons living in the U.S. is a refugee; in Kenya it's 1 in every 103 persons. The numbers are especially striking in the West Bank and Gaza Strip, where one out of every 2 persons is a refugee.[10]

The Bible describes a God who commands people to care for strangers and sojourners and aliens in their midst:

"Do not oppress an alien; you yourselves know how it feels to be aliens, because you were aliens in Egypt" (Exod. 23:9).

"When an alien lives with you in your land, do not mistreat him. The alien living with you must be treated as one of your native-born. Love him as yourself, for you were aliens in Egypt. I am the LORD your God" (Lev. 19:33 – 34).

"Do not take advantage of a hired man who is poor and needy, whether he is a brother

Israelite or an alien living in one of your towns. Pay him his wages each day before sunset, because he is poor and is counting on it. Otherwise he may cry to the LORD against you, and you will be guilty of sin" (Deut. 24:14 – 15).

Considering that our Father is explicit about how his people are to care for the aliens in their midst — which certainly include refugees, immigrants, visitors, and strangers — we ought to look at how we, as individual Christians and as members of local churches, care for people in these situations. Our responsibility is heightened by the fact that American-led wars in Iraq and Afghanistan have contributed to the number of refugees fleeing these countries. In fact, Iraq and Afghanistan generate more refugees than Sudan and Myanmar (also known as Burma), two of the most well-known refugee situations.[11]

Passing new refugee laws is probably not something most of us will have the opportunity to do. That said, advocacy — signing petitions, getting the issue on the ballot, and contacting congressional representatives and senators — is a tangible action that each of us can take. Additionally, many people have become involved with refugee resettlement

programs in their own regions. Many organizations encourage caring locals to "adopt" a single refugee or family of refugees, helping to ease their transition into a new life. Such care includes things we might take for granted — like how to use the local public transportation system, how to shop in a grocery store, or how to use a washer and dryer. Helping in these simple ways goes a long way toward making refugees feel more at home in a strange country.

A friend of ours has opened up his family's farm to take in refugees displaced by a horrific war in the northern part of his own country. To those who come, he offers land, seeds, and oxen for plowing — in short, the chance to start over again. It isn't easy by any means. Yet he is choosing to offer these displaced individuals a new home because theirs have been irrevocably stolen.

Some other friends of ours connected with a student from India studying at a university in their town. Since then, they have included him in their life by inviting him to Thanksgiving, learning how to cook authentic Indian food under his teaching, and learning about him and his culture. In doing so they've helped this man experience a bit of home, even while living far from his own country. While this man is not a political refugee, our friends are taking seriously God's command to care for the sojourner in their hometown.

Caring for refugees, strangers, aliens, and sojourners means being hospitable, and true hospitality — not the grudging, short-lived acceptance of an inconvenient stranger — is something that requires long, hard work. When we truly invite strangers in, we commit ourselves to help in whatever ways they need, whether it's with a home-cooked meal, assistance with a job search, a place to stay, or a listening ear. We are saying to the stranger, "I am willing to be part of your life and let you be part of mine."

The apostle Paul told Christians living in Rome to "share with God's people who are in need" and to "practice hospitality" (Rom. 12:13). Paul isn't suggesting — he's commanding. Hospitality is not optional for Christians. It is the basic social orientation of all who claim to follow Christ. The author of Hebrews exhorts us to "not forget to entertain strangers, for by so doing some people have entertained angels without knowing it" (Heb. 13:2). As you read the following field notes, consider what it means for you to actively practice and extend hospitality toward aliens, sojourners, travelers, and refugees. Such action is the natural response of people who were once strangers themselves, until welcomed by the God of hospitality.

A Peaceful Land

Saw Kaw Khu

My name is Saw Kaw Khu and I was born in July 1967, deep in the jungles of Burma (also known as Myanmar[12]). I came into the world in the middle of our people's fight for freedom. To this day, Burma is still under oppressive communist rule instituted by General Ne Win's military coup d'état in 1962. The results of a democratic election in 1990 were ignored by the oppressive junta.[13] Despite international condemnation and sanctions, the 48 million Burmese citizens continue to live without freedom.

My father was a Karen (one of the ethnic groups in Burma) freedom fighter, fighting against the illegal and oppressive Burmese government. He has told me about my humble beginnings while he and my mother were hiding out in the jungles during the fight for freedom. It was the rainy season. Buckets of rain fell and creeks were swollen with floodwaters. My parents were fleeing the approaching Burmese army, and I was born into the chaos of it all. There were no clothes or baby wrappings, so my father tore his old sarong into strips to wrap me in. I was the first-born and only baby in the battalion. My dad told me that all the other members of the resistance loved me — to them I was a symbol of life and hope amidst an awful, bloody struggle. One day my mom had to hold me above her head and flee across a river to escape. Yet with great confidence my father named me Kaw Khu — "peaceful land" in the Karen language. He hoped that one day his baby boy would lead his people in what my father had only experienced in his dreams: a land of peace, stability, and justice.

My entire childhood was spent on the run. After I graduated from a temporary high school in a refugee camp, there was no chance for further study. Instead of school, I joined the Karen Freedom Fighters and served in the medical department. I finished three years of medical training, and then I worked in both hospitals and on the front lines of fighting zones. I enjoyed the soldier's life and the chance to help my people with the training I'd received, but I never liked the killing. In some ways, though, we had no choice. Fighting was the only way to protect ourselves, our people, and our loved ones from the brutal military junta. I hated the war — everybody did — but survival demanded it. In 1984, the Burmese government troops destroyed all of the Karen villages and occupied the Karen military bases one by one along the Thai-Burmese border. Many thousands of Karen people were forced to become refugees.

After some time in Thailand, my wife, daughter, and I came as refugees to the United States of America in 1999. Although we were happy to live in the United States, everything was challenging to us when we first arrived. It was like starting over. From the food we ate to the jobs we worked to the home where we lived, everything was an adjustment. For people like us who have only known war, a peaceful country is an indescribable blessing. God has been merciful to my family and me. We no longer face daily atrocities and persecution like when we were living in Burma. At the same time, however, we face new temptations here: the deceitfulness of riches, the allure of sex and drugs, and so on. We have exchanged one form of warfare for another.

Now I am the mission director at the KING (Karen International Gospel) Revival Fellowship in Omaha, Nebraska. Our congregation has about six hundred members — Karen people who, like us, have come to the United States as refugees. There is a unique community amongst the displaced. I love my job, and I am so thankful for the chance to help lead my people deeper into relationship with Christ. It's tough being a good leader — a leader who loves righteousness and wants to serve his people rather than be served.

As a refugee, God is teaching me a difficult lesson about being his follower: I must love my enemies. Although the Burmese military came and killed our people and burned the villages, schools, and churches, I must forgive them. Some days this is overwhelmingly difficult, particularly when I remember all that has happened. But through the love of Jesus Christ, the impossible becomes possible. I know that hatred and revenge will not bring my people the freedom or peace we long for. Only God is powerful enough to bring such a mighty change. We must turn to him and trust.

Nearly fifty years have passed since the coup d'état and my people are still engaged in a difficult resistance against the Burmese regime. I don't know how many more years we will have to fight to gain our freedom. My family, my congregation, and I continue to follow closely as things develop in Burma. We hope, wait, pray, and trust that the Lord is in control and somehow working out his plan. Maybe someday soon we will have our own peaceful land, whether on earth or in heaven. Hasten the day, Lord.

BIO

Saw Kaw Khu, also known as "Rocky," was born in 1967 in the jungles of Burma. He graduated high school in 1985 from Huay Ka Loke Karen refugee camp in Thailand. After graduating, he received medical training from Aid Medical International (AMI). After this he served in the medical department of the Karen National Liberation Army for eight years. He then worked with the Asian Tribal Ministries as a youth leader and interpreter. In 1998, he married Salweena Khu in Thailand, and in the fall of 1999 Rocky and his family immigrated to the United States of America as refugees. In 2005, Rocky and his family moved with a small group of Karen people to Omaha, Nebraska, and began helping other Karen families resettle there. He is the founder and director of KING Revival Fellowship (Karen Christian Church) in Omaha and currently serves as the mission director. Rocky also serves as the chairperson of the Karen Society of Nebraska. Since 2006, Rocky has also been working full time for the Lutheran Refugee Services as a case worker for the Karen. Rocky and his wife now have three children.

A Functioning Heart

Rose Sore

The thing that comes to mind when I think about refugees is persistent faith. Written on the face and in the life of every refugee I've met is the same truth: the only thing that can supersede the pain they've endured is their drive to keep going. They cling to the faith that someday, somehow, all will be well.

This faith is hard for the rest of us to understand. Refugees experience what we only encounter in our nightmares. Stripped of everything they know and love, they are forced to rebuild their lives again. Some lose family, some lose property, and all lose a sense of home.

Refugees face myriad difficulties that are hard to quantify, but there are three that strike me as the most challenging. The first is economic. Meeting day-to-day needs such as food, clothing, and shelter is nearly impossible. Restrictive laws make it difficult for refugees to obtain work permits in host countries, and even a permit doesn't guarantee a paying job. The economic strain affects all other aspects of life: the education of their children, their living conditions, their medical care, and so on.

The second challenge is emotional. Refugees have great difficulty finding acceptance and consequently suffer a deep sense of loneliness. Separated from familiar territory and the comfort accorded by a sense of community, refugees often feel marginalized or ostracized from the new society in which they live.

The third profound challenge concerns the children of refugees. Most of their parents fled when they were adults, with a clear understanding of who they were. The children, on the other hand, are often born and raised in foreign territories under very strenuous circumstances. From early on, they have to deal with being different, and they have no clear sense of community or homeland to anchor them.

I live and work in Nairobi, Kenya. Following the elections in late 2007, the otherwise stable country quickly deteriorated into a violent state, and the notion of having to seek refuge elsewhere became a real possibility for me. I am thankful that I didn't have to flee my country, but many in Kenya — and millions around the world — aren't as lucky.

A dear friend of mine is married to a man who was an active politician in the Democratic Republic of Congo (DRC) in the early nineties. The political climate during the rule of Mobutu Sese Seko was not very friendly, and eventually it became altogether deadly. Friends and associates of theirs started to go missing and were never heard from again. One day my friend's family discovered that her husband's name was on a hit list.

They chose to flee the country with their one-year-old to Rwanda. Theirs was a double tragedy, because they had no way of knowing they were walking straight into the Rwandan genocide. They didn't realize that although they had left the DRC for fear of death and in hope of peace, they would now meet face-to-face with brutal ethnic cleansing. They literally stepped over bodies in their escape from Rwanda. This time they did not have the luxury of worrying about property; it was a miracle that their lives were spared. In 1994 they finally made it to Kenya where they have lived ever since. Their one-year-old is now fifteen and has lived in both Rwanda and Kenya as a refugee. They dream of going back to the DRC, but the political situation has yet to stabilize sufficiently.

Often we hear stories like this and sigh in sadness, feeling the pain of those who are distant from us — but a sigh is as far as we get. The issues surrounding refugees are highly complex, and I definitely don't want to offer simplistic answers. But I believe there is more that we can — and should — do. It is easy to wonder what kind of God would let anyone suffer as much as refugees suffer — what kind of God lets you lose everything? But God is the one who stays by the side of each refugee, and often he is the only one who does.

I was once asked if refugees can ever go back to normal life. My response is this: how normal is a life marked by the loss of loved ones? How normal is life within the confines of someone else's land? A refugee's life can never go back to *normal*. But I have witnessed how refugees can still live fruitful and rich lives, if provided with the right tools to put them onto a path of healing. These include tools of economic empowerment and tools of peace.

Amani Ya Juu ("Higher Peace" or "Peace from Above" in the Swahili language), the organization I work with, has been structured in such a way that it helps meet the biggest needs faced by refugee women. Amani Ya Juu provides a source of income for refugees by involving them in a unique training program. Besides merely meeting short-term solutions to day-to-day needs, Amani Ya Juu provides women with skills that continue to be economically fruitful long after they've left our care. More importantly, Amani is a harbor of peace for refugees. All of the women we serve come to us with visible and invisible burdens, and we help to shelter them within the warmth of a Christ-centered family. Gradually, their harsh wounds can begin to heal as they become part of this new family. It's not a "traditional" family tied by bonds of blood and nationality, but rather a deeper family bound by faith and love amidst great suffering.

Anyone who wants to help can support one of the countless organizations doing quality work to improve the lives of refugees. We have had a lot of support from people who want to make an impact in the lives of the ladies at Amani. These people don't have to come all the way to Kenya to help. Rather, they have demonstrated their support by purchasing the products these refugees make. They have told others, who in turn have lent their support. Perhaps it seems like a tiny step to take, but these seemingly minute efforts have far-reaching implications for the lives of refugees.

Compassion is the mandate for all humans. If we find ourselves blessed with peace and material possessions enough for today's needs, how can we not lend a helping hand to others who are victims of circumstances beyond their control?

BIO

Rose Sore is a twenty-five-year-old Kenyan single mother of a beautiful two-year-old boy named Antoine Lamor. His very name captures the fact that he is loved (Lamor is an intertwining of the French and Spanish words for love). Rose works as the export manager for Amani Ya Juu, based in Nairobi. Through Amani, Rose is able to work with incredible women who are typically disregarded because of their refugee status. Rose is also a communications major at Daystar University. Her passions include writing, reading, traveling, and collecting quotes. Though the world can be a dark place, Rose's hope is that people will continue to seek others' interests above their own, and through this, that light will creep into the dark places.

Grace

Dan Brose

There is an African proverb that captures the plight of refugees: "When the elephants fight, the grass is trampled." As conflict erupts between the "powers that be," common people are trampled.

December 1960: My Birth

The certificate reads "Ruanda-Urundi, December 1960." I was born and lived among refugees in a remote corner of what is today called Burundi. Though I was too young to really know what was going on, many of the people who lived and worked around my family and me were refugees. Most had fled ethnic violence and slaughter in what is today called Rwanda.

If I returned to where I grew up, most of those I knew would be gone — they're refugees. Again. They've had to abandon everything and move on. Again. As a young child, I was naïve to the issues that bred conflict. I spent my days hunting with sling shots, climbing trees, and playing soccer with the other kids. I didn't know a Hutu from a Tutsi or a Rwandan from a Burundian.

In Ruanda-Urundi, the year 1960 marked the beginning of decades of conflict, massive population migrations, and horrific genocidal wars. The small countries of Rwanda and Burundi were formed from the red-hot ashes of Ruanda-Urundi. Both countries have the same tribes and similar languages, history, and culture, and both countries are steeped in conflict. Rwanda is known for the genocide in 1994 — ninety days of killing and huge flights of refugees — while Burundi is somewhat forgotten by the international conscience. Even today, millions are still living outside both countries as refugees.

December 2000: My Life

Today, I live and work among refugees. Many of the visas and stamps in my U.S. passport say Rwanda and Burundi. The reason I've gone back is largely because of refugees — new and old alike, all innocent people in great need who have fled their homes because of conflict and power struggles. I work with families who have left all of their belongings behind to be plundered by neighbors and rebels, and with families who have lost children to enslavement (boys as soldiers and girls as sex slaves). HIV spreads through refugee camps like wildfire. Poverty is a constant companion and the source of innumerable other problems. Most refugees don't have birth certificates or passports. Many are not accepted

as citizens of any nation at all. They are invisible people. Everyone wants a home, but few refugees are able to return to theirs or create a new one.

Sometimes the refugee problem seems utterly overwhelming, but we try to help.

Grace Uwizera*

Grace is one of the people made invisible by circumstances beyond her control. With her husband and family members, Grace fled to the Democratic Republic of Congo (DRC) (formerly Zaire) after war and ethnic slaughters began in Rwanda. This is her story:

From April 1994 until September 1997, we experienced very hard and atrocious times. When war broke out in Kigali, Rwanda, in April 1994, we fled destitute and in panic, leaving behind all of our belongings. Along with hundreds of thousands of other Rwandans, we traveled on foot for almost a week, walking ninety miles to reach Bukavu, DRC. Upon arriving in Bukavu, the Congolese soldiers stole any valuables we were carrying with us — money, radio, mattress, clothes. Many Rwandan refugees died from starvation and diarrhea, and we thank God for protecting us, even though we were struck by extreme hunger and other ailments. By God's grace, humanitarian organizations came to rescue us, distributing plastic sheeting for shelter, food, and other basic materials to support refugees living in the camps.

After living in refugee camps for two years, in October 1996 the Rwandan military invaded all of the camps in the DRC. Many were killed. We escaped and managed to live by running west into the forests in the interior of the DRC, again leaving behind any belongings we had accumulated. In the forests, *many died* from war, disease, hunger, fatigue, and wild animals. Some refugees managed to cross the entire country by foot (more than *1,500* miles) to *seek* refuge in other countries. We stopped in the Équateur province, after traveling more than five hundred miles by foot, because a family member was seriously ill. After waiting for nine months, we finally decided to return to our home country of Rwanda, facilitated by the UN High Commission for Refugees.

Throughout this journey of three-and-a-half years, we were separated from many family members — some whom we know are dead, and others whom we have not heard from to this day.

Grace's story ends fairly well: A safe return to her home country, a reestablished life, a family, and a testimony of God's evident protection. Yet for each one who has been able to return home and rebuild life in Rwanda and Burundi, many others have disappeared and are either dead or still living outside of their home country as refugees.

I work and pray for governments that seek true peace, justice, and equity among people. In some of the most difficult moments I take solace in God's promise through Isaiah 9:6 – 7:

> For to us a child is born, to us a son is given, and the government
>   will be on his shoulders.
> And he will be called Wonderful Counselor, Mighty God,
> Everlasting Father, Prince of Peace.
> Of the increase of his government and peace there will be no end.
> He will reign on David's throne and over his kingdom,
> establishing and upholding it with justice and righteousness
> from that time on and forever.

For Grace, and the many millions of other refugees around the world who have seen their lives utterly shattered: May the Prince of Peace reign in our hearts *and* governments.

BIO

Dan Brose is a graduate of Oregon State University (BS ChE) and Stanford University (MS ChE). Dan is World Relief's Director of International Programs, providing leadership for the implementation of World Relief's international activities. Prior to serving in his present role, Dan was Regional Director for World Relief in the Great Lakes region of Africa (Rwanda, Burundi, and Congo). Dan also served as World Relief Country Director in Burundi (2003 – 2007) and Rwanda (2001 – 2005). Under Dan's leadership, World Relief's activities in the Great Lakes region of Africa focused on mobilizing the church to be active in preventing the spread of HIV/AIDS and to care for those who are infected and affected by HIV/AIDS; micro-finance and economic development; community health education; refugee assistance and resettlement; and encouragement of the church in its own self-initiated activities.

Visible Redemption

Richard Angoma

I've seen redemption in the flesh; his name is Geoffrey.

For over twenty years a civil war in northern Uganda has ripped apart the lives of the people there. Until recently this devastating war has raged almost unnoticed by the rest of the world. The conflict is between the Lord's Resistance Army (LRA), a twisted rebel group with astonishingly brutal tactics, and the government of Uganda. The LRA is capable of unspeakable cruelties: machete massacres, forced cannibalism, families burned alive in their huts, padlocked lips, and victims chained to trees and left to starve. Well over one million people have been forced to flee their homes to seek security at camps for internally displaced persons (IDPs), and thousands upon thousands of people have been killed and maimed.[14] Thousands of children have been orphaned, and many additional thousands have been abducted to serve as slaves — the boys as child soldiers and the girls as sex slaves for the soldiers. Though the situation has improved of late, it is by no means completely resolved.

Geoffrey, now seventeen, was abducted by the LRA when he was just eleven years old. On that horrible evening, Geoffrey and his brothers were asleep in one of the huts in the village of Kitgum. They were awoken abruptly by loud kicks on the door and harsh voices outside, demanding entry. Gripped by fear, the boys didn't move. Without warning, the door was suddenly kicked opened. It was the LRA. In the ensuing confusion, two of Geoffrey's older brothers were able to escape. Geoffrey and his youngest brother, however, were not so lucky. They were abducted by the LRA soldiers and marched hundreds of miles north to the LRA camp in southern Sudan. For the next two months the LRA brainwashed them, turning them into child soldiers. Geoffrey spent the next two years in the LRA camp until he finally escaped and returned home. Geoffrey has not heard from or seen his younger brother since he escaped.

There are few opportunities for families or people like Geoffrey who have been displaced by something as horrific as the war in northern Uganda. Many flee with absolutely nothing but the clothes on their back. They've left everything: their friends, fields, and even families as entire villages were burned to the ground by the LRA.

My family owns five hundred acres of fertile farmland in the northwestern district of Masindi. In 2000, against the backdrop of this brutal war, God made it clear that my calling was to help refugees. I started Family Empowerment Uganda (FEM) to serve those displaced by the war. We do this by empowering displaced families, widows, and orphans.

Empowering means not just giving someone what they need but teaching and equipping them to provide it for themselves. The best way to do this in northern Uganda is through sustainable and profitable agriculture. The displaced families use a plot of my family's land to begin farming again — free of charge. We share farming implements and seeds until the families have enough income to buy their own. Both crop and animal husbandry have yielded enormous economic benefits for the displaced families who arrived with nothing at all. Crops such as sunflower, sim-sim (sesame seeds), groundnuts (peanuts), and passion fruit have proven profitable. Animals such as goats, poultry, and cattle have also contributed to many families' income. The goal is that within a few years, the family will be able to save enough money to move from our land to their own plot.

Beyond sustenance, the need for education is great. For many, the LRA's presence has resulted in years (if not decades) of life in IDP camps, where children and adults alike have been denied formal schooling and vocational training. When many displaced families are struggling to provide food for their children, education quickly becomes a luxury instead of a certainty. Yet education is one of the strongest hopes for the future. With the proceeds from our agricultural projects, we are able to support the education of 174 orphans, providing materials such as books, pens, and pencils. For those who are not of school age, we have started a vocational training center.

Considering the past trauma that has been experienced by everyone who comes to FEM for help, we've learned that we can't meet physical and material needs without addressing the deep emotional and spiritual needs as well. The good news of Jesus Christ is that he can redeem unthinkable evil. It may sound trite, but if you could hear the stories of those who come to FEM, you would agree: only Jesus Christ can bring restoration to the traumatized. Weekly prayer meetings, Bible studies about God's forgiveness and unconditional love, and the evident work of the Spirit have helped to bring true healing where you would never think it possible.

Thomas is just one example. Thomas, twenty-five, was abducted by the LRA several years ago. Despite the unspeakable experiences of brainwashing, physical abuse, and forced murder, today Thomas is a joyful, vibrant member of our community. From a human perspective, that sort of healing isn't possible in just a few short years. But for God, everything is possible.

In the past eight years we've been able to help more than two hundred displaced families and five hundred orphans move away from trauma, poverty, and disease — and toward a hopeful future. Today, Geoffrey is back in school, continuing his education. Likewise, Thomas is a thriving member of our community. They both have plots of land on our farm and work diligently to provide what they need to survive. They are both leaders in our weekly worship meetings and have a vibrant passion for Christ.

Like the winter sweet shrub that lies dormant through the long, hot summers until it flowers in the unlikely months of December and January, even the most scarred and damaged life can grow once again when watered by the grace and love of our God.

BIO

Richard Angoma is the founder and executive director of Family Empowerment Uganda, a non-profit organization that brings hope and empowerment to families that have been ravaged by war, poverty, and disease in the East African country of Uganda. Born thirty-four years ago to parents from northern Uganda, Richard has lived and suffered through years of war and witnessed the brutal effects of it on children, widows, and families.

Love in the Desert

Janet Lenz

I made my way along a dusty passageway to the large metal door of the building. I had been delivered here late in the night and had yet to see the surroundings. Opening the door, I was hit with a blast of hot air, as if I had opened the door of an oven. As my eyes adjusted to the blinding sunlight, I took in the desert scene and gasped. I was in the Sahara Desert of North Africa, standing in a refugee camp. Covering the barren landscape was a sea of tents, seeming to move as waves of heat rose from the scorched ground. Figures draped in flowing robes leaned into the wind, shielded from the sun and blowing sand only by the gauzy fabric they held over their faces. A single question preoccupied me: "Who are these people surviving in this hellish place?"

Growing up as a pastor's daughter, and now a pastor's wife, my life had revolved around church. I have always been shy and fearful, and my sheltered history had not prepared me for this radically different world. I'd never met a refugee, never been to Africa, and never met a Muslim. But now I was standing before the Saharawi people, whose homeland of Western Sahara had been taken from them by Morocco in the early 1970s. This entirely Muslim people group had taken refuge in one of the most uninhabitable places on earth. I was here because I had agreed to escort nine Saharawi children to spend two months of the summer with families from our church. Having experienced an increasing sense of panic in the weeks before my trip, I was surprised at the deep sense of confirmation that settled into my heart just then.

That week, as I moved among the camps meeting families and hearing their stories, I experienced the Spirit of God in a new way. He was there as the Saharawi shared their tents, rations, and tea with me. He was there as they spoke of their longing to return to their homeland someday. Thirty years of peacefully waiting and hoping, repeatedly expressed in every parting with their words, "Please don't forget us …" I knew these people were forever sealed in my heart, as they are in God's.

One day I asked a bright, beautiful, young Saharawi woman what she remembered of her homeland. She described a day when her father had taken her little hand in his and led her through the doorway of her house. Not wanting to alarm her, he gently explained that her family had to leave quickly. As her little legs tried to keep up with her daddy's steps, she looked back at her house and the blue door that was now locked behind them. She sighed, then with a trembling voice, she said, "Someday, I will go back there, and I will look and look and look until I find that blue door. And then I will be home."

I write this while sitting in the little office of our church's English school, about one hundred yards from the place where I spoke with this young woman in 1999. Over two

hundred Saharawi children have now spent summers with U.S. families. Since that time, over four hundred followers of Christ have traveled to the camps, building relationships and conducting programs for youth. In addition to establishing our English school, we have led, at the request of the religious and political leaders in the camps, several worship concerts and seminars on the theme of "Who Is Christ?" Initial fear and suspicion have gradually matured into respect, favor, and outright honor as believers come here to live out their love of God with these Muslim people.

Today there are still approximately 150,000 Saharawi people living as refugees in the barren landscape of the Sahara. Sometimes it feels overwhelming; for a long time I was convinced there was no way a pastor's wife from Wisconsin could have an impact in this faraway place. But our church's advocacy on behalf of the Saharawi is beginning to yield results. God has opened up doors at the United Nations, allowing us to speak on behalf of those who have no voice at all. We are beginning to connect our work in the camps with the refugees' homeland of Western Sahara, where 200,000 Saharawi remain.

One step at a time, we're doing all that we can to bring that young woman closer to that blue door.

BIO

Janet was raised as a pastor's daughter. She married Bill Lenz in 1981, and together they founded Christ the Rock Church in Menasha, Wisconsin, where Bill continues to serve as the senior pastor. While raising their three sons, Janet served in many ministries in their growing church, including those focusing on worship, children, and women. For the past eleven years, Janet has led the Missions/Outreach ministry, where she has become deeply involved in working with the Saharawi people, a displaced Muslim nation living in exile in refugee camps in the Sahara Desert of North Africa. Through a wide range of programs, believers from across the U.S. and beyond are bridging the great distance and differences that have isolated the Saharawi from the world.

NOW WHAT?

Tens of millions of people live as refugees. Whatever the cause, these men, women, and children have been torn from their former lives and forced to move in order to survive. A stable, safe home is something most of us take for granted. Throughout the Scriptures, it is clear that refugees are close to the heart of God. Are they close to your heart? Spend some time reflecting on this question and consider how you might engage with the world's refugees.

Reflect

1. *What do you think?* How has this section been for you to read? Frustrating? Confusing? Enlightening? All of the above? Why do you think this section has evoked the feelings and response that it has? Take some time to journal about your experience reading this section. Include the thoughts and emotions that it called up, as well as anything new you may have learned. And don't be afraid to ask yourself some hard questions, and then work to find some answers.

2. *Put yourself in another's shoes.* Imagine that you wake tonight to the sound of machine gun fire outside your house. A war has just broken out in your country, and you must leave tomorrow and flee for safety. You must leave the majority of your possessions. This is life or death — what do you take? What is most important to you, and what will you need to survive on your own? What will be hardest for you to do without?

3. *How do you use the term "aliens"?* In this section, we've used the term aliens because it is one of the words used in English translations of the Bible to refer to people we now call refugees, immigrants, asylum seekers, strangers, and sojourners. It's a strange term — it's not like they're from another planet. But refugees often come from cultures and countries that are entirely foreign to us. They may speak different languages, have customs that you and I have never heard of, and tell stories very different from our own. In the past, how have you responded to aliens and refugees — others from different cultures? Have you extended hospitality and welcome? Have you treated them as if they

were from another planet? Have you surrounded yourself with people so much like yourself that you have simply never encountered an "alien"? Try to articulate the mind-set and paradigms which are at work in you under the surface. Does that mind-set hold up in light of Christ's great love? If not, how might you begin to tweak it?

4. **Contemplate minority status.** Have you ever been in the minority? The stranger in a strange land? The only one who doesn't speak the language? Have you ever felt like an alien? If you have, it probably taught you a lot about what to do and what not to do when you are in the majority. It is hard to imagine what it feels like to be the alien if you've never experienced it. If you've never been in this situation, think of a way that you can put yourself in this sort of situation. Fair warning: It probably will be uncomfortable, but you might learn something about compassion and hospitality. If you have experienced life in the minority, remember what it felt like. When did you feel comfortable? Welcomed? What felt alienating? Allow these experiences to shape your attitude and actions toward strangers you meet in the future.

Pray

Spend time praying for refugees and the situations that cause them to flee their homes. Write out your prayer to the Lord as the words come to mind. List a few countries that are affected by this — both the countries refugees are fleeing *from* and those they are fleeing *to*. Pray specifically for refugees and those who are helping them. Ask God to provide for this day's needs, but also to provide sustainable solutions that restore homes and bring God glory.

Respond

1. **Be hospitable.** Spend some time exploring how you can help refugees around the world. Connect with one of the organizations listed on the next few pages and see if it would be possible for you to help someone resettle in your area. You don't just have to help refugees either. If you know anyone who has moved into your neighborhood recently, have them over for dinner and ask them to tell you more about the life that they left behind (whether it was in a different country or a different county).

2. **Be a good consumer.** There are many opportunities to buy items made by former refugees. The next time you need to buy a gift, instead of heading to the nearest mall,

consider going online and ordering an item made by a refugee. Not only will the gift be unique and beautiful, you will be helping someone provide for their family and start afresh.

3. *Advocate politically.* Spend some time writing or calling your local officials, asking them to make policy decisions that benefit refugees who are attempting to seek asylum in your country. Go to *www.congress.org* (U.S.), *www.parliament.uk* (UK), or *www.parl.gc.ca* (Canada) for useful tools that let you contact your elected representatives directly. Let your voice be heard and get as many others involved as you can.

4. *Become a refugee co-sponsor.* Church World Service is an organization that connects refugees coming into the United States with congregations in more than twenty states across the country. Visit *www.churchworldservice.org* to see if your local congregation can help refugees coming to the United States. This means becoming friends, sharing resources such as time, knowledge, and money, and helping them however you can. It's a powerful way to show love to a stranger.

Spread the Word

It feels daunting to confront such a global problem on your own. But tremendous change can happen when we work together. Would you consider spreading the word about the need to extend hospitality and welcome those who are refugees, as well as the organizations that are doing something to make a difference? Now that you've read this chapter, it isn't "someone else's responsibility" — it's yours. Change begins with individual people deciding that they are going to live differently. What role can you play? Maybe it's inviting some friends to coffee, starting an action group at your church, or getting your youth group to hold a rally. Help change lives. Spread the word. To help you do so, we've designed a simple and effective tool: *www.zealouslove.org/spread*.

Share Your Ideas

Have a great idea about something other people can do to engage with refugees? Do you want to connect with others who are getting involved? Join the conversation at *www.zealouslove.org/share*.

Discover More

In the Field Notes you've heard from several contributors about the harsh reality of life as a refugee. You've also heard about the incredible work that's being done to address the needs of refugees, both on a personal and corporate scale. Remember, there is no "one size-fits-all" solution. It requires different organizations and different people working together. If you want to get involved in this area, check out the following organizations. Also, you can visit *www.ZealousLove.org/refugees* for updated information.

World Relief

Vision: For more than sixty years, World Relief has stayed true to its original mission to empower the church to serve the poor in the name of Jesus Christ.

Method: The church's strength in numbers, integration in the community, and moral authority make it an ideal agent for change in communities and societies. World Relief works through 7,000 local churches ministering to the poor around the world. World Relief's 31,000 volunteers testify to a global church that transcends geography, denomination, and ethnic affiliation. Our volunteers multiply our efforts twenty times over. World Relief's impact is permanent life change and sustainable community transformation from within, led by the local church.

Contact:
World Relief
7 East Baltimore St
Baltimore, MD 21202
Phone: (800) 535-5433
www.worldrelief.org

Church World Service

Vision: Church World Service works together with partners to eradicate hunger and poverty and to promote peace and justice around the world.

Method: Founded in 1946, Church World Service is a cooperative ministry of thirty-five Protestant, Orthodox, and Anglican denominations, providing sustainable self-help and development, disaster relief, and refugee assistance in eighty countries. Within the United States, Church World Service assists communities in responding to disasters, resettles refugees, promotes fair national and international policies, provides educational resources, and offers opportunities to join a people-to-people network of local and global caring through participation in CROP Hunger Walks, the Tools and Blankets Program, and the CWS Kits Program.

Contact:
Church World Service
28606 Phillips Street
PO Box 968
Elkhart, IN 46515
Phone: (800) 297-1516
www.churchworldservice.org

Family Empowerment Uganda

Vision: Family Empowerment Uganda exists to help refugees (individuals and families) displaced by the brutal Lord's Resistance Army (LRA) conflict in northern Uganda establish a new life.

Method: Located in northwestern Uganda, FEM-Uganda helps meet needs of families who are victims of war, poverty, and disease through four broad activities: agriculture, evangelism, formal education, and healthcare.

Contact:
  www.familyempowermentuganda.com

Additional Resources

www.amaniafrica.org

www.invisiblechildren.com

www.notforgotteninternational.org

www.unhcr.org

www.worldvision.org

Visit *www.zealouslove.org/ refugees* for more information and organizations.

HUNGER

No, this is the kind of fasting I want:
Free those who are wrongly imprisoned;
lighten the burden of those who work for you.
Let the oppressed go free,
and remove the chains that bind people.
Share your food with the hungry,
and give shelter to the homeless.
Give clothes to those who need them,
and do not hide from relatives who need your help.

Isaiah 58:6 – 7 NLT

It's easy for Christians to get caught up in their religious practices, which is exactly what God addresses here through the prophet Isaiah. He does not want us to go through the motions of fasting, worshiping, or praying without engaging our hearts. And if our hearts *are* engaged, not only will we fast, worship, and pray, we will "spend [ourselves] in behalf of the hungry (Isa. 58:10)."

What does it mean for us to "spend ourselves" on behalf of those who are in need?

BRIEFING

Danae and I recently had a layover in the Denver airport. Since we were hungry, we made a stop at the terminal food court. Soon it was clear that nearly every other person in the airport had the same idea — lines stretched across the tile floor, and people's patience was stretched to the breaking point.

Deciding what to eat was overwhelming. Five restaurants were open for business, and each restaurant advertised more than seventy options or combinations on their menu — it was a long layover, so I counted. That's more than 350 choices in one airport terminal food court. I don't remember what we ordered, but I do remember sitting at one of the sticky tables and looking around the food court in complete astonishment.

Hardly anyone *finished* all of their food that day, despite the inflated airport prices. As people came and went, sandwiches, salads, and soggy soda cups were pitched into fast-filling garbage containers, one after the other. Midway through our meal we heard an announcement that our flight was boarding. In a mad rush we tried to take a few more bites but ended up pitching the remains into the trash as we ran to our gate.

Memories like that always make me feel a little sheepish when I consider the hunger faced by others in our world. Most of us in the developed world have so much that we can throw away excess food without even a second thought. Or, we don't eat to survive; we eat because we like good food. Some of us even eat way too much. That's a big reason why tens of millions in developed countries like ours die from heart attacks, cancer, and diabetes every year. We spend billions overeating — and billions more on self-help books so we can work off the extra poundage. Just walk into a bookstore and you'll doubtless see a well-stocked diet section with subtitles like *An Owner's Manual to Waist Management* and *Train Your Brain to Think Like a Thin Person.*

In stark contrast, more than 923 million people around our world are hungry.[1] An undernourished or malnourished person is someone who is consistently unable to get enough of the calories or the right nutrients their body needs to be healthy. In the tiny country of Burundi, for example, two out of every five people are undernourished.[2] Nearly one-third of all children in developing countries are underweight or stunted because of a lack of food.[3] Worldwide, more than two billion people (nearly one-third of the world's population), are undernourished.[4] Every year some nine million people die from hunger and hunger related issues.[5] That means more than 25,000 every day, one every 3 seconds or so.

Those fortunate enough to not die from hunger may be unable to live the energetic, healthy lives God intended. Hunger weakens the body's immune system, making people more susceptible to opportunistic diseases which claim still more lives — more than half of malaria deaths are related to undernourishment.[6] Chronic malnutrition can have lifelong implications by impeding a child's mental and physical growth and thus irrevocably affecting life even if later adequate nutrition becomes available. An organization called Bread for the World says it well: "Hunger is, in essence, the most basic form of poverty, where individuals or families cannot afford to meet their most basic need for food."[7]

A terrible irony in our world today is that while the developing world struggles to feed itself, the developed world is killing itself with its eating habits. Cardiovascular disease is caused by (among other things) diets high in saturated fat and cholesterol. It is *the* leading cause of death in the United States.[8] According to the World Health Organization (WHO), heart attacks and strokes cause nearly 17 million deaths around the globe every year.[9] One doctor noted that cultures with significantly lower rates of heart disease usually have significantly different dietary patterns than those plagued by heart disease — namely, they consume less fat and cholesterol.[10] Astonishingly, coronary heart disease in the United States alone costs approximately $150 billion in direct and indirect costs each year.[11] By contrast, the World Food Programme's entire budget for 2006 was around $2.7 billion.[12]

> When someone steals a man's clothes, we call him a thief. Should we not give the same name to one who could clothe the naked and does not? The bread in your cupboard belongs to the hungry man; the coat hanging in your closet belongs to the man who needs it; the shoes rotting in your closet belong to the man who has not shoes; the money which you hoard up belongs to the poor.
>
> **Basil the Great**

Does God care about those who are hungry in our world? During the time of Moses, he provided manna to meet the Israelites' need for sustenance in the wilderness. He's opposed to hoarding, though — those who took more than they needed found it rotten and full of maggots the next day (see Ex. 16). We would do well to heed this lesson today in our culture of overeating and self-indulgence. In the New Testament we need not look any farther than Matthew's gospel for another indication of God's concern for those who are hungry.

"Bring them here to me," he said. And he directed the people to sit down on the grass. Taking the five loaves and the two fish and looking up to heaven, he gave thanks and broke the loaves. Then he gave them to the disciples, and the disciples gave them to the people. They all ate and were satisfied, and the disciples picked up twelve basketfuls of broken pieces that were left over. The number of those who ate was about five thousand men, besides women and children.

Matthew 14:18–21

Maybe a better question for us to ask is this: if God cares enough to work miracles both in the Old and the New Testaments so that people could eat, how should we care for those who are hungry in our world right now?

In one of my favorite Calvin and Hobbes comics, Calvin's parents order him to finish his

vegetables because there are starving children in China who would love to eat the food he's pushing around on his plate. After leaving the table, his vegetables still uneaten, Calvin finds a large box, tape, and a marker. A few days later, much to his mother's chagrin, a box full of moldy, decomposing vegetables is returned to her front door with "INSUFFICIENT POSTAGE" stamped on the top. Calvin had addressed it to "The Starving Children of China."

Caring for those around the world who are hungry is not about rummaging through our pantries and sending expired cans of lima beans to some faraway land (although giving our extra food to a local organization would be a good start). Today's world food scene is complicated. Food is transported on massive cargo ships. Government subsidies and trade negotiations artificially increase or suppress the price of staple commodities. UN helicopters drop 100-kilo bags of rice to desperate families in desolate places. At the time of this writing, high gas prices are crippling aid agencies' ability to transport life-saving wheat, rice, and corn to those in need. No wonder it feels as if people like us are too small to do anything meaningful.

Rather than becoming discouraged, however, we can begin with small steps, knowing we will one day be asked what we *did* — not what we *thought* about doing. A good start is being thankful for the food we *do* have. Imagine a child eating half the sandwich her mother made her and then throwing the rest out the car window because she was "finished." Any parent would be understandably frustrated. Is it any different with God? The idea that my food is *mine* to waste as I see fit (because I bought it, made it, or grabbed it from the fridge) falls apart when we remember that "every good and perfect gift is from above" (James 1:17).

Beyond thankfulness, there are other ways to get involved in helping those who are hungry. Possibilities range from writing politicians about agricultural laws to changing how you buy the food you eat. Supporting local farmers' markets and even growing your own vegetables can help you appreciate how food makes it from soil to supper. Many organizations have programs designed to remedy hunger in the short term (relief) and address the long-term causes (development). Given the disparity between what happens with food in developed countries (waste and over-indulgence) and in developing countries (malnutrition and undernourishment), inaction really isn't an option. Working to end hunger is a long road, but surely we can do no less than start walking, trusting that the Lord will lead us.

Remember Sodom?

Debbie Diederich

For years I've obsessed about my weight. Since I was twelve, I can't remember a single day when I didn't think about what I'd eaten — and either regretted it or felt encouraged that I'd finally stuck to my daily promise of "being good." Last night, again, as I lay in bed reliving the day, I took the usual inventory of the food I'd consumed and the latest exercise program I did or didn't follow. I'm not alone.

Did you know that Americans spend $50 billion a year on weight loss and nutritional products?[13]

So what's the answer? Should we stop eating? Or stop exercising? No, but a good place for us to start is to begin sharing what we have with those in need. The Bible is clear about this. Ezekiel 16:49 says, "Now this was the sin of your sister Sodom: She and her daughters were arrogant, overfed and unconcerned; they did not help the poor and needy." Do I need to remind you what happened to Sodom?

I remember the day this first hit home. I was doing a radio interview about the 30 Hour Famine, a hunger awareness program I manage for World Vision. During the interview, I was asked if I ever got discouraged knowing that 14,000 children die every day from hunger.[14] The simple answer was "Yes!" but what came out of my mouth was, "Yes it's discouraging, especially when I know that if we Americans ate just a little less, we could stop spending so much on weight loss, and instead give more to feed people who really need it!"

Every day in my job at World Vision, I struggle to find new and creative ways to wake up a nation that is self-consumed — and it's a wake-up call that I need as well. I wonder how we would feel if our children were wasting away before our eyes and we were helpless to do anything about it. Would we keep spending billions on overeating, then follow it up by going on the latest weight loss fad while they starved?

It sounds bleak, doesn't it? This is the kind of information no one wants to hear. But there is good news! There is a generation that has heard these awful statistics — in fact, they embrace them, write them on signs, T-shirts, websites, anywhere that will draw attention and cause people to get involved. Every year, half a million teenagers raise millions of dollars through World Vision's 30 Hour Famine to help feed and care for hungry people around the world. They pledge to go thirty hours without food and get friends and family to sponsor them. During their thirty-hour fast, many of them go out into their communities and serve.

Not long ago I visited a youth group at a church in Spokane, Washington. They had decided to open up their church to local homeless men and women during their Famine event. Even though the youth were hungry, they didn't complain as they prepared sandwiches and soup for their guests. Then they did the most important thing of all — they sat and visited with their guests while they ate. I watched in amazement as young people explained why they were going without food. I expected the homeless men and women to react with surprise, but instead there was nodding of heads and tears of appreciation as they listened to what these teenagers had to say. In return, some of the homeless shared their own stories. Over time, friendships were formed and the youth group committed to extend another invitation soon.

Later the teenagers told their youth pastor they wanted to start feeding the homeless every week. But how would they pay for it? First, they found out how much the church was spending on disposable cups and plates each month. They calculated that if the church purchased reusable cups, plates, and silverware — and if the youth washed them after every church function — the savings would be plenty to prepare food each week for the homeless!

I still obsess about my weight and feel guilty that I don't exercise enough. Like many of us, I have the best of intentions, but unfortunately my priorities are not always in line with God's. Caring for our bodies *is* important — don't get me wrong — but not at the expense of caring for *the* body of Christ. God's children around the world are calling us out of our easy lives to share our excess food, lest we be condemned as Sodom was before us.

BIO

As Youth Marketing Director, Debbie Diederich oversees the 30 Hour Famine at World Vision. Debbie has been involved with the Famine since its second year in existence and has helped to make it into an international movement. Since its inception, Famine teams have raised more than $100 million to support World Vision's global aid and development programs. Debbie lives in Auburn, Washington, with her husband, Paul. They are the proud parents of four sons and have three grandchildren.

We're Farmers, Just Like You

Laurie Kaniarz

It's traditional for American farmers to help neighbors in need: building barns, bringing in crops, lending tools — whatever needs to be done for another farm family to get them on their feet again. Through Foods Resource Bank (FRB), many farmers across the country are carrying on this tradition — it's simply that their "neighborhood" now includes the developing world.

Agricultural projects from Maryland to Oregon produce a crop, market it, and make the funds available to FRB. Working through the in-country presence, infrastructure, and experience of its member organizations (fifteen Christian denominations and their local partners), FRB's overseas programs enhance food security. We try to "help people feed themselves" in some of the world's poorest communities in places like sub-Saharan Africa, Asia, Eastern Europe, the Middle East, Central and South America, and the Caribbean.

Americans are generally aware that we are a wealthy nation. Yet most are amazed to learn about the challenging environments in which "non-wealthy" people live — and survive — around the world. In the Bamba and Machakos regions of Kenya, for example, temperatures are searing and water is scarce. Women and children are often forced to walk more than eight hours a day in search of water to carry home in back-breakingly heavy five-gallon jerry cans. Never mind irrigating crops — there isn't enough available water to do that.

Separating particular aspects of poverty is nearly impossible. Think about it: hunger is related to food, food needs water to grow, so a lack of food is compounded by a lack of water, which causes people to travel great distances, which undercuts health and education, and so on. Through food-for-work programs aimed at making sustainable water available (dams, numerous water pans, handmade water jars for rooftop collection), the average distance to water points has been reduced significantly for people in the Bamba and Machakos regions. This improves health and hygiene and frees up residents to care for their families, crops, and livestock.

Not only has nutrition improved, families are saving extra money to buy basic medicines and enroll their children in school. Drought-tolerant crops such as amaranth and animals like goats and cows make it easier to produce food in this parched land. People are being trained in how to market their crops and animal products to increase their income. Environmental conservation efforts — terraces, tree planting, and dry-land farming — are improving yields and making communities more resilient in times of crisis.

A Machakos resident named Luki, who received a cow from our program, now has monthly income from the sale of milk. Because of this Luki has been able to welcome five needy youngsters into her family. Her mango trees, planted in holes to make better use of scarce water, will bring additional income. Luki says she now has a clear way to get out of poverty that, until now, has always been an inescapable reality.

Similar efforts are being made in the Western Hemisphere. The daily struggles of those living in the highlands of Guatemala would overwhelm most of us reading this book. Steep, mountainous, often eroded terrain is a challenge to farm. More than thirty years of armed conflict has taken a profound physical, psychological, and economic toll on the poor. The highland population consists mainly of women, children, and the elderly; most of the able-bodied men and boys have no choice but to travel north on foot to seek work. Yet in the words of Roberto Muj, part of FRB's program, "The farmers take what they have, what the land has given them, and use it to their best advantage. They use what they have instead of complaining about what they don't have."

FRB and its partners supply tools and training, assisting communities with improvements such as water recycling and greenhouses to guard against the killing frosts so common at high altitude. Using discarded tires for contained patio gardening makes it possible for the very old and the very young to grow food without having to travel far from home.

All over the world subsistence farmers and their families are hard at work improving their lives and experiencing hope for the future — strengthened in part thanks to the compassionate support of FRB's U.S. agricultural growing project communities and volunteers.

When Kenyan farmers recently asked a visiting farmer from Ohio to thank all those who supported them in raising their own food, he replied, "Oh, it's nothing special. We're just farmers like you."

BIO

Laurie Kaniarz has been an administrative assistant at Foods Resource Bank since 2000, witnessing the enthusiasm of the people who make up the growing projects across this country and the joy of the program participants around the world. She taught English in Spain and Ecuador for six years; worked as customer service liaison for Latin America in the surgical instruments and vegetable-seed sectors; and now lives in Kalamazoo, Michigan, with her husband.

Speaking Up for the Hungry

Rev. David Beckmann

Around the world, more than 923 million people are undernourished. Nearly ten million (9.7 million to be precise) children younger than five die each year mostly from preventable causes.[15] Many of these deaths are directly linked to malnutrition.[16] Even in my own prosperous country, the United States, government data shows that 35 million people live in households struggling to put food on the table.[17] More than 12 million of those affected are children.[18]

Yet there has been progress. In the past decade, the United States has dramatically increased funding for programs that help people in poor countries feed their families and build a better future for their children. Globally, one child in three was malnourished forty years ago; today, it is one in six. The truth is that God has made it possible in our time to reduce hunger and poverty dramatically.

Bread for the World is a collective Christian voice to end hunger at home and abroad. Each of our faithful members has a personal story of advocacy. We are stronger when we act together in Christ's name to help our neighbors, whether they live in the next house, the next state, or on the next continent.

As one Bread for the World advocate put it, "Once the 'why' question is answered, the 'how' question is not hard to get past." Here is our approach: Bread for the World members work together to urge our nation's decision makers to end hunger at home and around the world. With the stroke of a pen, policies are made in Washington, DC, that redirect millions of dollars and affect millions of lives. Year after year, Bread members have won far-reaching changes in Congress on behalf of hungry people. We make our voices heard so that our laws are more just and compassionate to people in need.

Right now we're working to increase poverty-focused development assistance overseas and to pass the Global Poverty Act, which will make our assistance more effective. We write personal letters and emails to our representatives in Congress. Through "Offerings of

Letters," church members place the letters in the offering plate, dedicating them to God and saying prayers for those who are hungry and poor. Again and again, we have heard from members of Congress that the letters they receive from constituents have influenced specific votes or decisions. We also meet with our representatives and senators to discuss policy changes that could help end hunger and poverty. Each June, our members join together and make the journey to Capitol Hill to give their elected representatives this message in person.

We all need to connect advocacy to our local communities, personal relationships, and the wider world. Recently, Bread for World members organized a poverty-simulation experience for young people at a church in Waco, Texas. Special opportunities to participate in the church's food distribution program were offered, and a short series of discussions with guest speakers took place afterward. The guest speakers included an organizer from Bread for the World, the educational director of a sustainable agriculture farm, and the coordinator of a local community garden. Through experiences like this, the younger generation becomes knowledgeable and active against poverty and hunger in the world they are inheriting.

God's grace in Jesus shapes our lives. It moves us to reach out to others in love and seek justice where human dignity is at stake. The Bible is clear: love for God and neighbor requires both charity and justice. Jesus challenged his apostles and disciples two thousand years ago just as he challenges his disciples today: we must love our neighbors. Personal letters, emails, phone calls, and visits to our nation's decision makers go a long way toward providing help and opportunity for 923 million hungry neighbors around the world.

BIO

Rev. David Beckmann is the president of Bread for the World, a collective Christian voice urging our nation's decision makers to end hunger at home and abroad. He has served in this role since 1991, leading large-scale, successful campaigns to strengthen U.S. political commitment to overcoming hunger and poverty. Before that, he served at the World Bank for fifteen years, overseeing projects and driving innovations to make the Bank more effective in reducing poverty. Beckmann is a clergyman as well as an economist and is ordained by the Evangelical Lutheran Church in America.

Really "Cheerful" Givers

Francis Chan

It was my first trip to Africa, and I felt like I was living in one of those famine commercials on television. Naked children ran in and out of mud huts, obviously malnourished and underfed. I always thought I had compassion for the hungry, but the shocking reality of their predicament made me wonder if I'd ever really cared. It's one thing to be saddened by pictures; it's quite another to interact with people who eat less in a week than I do at one sitting. As I began to form friendships, my so-called compassion became a zealous determination not to ignore the needs of my new brothers and sisters.

I kind of knew I would cry when I first met victims of hunger — what I didn't expect was to fall in love with them. I also didn't expect to make a connection between those kids and my own. "Love your neighbor as yourself" translated to "love those kids like your own." I began to ask myself questions like *What would I want someone to do for my kid if she were the one starving, naked, and crying?*

But this story isn't about me. It's about the power of a loving church. All I had to do was come home and share my experience with a Spirit-filled congregation. The members of Cornerstone Church were quick to respond with several hundred thousand dollars in aid. Hundreds of orphans were sponsored, a school was started, and orphanages were built.

One of the greatest moments of my life was returning three years later to what used to be a bare jungle. Now it was a classroom filled with hundreds of healthy children. These kids were receiving meals, shoes, clothes, vitamins, and an education. I listened as they sang praise songs to Jesus with huge smiles on their faces. The teacher at one point interrupted her class, pointed to me, and told the kids, "This is Pastor Chan. All of you are sponsored by someone from his church." The kids erupted in cheers and applause.

I never thought of holding back my tears — this is the good stuff. I'm not exaggerating when I say it was one of the most joyful moments of my life. I don't know when I've ever felt happier or more fulfilled.

That experience changed my attitude toward giving. All my life, I thought of giving as something I was supposed to do. I even felt a bit self-righteous when I made sacrifices. I saw it as "suffering" for the sake of the Lord. I had no idea what Christ meant when he said, "It is more blessed to give than to receive" (Acts 20:35). You see, he meant it *literally*! He means that the givers will be *more blessed* than the receivers. That's a hard truth to peddle these days in our materialistic, self-focused culture. (You're probably thinking, "Here's where he asks for my money ...")

Before that trip back to Africa to see a classroom full of healthy kids, I was only thinking about the joy we'd bring to orphans when I asked a bunch of rich Americans to give. I had no idea this would be the very thing that caused our church to come alive. The result is a body of believers in Simi Valley, California, that is addicted to giving and has never been more joyful. When opportunities for giving are announced, our congregation gets excited. They literally cheer when we write checks. They cheer over the millions of dollars we send out annually. There's more cheering at Cornerstone than ever. Maybe that's what Christ meant by "cheerful givers."

BIO

Francis Chan is the pastor of Cornerstone Church and the president of Eternity Bible College in Simi Valley. He speaks to youth throughout the U.S., challenging them to deeper commitment. He is on the board for Children's Hunger Fund and World Impact. He recently authored his first book, *Crazy Love*. Francis and his wife, Lisa, have been married for fourteen years and have four children: Rachel, Mercy, Eliana, and Ezekiel.

Andy

Brad Meuli

The first time I met Andy, he was crying. I was relatively new to the Denver Rescue Mission, but I had heard about Andy. He'd been eighty-sixed by the mission staff for various reasons: fighting, swearing, belligerence, and so on. Some would say he was a mean drunk. The suspensions were always temporary because we knew he didn't have anywhere else to go — but that didn't make it any easier to put up with him.

I met Andy at our annual Great Thanksgiving Banquet, so I knew he wasn't crying because he was hungry — he'd just eaten a gourmet dinner complete with turkey, mashed potatoes, pumpkin pie, and all the trimmings. Each year we also hand out a "Thanksgiving Banquet" food box — a complete meal that includes a frozen turkey — to over a thousand needy families. Slightly intoxicated, Andy was crying because we wouldn't give him a frozen turkey. Steve, our director of programs, tried to comfort him, but Andy left feeling pretty depressed about his lack of a raw, frozen turkey.

It's not like he could have cooked it — Andy slept in our shelter most nights. For the last eight years, Andy had been coming to the Denver Rescue Mission, hungry, homeless, and most often intoxicated. For eight years our staff and volunteers prepared and served him food, loved him, prayed for him, and tried to encourage him to join our New Life Rehabilitation Program. Sometimes the result was a string of curses that would have made a sailor cringe.

Why did we keep trying to help him? We often say at the Denver Rescue Mission, "It all starts with a meal." Reaching out to the hungry that walk our streets shows that we care. It allows us to earn the right to be heard, to be able to share the Good News of Christ. When we take on the title of "servant" and serve a meal, we demonstrate our belief in Christ's ability to reach into the horrible depths and pits of our society and change someone's life — even one like Andy's.

After eight years of being on the streets and staying alive because of the meals he received at our mission, Andy's heart began to change. I'll never forget his words: "I want to change, I don't want to live like this anymore. I'm tired of being hungry, addicted, and alone on the street. I'll even try Jesus." On that day, thanks to the encouragement of countless volunteers and patient and dedicated staff, he entered our New Life Rehabilitation Program.

A year later, I asked Andy, "What are you the most thankful for?" Well dressed, sober, and changed forever by the love of Christ, he responded, "I'm just thankful I can just remember the last twelve months of my life. I can't remember the eight years before that. I cannot believe I was on the street all that time. The mission saved my life."

It all started with a meal — eight years of meals, as a matter of fact.

BIO

Brad Meuli joined the Denver Rescue Mission (DRM) in 1999 and was named president/CEO in January 2001. Before joining DRM he enjoyed a seventeen-year career in banking and served as a major in the Marine Corps. He is a licensed minister and a graduate of Denver Seminary. Brad currently serves on several boards including the City Mission World Association, an international organization for Rescue Missions. Brad is married and has five children and three grandsons.

NOW WHAT?

Those of us who can buy books (and thus, most people reading this book) generally don't have to worry about their next meal. Sure, you might not have any stellar ideas yet about what to cook, but remember — at this moment there are 923 million hungry people in our world. That kind of puts questions like "soup or spaghetti?" in perspective, doesn't it? Read through the following and consider how to engage the hunger issue and love your neighbor in the process.

Reflect

1. *What do you think?* What have you learned in this chapter on hunger? Were there any moments when you felt a long-held idea shift a little? Maybe you didn't know so many people were hungry in our world today. Maybe you've never before realized that you can play a role in helping people get the food they need. Has hearing about people who are starving to death changed how you think about your food? Does it make you feel guilty about eating? Or does it fill you with gratitude for the food you eat? Reflect on why you held this paradigm in the past, and how this has changed. Then consider what you think a healthy, sustainable response might look like.

2. *Imagine if you were hungry.* Do you think God feels differently to someone who is hungry? Someone once said, "There are people in the world so hungry that God cannot appear to them except in the form of bread."[19] How might your concept of God change if you were hungry? Would your prayers be different than they are now? How might your faith grow by thinking about your life from this perspective? What might your prayer-life be like if you were physically and tangibly desperate for God to provide?

3. *Examine your rhythms.* What are some habitual patterns in your life that you might need to reconsider after reading this section? What are some habits you might want to cultivate? It could mean eating a simpler meal once a week, choosing to buy fairly traded coffee, or making your lunch several times a week instead of eating out and then using that money to support an organization helping hungry people around the world.

4. **Who are you?** What is something you've discovered about yourself while reading *Zealous Love*? Is there an aspect of your character that you are proud of and want to cultivate more? Or perhaps you've discovered something that you are not proud of and hope to change? Dwell especially on the issue of what you consider "needs" in your life. Are they really needs or, in the context of the hundreds of millions of people who don't even have enough food, are they luxuries?

Respond

1. **Cultivate thankfulness.** Practice being thankful for the food and provision you have in your life. Practice being thankful for the small things — the crispness of an apple in October, the smell of garlic cooking, the satisfaction that comes after a delicious meal. Let each meal become an opportunity to give thanks. And may thankfulness lead you to generosity and action.

2. **Fast.** Try going without food for a while. It might be for one meal or one day. Or you might choose to fast from another aspect of your life that you enjoy — like television, dairy products, chocolate, or your cell phone. The process of going without has strong spiritual ramifications, but it also can help you better identify with some of the 923 million people around the world who are hungry right now. As you fast, think and meditate on the reality that you have the luxury of choice — you are fortunate enough to *choose* to go without, rather than having no option. Don't fast out of guilt or to lose weight or any other misconstrued motive. As you fast, allow the process to make you thankful for the abundant provision in your life, but may you also seek to empathize — to stand in solidarity, even for a short time — with hungry men, women, children, and families around our world.

3. **Eat simply.** This is a powerful thing to do with your family or a larger group. Determine to eat a very simple meal for dinner three nights in a row. Perhaps beans and rice with no extra condiments or flavorings, or maybe just rice if you truly want to experience what many others in the world consider normal. Interact with the people you're eating with, and try to listen for what the experience might teach you.

4. *A variation of this exercise that works with larger groups is to feed 15 percent of the people a gourmet dinner, complete with drinks and dessert.* Then feed 25 percent a very simple meal like a bowl of rice and beans. The final 60 percent get a small bowl of

rice or a single slice of bread. It will be uncomfortable and unfair — that's the point. This is roughly a microcosm of the global situation. Just because we can't literally see all our neighbors struggling with this hunger, it doesn't mean they're not there or that we don't have a responsibility to help.

5. *Add to your shopping list.* Next time you're at the grocery store, make a point of purchasing a few nonperishable food items to donate to your local food bank or soup kitchen. As you learn more about the needs in your area, make it a habit to add a few more items to your cart every time you are at the store. You might think that a couple of cans of beans or packages of pasta won't make a difference, but if it becomes a habit for you, that food will add up over the months and years, not to mention the change it will make in your own heart.

Spread the Word

It feels daunting to confront such a growing, worldwide evil on our own. But tremendous change can happen when we work together. Would you consider spreading the word about the world hunger crisis, the people whose lives are affected, and the organizations that are doing something to make a difference? Now that you've read this chapter, it isn't "someone else's responsibility" — it's yours. Change begins with individual people deciding that they are going to live differently. What role can you play? Maybe it's inviting some friends to coffee, starting an Action Group at your church, or getting your youth group to hold a rally. Help change lives. Spread the word. To get started, we've designed a simple and effective tool: *www.zealouslove.org/spread*.

Share Your Ideas

Have a great idea about something other people can do to engage the issue of hunger? Do you want to connect with others who are getting involved? Join the conversation at *www.zealouslove.org/share*.

Discover More

In the Field Notes you've heard from several contributors about the dire consequences of hunger. You've also read about the incredible work that's being done to address the issue, both on a personal and corporate scale. Remember, there is no "one-size-fits-all" solution. If you want to get involved in this area, check out the following organizations or visit *www .zealouslove.org/hunger.*

Bread for the World

Vision: Bread for the World is a collective Christian voice urging our nation's decision makers to end hunger at home and abroad.

Method: By changing policies, programs, and conditions that allow hunger and poverty to persist, we provide help and opportunity far beyond the communities where we live. God's grace in Jesus Christ moves us to help our neighbors, whether they live in the next house, the next state, or the next continent. We can end hunger in our time. Everyone, including our government, must do their part. By making our voices heard in Congress, we make our nation's laws more fair and compassionate to those in need. Bread for the World's downloadable brochure "Advocacy 101" offers more tips and examples for new advocates. The web site also provides links to hunger resources and lists Bread for the World regional organizers and upcoming events.

Contact:
Bread for the World
50 F Street, NW
Suite 500
Washington, DC 20001
Phone: (800) 82-BREAD
www.bread.org

Children's Hunger Fund

Vision: Serving children in need ... across America and around the world.

Method: Thousands of compassionate families fill Food Paks with nutritional food, which are delivered directly into the homes of families they have never met. Trained ministry partners pick up food from our warehouse and operate distribution centers, feeding nearly 30,000 people every week! Faithful volunteers package and prepare food, or wrap the thousands of toys given to children during the holiday season. Generous donors with a heart to feed and clothe the hungry write monthly checks, enabling our efforts to continue around the clock. Caring corporations give truckloads of quality products to those who could, otherwise, never afford them. In countries around the world, CHF builds strong relationships with indigenous leaders who have a passion for their own people, and provide food and other aid to support their ministries.

Contact:
Children's Hunger Fund
PO Box 7085
Mission Hills, CA 91346-7085
Phone: (800) 708-7589
www.childrenshungerfund.org

30 Hour Famine / World Vision

Vision: The 30 Hour Famine is an international youth movement to fight hunger.

Method: Since 1992, U.S. Famine participants have raised more than $100 million, saving lives and helping communities worldwide break the cycle of poverty to become self-sustaining. The Famine encourages and empowers teenagers to raise funds to help fight world hunger and poverty. During the Famine, teens go for 30 hours without food (consuming only juice) while they learn more about hunger through resources, games, and activity ideas provided by World Vision. They also perform service projects in their communities in response to the needs of the less fortunate. The 30 Hour Famine is the largest program of its kind and includes more than 21 participating countries annually. This year, an estimated $13 million will be raised in the U.S. alone.

Contact:

World Vision's 30 Hour Famine
PO Box 9716
Federal Way, WA
98063-9716
Phone: (800) 7-FAMINE
www.30hourfamine.org

Foods Resource Bank

Vision: A Christian Response to World Hunger.

Method: Foods Resource Bank (FRB) is committed to providing food security in the developing world through sustainable small-scale agricultural production, thereby allowing hungry people to know the dignity of feeding themselves. Member organizations are Christian denominations and/or their relief and development agencies. Revenues to support sustainable food security programs are generated in the U.S. through community growing projects involving landowners, farmers, agribusinesses, and churches.

Contact:

Foods Resource Bank
75 Remittance Drive, Suite 6539
Chicago, IL 60675-6539
Phone: (888) 276-4FRB (4372)
www.foodsresourcebank.org

Association of Gospel Rescue Missions (AGRM)

Vision: AGRM exists to proclaim the passion of Jesus toward the hungry, homeless, abused, and addicted.

Method: AGRM fosters and feeds a movement of diverse, energetic disciples who will see the practice of hospitality to the destitute as both a catalyst for life transformation in Jesus and a fundamental expression of their Christian faith, thus propelling the church into the lead role in society's quest to alleviate homelessness.

Contact:

Association of Gospel Rescue Missions
1045 Swift Street
Kansas City, MO 64116-4127 USA
Phone: (800) 4-RESCUE (624-5156)
www.agrm.org

Additional Resources

www.fao.org/wfd

www.feedingamerica.org

www.fh.org

www.freedomfromhunger.org

www.lifewind.org

www.wfp.org

Visit *www.zealouslove.org/ hunger* for more information and organizations.

LACK OF EDUCATION

"Then these righteous ones will reply,
'Lord, when did we ever see you hungry and feed you?
Or thirsty and give you something to drink?
Or a stranger and show you hospitality?
Or naked and give you clothing?
When did we ever see you sick or in prison and visit you?'
"And the King will say,
'I tell you the truth,
when you did it to one of the least of these
my brothers and sisters,
you were doing it to me!' "

Matthew 25:37–40 NLT

Jesus is talking here about the basics: food for the hungry, water for the thirsty, clothing for the naked, and companionship for the lonely. In some unfathomable way, the King of Kings views service rendered unto the "least of these" as service rendered unto him. When we serve those in our world who are in need, we are actually serving Christ himself. Inversely, when we close our eyes to the need, hunger, and pain of those in our world, we are not merely ignoring them, but also Christ himself.

Education is one of the best ways to create lasting change. By empowering the next generation with the tools they need to understand their world and perhaps shape it for the better, we are addressing a wide range of social injustices. Inversely, if we fail to care about the lack of education which exists in our world, we allow billions to remain trapped in cycles of poverty which have held captive generations before them.

BRIEFING

Education is not just about passing exams, getting good grades, or improving comparative national averages. It is about teaching people to think and equipping them with the tools necessary to improve the quality of life globally, nationally, regionally, and personally. Studies have shown that for every year of schooling someone has, there is a corresponding ten percent increase in that person's wages.[1] In East Africa, a person with at least some secondary schooling is significantly less likely to contract HIV than someone with no formal education.[2]

On the other hand, a lack of *quality* education keeps people entrenched in poverty. Of the more than 800 million illiterate adults in our world today, approximately 70 percent live in some of the world's most impoverished areas — namely, sub-Saharan Africa and East and South Asia.[3] If you live in America or Western Europe, you are likely to receive five or six more years of formal schooling than the typical person living in sub-Saharan Africa.[4] If we want to combat poverty — if we hope to see long-term, sustainable development improving the lives of those in need — then we must note the lack of education in our world. It is undeniably linked to the dismal quality of life endured by so many others.

Danae and I had the chance to connect with some missionary friends in Uganda not long ago. Over a meal one evening, they shared how they connect evangelism and development. "One without the other doesn't really make sense," they explained. It's like trying to clap with one hand.

Vocational training is part of this couple's ministry, along with Bible training, worship services, and church planting. In other words, they are educating people — empowering them with the knowledge needed to start their own businesses and improve their quality of life. One of the vocational endeavors is a baking school, where men and women learn how to create simple, nutritious bread that can be made without relying on industrial ovens.

One day during a baking class, the flour began to run low. Instead of canceling class, the students were instructed to cut the recipe in half. Unfortunately, none of the students, despite being secondary school graduates (roughly the equivalent of a high school diploma in the U.S.) knew how. Dumbfounded, the missionaries inquired further. While everyone in the class knew that "four divided by two is two," when it came to putting that knowledge into practice, nobody knew what to do with four cups of flour. A recent UNESCO report describes this kind of situation as a failure to "master a minimum set of cognitive skills."[5] It has everything to do with the environment in which a person is educated. Factors beyond a child's control — such as nutrition, the teacher's ability, and the teacher to pupil ratio — largely determine the outcome of the child's education.

A few days later, we visited some rural schools near Lira Town in northern Uganda. These were mud or brick buildings, with anywhere from 500 to 2,000 students at each. As we approached one of the schools, we noticed that the roof had collapsed over a classroom. When we asked the head teacher about it, he just laughed and shrugged. "It collapsed several years ago. We don't have money to fix it." Students who otherwise would have used that classroom instead gathered in the shade of a large tree on the school grounds, their class progressing with the aid of a chalk board propped against the trunk.

Continuing our tour of the school, we approached one of the noisier classrooms. Given that 93 million children[6] don't get to attend primary school, it was encouraging to see more than two hundred students crowded into this particular classroom. Unfortunately, it was only a 20-foot by 20-foot room, with no desks. Despite the conditions, the students paid close attention to the teacher.

> Living as we do in a world that suffers so much, two opposing possibilities can easily tempt us: either to turn our backs and live oblivious to the pain or to allow the pain to overwhelm us and despair to take up residence in our hearts. The truly faithful option is to face the pain and live joyfully in the midst of it. Those who suffer most remind us of how tragic and arrogant it would be for us to lose hope on behalf of people who have not lost theirs. They are teachers of joy.
>
> **Joyce Hollyday**

While their discipline and flexibility were admirable, such a high pupil-to-teacher ratio cannot help but negatively impact their quality of education.[7] Individual children will likely never receive one-on-one help with a new math concept or a rule of grammar, no matter how well behaved they are. And such classrooms are unable to make allowances for children who have learning disabilities or physical challenges.

A friend of ours is a Peace Corps volunteer in the tiny Central American country of Belize. One of his primary tasks is helping at a primary school in a rural village. The situation is bleak. Most of the children in Belize will never progress beyond the equivalent of a fourth grade education.

Upon realizing that students were performing poorly on a standardized national examination, the government of Belize decided to test primary school teachers to see how *they* performed on the same test. Many of the teachers didn't pass[8] — not exactly a great foundation for education.

Imagine, for a moment, that you had only received a fourth grade education — or worse yet, that you couldn't read or write at all. Where might you go for dependable information? How would you learn about improving your child's health? What job prospects would you have? How would you improve your family's situation?

If you have a college degree, consider how different your life would be if you had quit your education after high school. If you didn't go to college, consider what it would have been like if your family had run out of money for school fees when you were in the fifth

Courtesy of Micah Albert

grade. Consider what your job would be if you had to quit school at age ten to support your family. Those "imagine ifs" portray the reality faced by literally millions of children who have little or no formal education.

This is not just a problem in developing countries either. Some of the "Field Notes" contributors in this section are working to make a difference in the United States. Most of America's poorest citizens live in cities, where the public schools are often notoriously worse than those in wealthy suburbs. Nearly a quarter of all students in the United States do not graduate from high school on time, if at all.[9] More than two-thirds of those in the U.S. prison system do not have a high school diploma.[10] Even in developed countries, there is much work to be done in the area of education. After-school programs, tutoring opportunities, and mentoring programs can dramatically affect the education and ultimately the lives of students across the U.S.

A quality education dramatically alters a person's life. Literacy empowers people not only to read the Scriptures, but to gain access to a world of human knowledge that includes everything from nutrition and poetry to entrepreneurial insights and cultural expression. In addition, educated parents are more likely to educate their children, thereby helping to create a better future for the next generation.

The education of women is especially important. A study done by Oxfam showed that in Pakistani homes where the mother had no education, the infant mortality rate was 60 percent higher than in homes where the mother had had at least some education.[11] When a woman becomes educated, even at a basic level, it improves her entire household's ability to function. In the book *Three Cups of Tea*, Greg Mortenson quotes an African proverb he learned while growing up in Tanzania: "If you educate a boy, you educate an individual; if you educate a girl, you educate a community." What he has seen in his work in northern Pakistan and Afghanistan, where he builds schools for Muslim children, is that educated boys often leave their villages for the cities in search of better jobs, but educated girls stay, raising healthier children and prioritizing education for the next generation.

Despite the proven long-term impact of educating women, they still remain at a greater risk of illiteracy than men. Worldwide, there are just 88 literate women for every 100 literate men. In some countries, the disparity is much worse — 62 women for every 100 men in Bangladesh, while in Pakistan the ratio is 57 to 100.[12]

Despite the frustrating numbers, good things are happening. The number of children

Courtesy of Micah Albert

not attending primary school has dropped from 115 million in 2002 to roughly 93 million in 2006.[13] Although the responsibility of educating people falls largely on the shoulders of governments, we can help bring important changes. As citizens of countries with the resources to provide aid to developing countries, advocacy plays a vital role in addressing the global need for education. Additionally, many smaller organizations work to provide alternative and supplemental educational opportunities for students. From after-school tutoring programs in the United States to private, donor-funded scholarships in developing countries, we can love others by working to provide a quality education for the next generation.

What's a Hero?

Naomi Zacharias

From the time I was young, I have been a dreamer. I adored fairy tales like the story of Cinderella being rescued from injustice and taken to a world perfected by her fairy godmother, or tales of heroes on stallions whisking someone away from a troubled life to "happily ever after." I would daydream about my own story, always imagining a hero who would rescue me from whatever injustice or battle I was fighting and carry me away to a perfect, safe world. Once I grew up, I wondered if "happily ever after" even existed, or if fairy tales were only the stuff of children's stories. Now that I'm a few years older and a bit wiser, I think perhaps my problem was how I defined heroes and "happily ever afters."

She sat directly across from me, shifting nervously in her seat and absentmindedly moving the same piece of hair she had adjusted several times. For what must have been the tenth time, I reminded her she did not have to go through with it, and again she told me she wanted to. She needed to, she said. With that, she gave a nod. As the camera began rolling, she poised herself beautifully — though not entirely composed.

I'll call her Eva. She looked into the lens and told her story, how as a teenager she found herself on the street, living a life of prostitution in South Africa. Soon she found herself trapped in a world she never would have chosen. Drugs were at first a form of self-medication and then an addiction. Over the years she gave birth to two children, neither of whom she could afford to care for herself.

As Eva told her story, my mind flashed back two years to when first I met her. I was visiting South Africa on behalf of Wellspring International, the nonprofit initiative I worked for. I enjoyed my work, deciding which projects the nonprofit could adopt. But I fell in love with the people. Along the way, I met women whom I will never forget — women who were abused, abandoned, hardened, and broken. Some were rough around the edges, while others showed a vulnerability that melted me. Some were in prostitution; others were in hospice care; still others lived in shelters or raised their children amid desperate circumstances.

I realized how little separated me from these women. I couldn't possibly understand the depth of their pain, but I saw myself in their choices and their fragility. I saw the tough exterior that masked a longing inside to be known, protected, and loved. I saw the unrealized dreams that had long since been abandoned. These women maintained, somehow, a fervent desire to embrace life — to *be someone*, despite the crushing reality of their circumstances.

I couldn't look down on their choices because, standing face-to-face with these women, I wasn't convinced mine would be any different if I had been in their place. As Jacqueline Kennedy Onassis said, each of us is "a woman, above all else." And so while our stories were different and our specific hurts unique, we were, at root, connected.

I remember shaking Eva's hand when we met. On that particular trip I was visiting a rehabilitation home for women who previously had been engaged in prostitution. Eva had just moved in — for the eighth time.

Seven times she'd tried to escape her previous world, and seven times she found herself back on the street. She had no alternative means of support, but more importantly, she found that the familiar was less frightening than the unknown, regardless of how destructive the familiar was. With her success in the program would come freedom, but freedom to do what? Her previous identity and vocation might be removed, but replaced with what? You cannot create a void in someone, then choose not to fill it and expect her to become a whole, stable person. So seven times Eva returned to what she knew, an identity that she accepted even while loathing it, a place where at least she knew the terms of survival.

I knew that Eva and I probably would have been friends if we had met under different circumstances. I asked her what she would be if she could do anything in the world. She didn't hesitate; her eyes lit up as she exclaimed, "I would be a chef!" She loved to cook and always tried to switch with her housemates for kitchen duty. "I'm good at it," she said confidently. Cooking represented a new identity — one she might understand, claim, and feel proud of. It was one that could fill her void.

Soon after that conversation, we identified a culinary school near where Eva lived. She applied, was accepted, and our organization awarded her a scholarship. Two years later, Eva graduated at the top of her class and accepted a job in a four-star hotel in Cape Town.

Now I was back to visit and to give her a graduation gift. She wanted to do an interview and share her story with the donors who had made her education possible. I was hesitant because her story belonged to her; she didn't owe it to anyone. But she told it willingly, as a gift and testimony, with conviction and tears. At the end, she looked away from the camera and directly at me, where I sat on a stool right next to the tripod. "Thank you," she said. I began to protest that I was not the one deserving her thanks, but she waved her hand to stop me. "I know it was God, but you all were the hands, and I need to thank you. You see, now I am no longer a prostitute. I am a chef."

Wellspring International wanted to help Eva gain an education. We wanted this for her because, as an individual daughter of God, she mattered. If all our efforts and prayers were only for her, it would be worth it. How can we know the widening ripples of grace that would encircle the changed life of one woman? Because of Eva's education, she is much more likely to be healthy and productive. She will be a leader, a force for positive change among her family and community. Most importantly, any future children she has will have a greater chance for success and health. Her education — and her changed life — will bless generations yet to be born.

The word hero often refers to sports figures, musicians, celebrities, and world leaders. My hero, however, is a South African prostitute-turned-chef named Eva. Happily ever after — for Eva and for me — isn't about a *perfect* life, but a *significant* life in which, through the grace of God, our relationships draw us closer to a just and beautiful world.

BIO

Naomi graduated from Wheaton College with a degree in business and economics. Following an internship in development with Children's Healthcare of Atlanta, she accepted an internship as program director of a children's orphanage in the Dominican Republic. At her next job, Naomi's passion for global issues concerning women and children led her to launch a new initiative, Wellspring International, to research and identify key efforts internationally, working with women and children at risk and providing financial grants to efforts already underway. She has spent time in red light districts in Amsterdam, Bombay, and Bangkok, foster homes for children who have been orphaned by AIDS and those who are HIV-positive, women's prisons in South Africa, displacement camps in Uganda and Aceh (Indonesia), and parts of India and Indonesia that were devastated by the tsunami of 2004. Naomi currently works with Invisible Children, a San Diego-based nonprofit organization promoting youth activism in the United States and long-term development for the war-affected region of northern Uganda.

Painting Dreams in the Sky

Don Rogers

Three years ago, Peter Akuch woke up on the hard Sudanese ground, next to the cows. With his eyes to the sky, he remained on his typical bed of soil and cow-manure ash, thinking about his future, and straining for memories of the family he had lost during the war.

His closest companions during his thirteen years of life have been the village cows that provide warmth during cold nights, some milk if the owners are kind enough, and manure ashes that make his dark skin turn dusty gray but send the mosquitoes to dine elsewhere. Though he has been without a family, he has not lived alone. Countless other Dinka children who have suffered similar tragedy find a place of refuge and companionship in the cattle camps that move and graze near the Nile River.

As Peter lay there, his gaze was captured by a single white streak being painted on the sky near the rising sun. He pointed, and alerted some of his orphaned friends who slept nearby. "Do you see? At the front of that line is a plane! I hear that people ride inside, and my dream is to one day be the driver." No one responded. These kinds of dreams, dreams that required an education, were seldom talked about. Peter and the others with him were well aware that all the schools had been destroyed a decade before they were even born. Peter's dream was further out of reach than the plane that had inspired it.

More than twenty years of war pushed millions of people into other countries or into eternity. Those who stayed in Southern Sudan fought daily for survival and safety — hiding for weeks or walking for years. Schools, homes, farms, and dreams were smashed by bombs and torched with fire, leaving villages crushed, hope drained, and countless families separated.

I began learning about the challenges and dreams of the Sudanese from a man named Stephen. Years ago, Stephen had walked across the desert to reach the safety of neighboring Kenya. He had come to know Christ in Sudan while attending a Christian school as a boy. Now his school is a pile of rubble. During his years in exile, Stephen sought every educational opportunity he could, hoping someday his dream to establish a school and training center in his home village would become a reality.

In January 2005, a peace agreement between the warring factions in Sudan inspired Stephen to pack his bags. Armed with a passion for God, a relationship with our ministry (Empowering Lives International), and a vision to see lives transformed by education, Stephen returned home. Now, having established strong relationships with the community, Stephen has put God's love and vision into action.

These days, Peter still wakes up among the cows, but he knows just when he needs to begin his walk in order to get to school on time. Last year, for the first time in over twenty years, Peter and nearly two hundred other children between the ages of five and fifteen stepped out of a nightmare and into the first grade. Now, because of the

Courtesy of Micah Albert

prayers and support of caring people from around the world — and because of Stephen's leadership — children are being educated, encouraged spiritually, and provided nourishing meals and clean water from a newly dug well. During a ceremony attended by the whole village, several children read Bible verses slowly but clearly. The village leaders sat in amazement — these students were reading! The parents cheered. Some shared testimonies and told the village about their fresh hopes for the future.

The vision for education and transformation is still growing. The school is moving toward greater self-reliance as it farms the property, plants trees, generates income, and teaches appropriate agricultural practices to neighbors, pastors, and returning refugees.

Though the school still lacks desks, there is no shortage of dreams among the students. Zachair (11) wants to be a doctor. Keth (8) wants to be a teacher. Mary (9) dreams of becoming a pastor. David (12) has a dream to be the president of Sudan someday, so he can "gain respect and give things to people in need." Ajok (11) lives with her grandmother — her father, pregnant mother, and baby sister were killed by militia — and besides wanting to be a doctor, she just wants to own a pair of shoes someday. Through God's provision of education, these children's dreams now have a chance to become reality.

As for Peter — well, someday you may travel to Africa. Imagine the delight of heaven and your own heart when a voice comes on over the PA system. "Good afternoon, ladies and gentlemen. We have now reached cruising altitude over Southern Sudan. I am Captain Peter Akuch, and I will be your pilot today. Sit back, relax, and dream big as we journey together for a little while."

BIO

The life mission of Don Rogers is reflected in Empowering Lives International, the organization he founded fourteen years ago. During a short-term trip, Don and a Tanzanian friend converted a metal drum into a bread oven to help a suffering woman start a business. Other successful projects followed, and ELI was born. Today, Don and his wife, Amy, love serving among the African people as well as motivating people from the West to serve among the poor. Don and Amy have two sons (Joshua and Nathaniel) and serve ELI in Eldoret, Kenya, and in California, where Don often speaks for church and missions events.

A Mountain of Misery

Leanne Patterson

I'm learning that God calls us to live faithfully in seemingly hopeless situations. When God's own son came to this world, he ended up hanging on a cross. In light of that, I wonder what in the world I'm supposed to do. I believe that God wants us to have hearts that are willing to feel the pain and misery of humanity, because this is the way his own heart beats for us.

After graduating from Wheaton College, I served in a church plant in Mexico for two years as part of Christ for Children International. Later, I journeyed to New York City, where I lived and taught in Spanish Harlem and Platano City, Washington Heights. Now I find myself three miles from where I was born in Santa Barbara, California. I work with the Latino population on the east side, one of the city's roughest neighborhoods. Even after Mexico and Harlem, it's the most challenging situation I've encountered yet.

Every day I try to chip away at the overwhelming mountain of human misery that exists here. Cycles of poverty, infidelity, alcoholism, gangs, and teenage pregnancies are just a few of the realities I encounter every morning. I consider myself a *pajaro carpintero*, a woodpecker, attempting to bore a hole through the hopelessness. How? By being faithful in the small things of life, day in and day out. I advocate for marginalized children in the name of Christ. I give his children dignity.

Pablo was a student in my fourth grade combination class at Cesar Chavez Charter School. The first day of school, we were sitting in a circle as I asked the students about their summers. Pablo responded by hitting his fists against his head and rocking his body aimlessly back and forth.

Over the next few months, I watched Pablo spiral downward. Not a single hour would pass in which he did not scream that he hated himself, that he couldn't do the task, or that he was going to kill himself. Nearly every day he banged his head against his desk or the wall, usually during a new activity or learning procedure. Pablo needed a different setting. He needed an advocate.

We looked into his family situation, attended special needs and counseling meetings, and set up an advocacy program and home visits. What we found was alarming. Pablo was witnessing — and suffering from — verbal abuse against his mother. Almost daily he would either shut himself up in the family's wardrobe or turn up the television volume so he couldn't hear anything. His mother was enduring constant abuse at the hands of her boyfriend, and Pablo didn't know how to cope. He was out of control.

Today, Pablo is no longer in an abusive home. The necessary transition toward healing and wholeness in his family has begun. I had a chance to stand up as Pablo's advocate; now he is receiving the special services that he needs. He comes by and visits every now and then, and his doing so reminds me that even the bleakest of situations aren't impossible. Today, he gives love back with the warmest of hugs.

When we engage injustice, the situations we face often seem hopeless. But we are not alone. That's the hope we have. The apostle Paul says, "Let us not become weary in doing good, for at the proper time we will reap a harvest if we do not give up" (Galatians 6:9). We shrug off our weariness, and ask our brothers and sisters to help us continue, even when everything looks hopeless. Through Pablo, God showed me that he's much bigger than we are. He's always working because he's always loving. And he asks us to keep on, even when the mountain of human need seems insurmountable.

BIO

Leanne Patterson was born and raised in Santa Barbara, California. She is thankful to have been raised by two loving Christian parents and influenced toward missions and prayer by her grandparents. After graduating from high school, she went to Wheaton College, where her passion for missions and intercultural communication developed. Leanne studied Spanish and communications and spent many weekends and evenings translating at a community health center in inner-city Chicago. After graduation, Leanne spent two years in Zacatecas, Mexico, serving as a missionary with Christ for Children International. Her passion for teaching became apparent to her, and she decided to head back to the States to earn a master's in education through the New York City Teaching Fellows. She taught for two years in the mostly-Latino East Harlem. Today she teaches fourth grade at Cesar Chavez Charter School, a dual-language immersion school on the east side of Santa Barbara.

Spider-Man

Justin Little

It's spring in Los Angeles. The clear, rain-washed sky is reflected in the windows of shining skyscrapers rising from the grid of streets and sidewalks below. A river of cars and buses stops at the corner as busy people in suits and shirts and polished shoes fill the crosswalk. It's 9 a.m. in the Business District — the financial epicenter of downtown — and the work-day has just begun.

Not far from the gleaming windows of downtown — just a few blocks east and south, where the buildings aren't as tall and the sidewalks aren't as clean — are the sounds of laughter, shouting, and balls bouncing. The children of Towne Elementary School are at recess.

A group of first-grade boys in identical white-collared shirts and blue slacks play teth-erball by the fence. One boy in line is crying, because he was caught brandishing a piece of sharp plastic like a knife, and his teacher has promised him that his mother will hear about it. Some of the fifth-grade girls stand together by the wall-ball court, chatting about boys and about how they are in love with every member of the band, the Jonas Brothers.

Juan is a five-year-old kindergartner. He plays with the rest of the kindergartners in their own private playground, and today he wheels a tricycle around a newly painted track in the pavement. Eduardo is close behind him. The boys take the corners too fast, and their tricycles threaten to toss them as the inside wheels spin dangerously high off the ground. The thrill kindles their joy and they ride harder, going non-stop until recess ends and they return to the safe pace of the classroom.

Juan and his older brother live with their mom in a hotel two blocks north of the school. Their room is a box. It's so small that the bunk beds fill most of the space, stopping the door a foot from its frame when it opens inward. Juan's mother insists that he studies in his spare time, practicing his writing on weekends while she studies English. Juan is smart; homework comes easily for him. But he's always getting into trouble for breaking rules in class. Still, he reads at a first-grade level, even though he's only five.

Juan's father is in Mexico. Juan never sees him, so Juan idolizes Spider-Man instead.

Spider-Man is free to climb on walls and jump off buildings, even the ones downtown. Juan feels that kind of freedom only at recess on his tricycle. Between his hotel box and school, there aren't any parks where he can run or play soccer or climb a tree. He lives in a world of metal and electricity, concrete and glass, where you always have to wear shoes and stay on the sidewalk. If only Juan were free to summit the buildings that surround his world instead of being trapped below!

Spider-Man could do that. If only Spider-Man would come and help Juan learn to be free. Spider-Man would defend the city from gangs, protect the busy people in the Business District from muggers, plant gardens with trees big enough to climb, help Juan's mother learn English, and even teach the children to climb and jump and swing. Then the skyscrapers would no longer be impenetrable castles against the blue, but rather anchors for hands and feet and webs to swing Juan into the sky, his joy kindled with the thrill of freedom.

Juan loved "freeplay," a time on the weekly schedule for kids to just be themselves and play with our staff and volunteers in the sanctuary. Early in the school year, we started playing Spider-Man together. I would pick him up and fly him from one wall to the other, while he would use his hands and feet to "stick" to the walls. He never touched the ground. His laughter was wild and joyful. Juan found freedom in that game — a glimpse of the freedom God has in store for him in Christ. Recently, his family moved out of Skid Row.

Though I haven't seen Juan for a while, I hope I will not forget the chance I had to be involved in a life on the margins of our world.

BIO

Justin Little grew up in central Oregon. He spent his first year after graduating from Azusa Pacific University working as the kindergarten and first grade teacher at the S.A.Y. Yes! After School Program, a ministry of Central City Community Outreach in Los Angeles. Justin currently lives in Southern California and is pursuing his vocation in ministry and songwriting.

A Village Called Armenia

Michael Thoeresz

My name is Michael. I'm a Peace Corps Volunteer in Armenia Village, Belize. Armenia is a beautiful village nestled in the rain forest, eight miles south of Belize's capital, Belmopan. During my first year here, I taught eighth-grade composition at the village primary school. Halfway through the year, I began asking students what their plans were after graduation. The response floored me. Very few planned to attend high school in neighboring Belmopan. The main reason? Lack of money.

I felt I needed to find out more, so I visited my friend Cruz. His son Alex was one of my best students. Cruz confirmed what my students had said. With his salary, Cruz can feed and clothe his immediate family and even help his wife start a small corn-grinding business. But it's another story for him to pay for transportation, registration, books, uniform, shoes, and lunch so Alex can attend high school. And Cruz has three other children besides Alex.

Cruz explained how badly he had wanted an education for himself, yet due to his family's financial constraints, he never attended high school. He had always aspired to teach first grade, and due to some unusual circumstances, he'd been able to for two years. He loved it. But since he lacked formal credentials, he was forced to stop, and found work in a lumberyard instead. Cruz desperately wanted Alex and his other children to have the opportunity to attend high school. That's why he organized meetings with the principal, teachers, and other parents. It's why he checks his children's homework every evening, even after a long commute home from a nine-hour day of manual labor. And it's why he has instilled a belief in the importance of education in all his children.

Cruz is a charismatic speaker. He preaches at one of the largest churches in the village, and he's a dedicated community activist. I've never heard him speak so passionately as when he speaks about the education of his children. Perhaps it's because he knows that education is the best way to improve the future of the village he loves.

Around the same time that I was becoming aware of the lack of educational opportunities in the village, I heard that a nearby nonprofit, PathLight International, had undergone a change of management. I decided to introduce myself to the new directors and see if they would be interested in collaborating on a scholarship program for students in Armenia. The directors and I spent the next few months developing the program. That May, the program was announced to the eighth-grade class, and seventeen students applied for a scholarship — fourteen of whom were accepted to a nearby high school and given full scholarships. One of the scholarship recipients was Alex, my friend's son. We worked with

the other three students to find alternatives such as 4-H training and vocational school. The scholarships were extended to cover these educational opportunities as well. Recently, PathLight International hired someone from Armenia Village to handle the day-to-day administration, making the program self-sustaining.

Would Cruz have been able to send Alex to high school without the scholarship? It's impossible for me to say for sure. I know he would have tried, since he values education so highly. But the scholarship that Alex received has shown both he and Cruz that what may seem impossible can indeed be acheived. They recently asked me about the requirements and scholarships available to attend a university in the United States. Even though Alex is only a freshman in high school, he has already acquired a book to help him prepare for the SAT. His hopes, and the hopes of the entire village of Armenia, have never been higher.

BIO

Michael is a twenty-six-year-old Peace Corps Volunteer in the rural village of Armenia, Belize. He is currently finishing his two years of service and will then return to Portland, Oregon, his hometown. Prior to Peace Corps service, Michael traveled around North America and Eastern Europe, visiting family and friends and volunteering wherever he could. He was the assistant coach of a college tennis team in Southern California. Michael earned his BA in sociology from the University of Redlands. His hobbies include reading (especially Russian literature), tennis, and jumping off elevated rocks into rivers and lakes.

NOW WHAT?

Education is more than simply helping students pass tests. Education is equipping people of all ages with the skills they need to improve not only their own lives, but also the lives of their children, grandchildren, and neighbors. As we seek to love our neighbors as ourselves, creating and supporting effective education is one of the best ways to reduce poverty.

Reflect

1. *What do you think?* How has this section been for you to read? Frustrating? Confusing? Enlightening? Why? Did it shock you to learn how many adults are illiterate in our world today? Did it make you feel thankful for your ability to read and write? Take some time to journal about your experience reading this section. Be sure to include the thoughts and emotions that it evoked.

2. *Put yourself in another's shoes.* Imagine you were born in a developing country and you never had the chance to go to school. You don't know how to read, how to write, or how to do basic math. Spend some time listing various things that you wouldn't be able to do in your daily life. How would you feel, knowing there are people around the world who are literate and educated? What would you want them to do about your situation, and why?

3. *Make a change.* What small (or big) changes can you make in your life to reflect what you have learned in this section? Are you willing to make a commitment to support an organization that focuses on education in developing countries? Or would you like to contribute to quality education in your own community by serving as a tutor, mentor, or as part of an after-school program? Do you feel yourself being called to teach overseas, either on a short-term or long-term basis?

4. *Re-figure.* How we spend our money reflects what we value. In America, we pay professional athletes, models, Hollywood stars, and hedge fund managers a whole lot more than we pay teachers. This has always saddened me, because it says a lot about

what is important to us as a country. As much as we talk about the importance of education, we don't seem to back up our words with our money. What would others say you value if they had only your checkbook or your credit card statement to go by? What do you really value? Do your spending habits reflect what you believe is right? Do you need to make some adjustments in how you spend your money?

Respond

1. *Get involved.* There are many opportunities for non-teachers to change the face of education in our world. This includes donating money for scholarships to make education more affordable, supporting families who otherwise would have to put their children to work instead of letting them go to school, teaching English (a very useful skill to teach in places like Central and South America), empowering teachers with additional skills or teaching methods, building the educational infrastructure (schools, libraries, sanitation facilities), tutoring, helping children with special needs, counseling, or providing special workshops in the arts or music or sports or other subjects that are rarely available in poor countries (or even poorer parts of your own city).

2. *Become illiterate.* You might have to get creative on *how* to do this, but it's worth the effort to help you understand a bit of what it must feel like to be unable to read or write. Pretend for a day (or even an hour) that you can't understand any written words. Street signs, magazines, newspapers, books, computers, bus rules — they're all inaccessible to you. How will you learn to navigate the world around you? Consider being unable to write. No emails, no texting, no journaling, no letters. How might you connect with the people far away from you? Spend some time identifying habits you currently enjoy that would be impossible if you couldn't read or write. If you live in a city where there is a Chinese, Vietnamese, or Hispanic district, go there and visit a grocery store where minimal English is written or spoken. Understanding what it's like to be illiterate, even if it's just for a few hours, will drive your compassion and your action.

3. *Volunteer.* Nearly every public school has students who are struggling with some aspect of their education. By giving just a few hours of your time each month, you can have a profound impact on a student's abilities and future. Contact your local school, or search online to discover what opportunities might exist in your community.

4. *Organize a school supplies drive.* Many students in developing countries do not have adequate school supplies. Imagine trying to learn your multiplication tables or the alphabet without scratch paper or a writing utensil. Many students in developing countries have no option but to write in the dirt with their fingers. Contact an organization listed in the following section to see how you can help with a supplies drive.

5. *Sponsor a child.* There are many organizations that offer child sponsorship, which usually provides educational assistance like school fees, uniforms, and supplies — along with other kinds of help. It's a great way to ensure that a child gets an opportunity to be educated. Another way to do this is to find an organization that offers scholarships for students in developing countries to go to high school or college. Pledge a consistent amount of money. Friends of ours recently committed to financing a husband and wife in Africa who are pursuing their university degrees. No matter your financial situation, there are ways you can contribute to education around the world and in your own community.

Spread the Word

It can feel daunting to confront such a growing, worldwide problem on your own. But tremendous change happens when we work together. Would you consider spreading the word about the worldwide lack of quality education, the people whose lives are affected, and the organizations that are doing something to make a difference? Now that you've read this chapter, it isn't someone else's responsibility — it's yours. Change begins with individuals deciding they are going to live differently. What role can you play? Maybe it's inviting some friends to coffee, starting an action group at your church, or getting your youth group to hold a rally. Help change lives. Spread the word. To get started, we've designed a simple, effective tool: *www.zealouslove.org/spread.*

Share Your Ideas

Have a great idea about something people can do to engage the global challenge of education? Do you want to connect with others who are getting involved? Join the conversation at *www.zealouslove.org/share.*

Discover More

In the Field Notes you've heard from several contributors about the harsh reality of insufficient education. You've also heard some about the incredible work that's being done to address the issue, both on a personal and organizational scale. Remember, there is no "one-size-fits-all" solution. If you want to get involved in this area, check out the following organizations or visit *www.zealouslove.org/education*.

PathLight International

Vision: PathLight International serves at-risk children by providing educational opportunities that integrate faith and learning.

Method: Through service teams, scholarships, and teacher placements, as well as connecting needs and resources, PathLight helps vulnerable children become the self-reliant leaders of tomorrow.

Contact:

PathLight International
3037-T Hopyard Road
Pleasanton, CA 94588
Phone: (925) 426-7284
www.pathlight.org

Empowering Lives International

Vision: Empowering Lives International is a Christian non-profit organization working among the impoverished of Africa to provide training, resources, and encouragement to break the cycle of poverty and help people recognize their importance in the eyes of God.

Method: Strategically developed Skills for Life Training Centers, Christian Schools, Orphanages, HIV/AIDS awareness campaigns, Home Based Caregiver Training, business ventures, and programs to reach village alcoholics are part of an overall strategy to remove the barriers that hinder spiritual transformation, health, education, and economic progress. Passionate, godly national leadership is the key to ELI's strategic mission that now operates in Eastern DR Congo, Southern Sudan, Tanzania, and Eldoret, Kenya.

Contact:

Empowering Lives International
PO Box 67
Upland, CA 91785
Phone: (909) 931-1311
www.empoweringlives.org

Teach for America

Vision: Teach for America aims to end educational inequity. We are the national corps of outstanding recent college graduates and professionals of all academic majors and career interests who commit two years to teach in urban and rural public schools and become leaders in the effort to expand educational opportunity.

Method: We recruit aggressively to attract outstanding recent college graduates of all majors and career interests to commit two years to teach in urban and rural public schools, and we invest in the training and professional development necessary to ensure their success as teachers in our highest-poverty communities. Our teachers, also called corps members, go above and beyond traditional expectations to lead their students to significant academic achievement, overcoming the challenges of poverty despite the current capacity of the school system.

Contact:

Teach for America
315 West 36th Street
7th Floor
New York, NY 10018
Phone: (800) 832-1230
www.teachforamerica.org

World Vision

Vision: World Vision is a Christian humanitarian organization dedicated to working with children, families, and their communities worldwide to reach their full potential by tackling the causes of poverty and injustice.

Method: World Vision's goal is to ensure that all children receive access to basic education that will help them become fulfilled, productive members of their communities. We work to accomplish this through financial assistance to children's parents, specific programs for disadvantaged children, a school supplies program called SchoolTools, and advocacy.

Contact:

World Vision
PO Box 9716, Dept. W
Federal Way, WA 98063-9716
Phone: (888) 511-6548
www.worldvision.org

Compassion International

Vision: Compassion International exists as a Christian child advocacy ministry that releases children from spiritual, economic, social, and physical poverty and enables them to become responsible, fulfilled Christian adults.

Method: Compassion International's Learning for Life program focuses on a child's life from school age until program completion, aiming to prepare each sponsored child with the skills and knowledge required to assume adulthood, including those activities that will make the community a better place to live. We focus on preparing children to:

- Follow Jesus Christ in faith and deed as part of their spiritual training.
- Support themselves and share with others in need as part of their economic training.
- Be responsible members of their family, church, community, and nation as part of their social training.
- Maintain their own physical well-being.

Contact:

Compassion International
Colorado Springs, CO 80997
*No street address necessary
Phone: (800) 336-7676
www.compassion.com

Additional Resources

www.care.org

www.one.org

www.roomtoread.org

www.wr.org

Visit *www.zealouslove.org/
education* for more information
and organizations.

CREATION DEGRADATION

The wolf will live with the lamb, the leopard will lie down with the goat,
the calf and the lion and the yearling together;
and a little child will lead them.
The cow will feed with the bear, their young will lie down together,
and the lion will eat straw like the ox.
The infant will play near the hole of the cobra,
and the young child put his hand into the viper's nest.

Isaiah 11:6–8

After every step of the creation process, God "saw that it was good (Gen. 1:40)." Then, near the end of the creation account, God takes a wide-angle view, looking over all that he has made, from galaxies and gravity to ecosystems and DNA. And the text says, "It *was very good*" (Gen. 1:31 emphasis added).

But it doesn't last. The fall happens, and humanity is separated from itself, from creation, and from its creator.

Then from the prophet Isaiah, we get a look ahead — a prophecy about the day when unity will be restored. A glimpse of the peace and the camaraderie that will fill the land — harmony among all the Creator's creatures, even us humans. It's almost too good to be true, especially when you consider all the violence and death and turmoil and suffering in our world today.

But with God all things are possible.

Jesus is the great reconciler (Col. 1:19 – 20). Because he came, bled, died, and rose again, we can be reconciled to God, to one another, and with all of creation.

BRIEFING

You might believe that caring for the environment distracts Christians from the more important work of loving people and saving souls. You might even be wondering why creation care is being covered in a guide to social justice. If so, you are certainly not alone. Mike and I have had many conversations with good people who don't see the value and purpose of creation care, especially when compared to addressing hunger, fighting human trafficking, or straight evangelism.

Or maybe you are reading from a different perspective. Maybe you believe that a vital way to love people is through caring for the environment in which they live. You believe that a book on social justice must address the injustice we've termed "creation degradation." You maintain strongly that, for better and worse, the poor are undeniably affected by the quality of the environment.

Or maybe you are somewhere in between. Perhaps you think both stewarding the environment and directly caring for people are important, but you are not sure exactly what that looks like in your life. You might consider yourself a casual recycler, and you try to turn off the water while you brush your teeth. But when it comes to sending a check to an environmental group — even a Christian one — or volunteering to spend a Saturday cleaning trash from a local creek, you prefer to focus on church planting or relief efforts instead.

Mike and I are about as far away from being experts as you can get. This briefing is not about scientifically proving that we should do more for the environment. What we're going to do is share some stories from our lives to illustrate how we came to discover God's call to creation care in our own life.

My mom and Mike's dad are both passionate gardeners. My mom cultivates flowers, herbs, and berries, while Mike's dad grows vegetables. Growing up, neither of us paid any attention to our respective parents when they talked about their gardens, and only on rare occasions did either of us help out in the garden. Since we were married a few years ago, we have developed quite an interest — you could almost call it a passion for gardening. Suddenly, both of us wish we'd paid more attention growing up!

For us, gardening is something we do because we love the vibrant taste of home-grown tomatoes, the joy of picking squash from the vine and eating it an hour later, and because herbs from the windowsill pots are always fresher and more flavorful than the dried, store-bought variety. We garden because we want to understand where our food comes from. We garden because the miracle of a tiny seed sprouting and becoming a fruit-bearing plant never ceases to amaze us. We garden because it helps us to purchase less food that had to be transported halfway around the globe in order to get to our table.

For us, gardening is a luxury. If our plants all freeze in a mid-June cold snap, we'll be disappointed, but we won't go hungry. If the rain floods our garden and washes away our bean plants, we can just head to the grocery store.

But for many of the world's poor, gardening and farming are not luxuries — they are necessities. It's easy for us to dismiss the potentially disastrous effects of creation degradation, if our livelihood generally is not affected (or at least it doesn't seem to be). But, in the words of Ban Ki-Moon, Secretary-General of the United Nations, this situation "is having a disproportionate effect on the world's poor, and is also hindering efforts to achieve the MDGs [Millennium Development Goals]."[1] A growing number of people are convinced we have to take responsibility for how our decisions affect the environment, and ultimately, the human lives that depend on it.

Mike and I spent nearly six months of the past year visiting developing countries in Central America, South America, and East Africa. In each of these places we spent time among farmers. Now, when you picture their farms, don't think of acres and acres of corn fields owned by a faceless corporate entity. Picture small, subsistence-level family farms that (hopefully) provide enough food for one family to survive, and occasionally (if they're lucky) enough surplus to sell at the local market to buy some medicine, school books, and perhaps a few other necessities. We encountered these farms in rainforests, on mountains, and along arid plains. I was impressed by the determination it takes to grow food on a steep mountainside in Ecuador, by the resiliency it takes to hang in there when monsoon-like rains destroy crops and upend fruit trees in Belize, and by the courage needed to be thankful for a meager harvest from shriveled crops that didn't get enough rain in Uganda.

Though climate varies from place to place, the stories we heard from subsistence farmers around the world were strikingly similar. Most of these men and women grew up farming, learning from their parents and grandparents when to prepare the ground, when to plant, and when to harvest. Without us mentioning the debate raging around the notion of climate change, farmer after farmer told us that the weather has been changing — that dry seasons last longer than they used to, and that farmers no longer know when to plant because they can't trust the rains to arrive. And when they do arrive, often they produce torrential floods. Essentially, they told us the methods and rhythms they've depended on for generations are breaking down. These farmers don't know a lot about science, but they do know about farming — and across three continents, they told us the same story.

It's unsettling to hear such alarming news from people who possess the combined agricultural wisdom of countless generations. These people know the land because they *need* the land. Buying food from the supermarket isn't an option — they survive on what they grow and sell what little surplus they may have to purchase other essential items. This isn't a political debate about regulations or carbon caps. This is about children who die when the rains don't come.

While reading a summary of the UN's 2007 – 2008 Human Development Report, I was struck by the way increased exposure to droughts, floods, and storms is already impacting the lives of the poor around the world. It is a grave and tragic mistake to argue that the environment does not impact the poor.

Consider that each year between 2000 and 2004, more than a quarter of a billion people were affected by climate-related disasters. Over 98 percent of them were in developing countries.[2] While it would be unfair to put all the blame on human-initiated climate change, more and more scientists worldwide are concluding that human activity is very likely a contributing factor. The fourth report from the Intergovernmental Panel on Climate Change (a widely respected panel) concluded that, "There is a very high confidence that the global average net effect of human activities since 1750 has been one of warming."[3] But regardless of how much human activity is a factor in a particular hurricane or drought, it is beyond argument that human activities in the developed world — including large-scale pollution, deforestation, irresponsible waste disposal, and disproportionate consumption of resources — make it difficult (and sometimes impossible) for the poor to live off the land.

Wherever you stand on the issue of climate change, to get mired in debate is to miss the larger opportunity to care about what God cares about — the creation he called "very good" and the immeasurably valuable humans who depend on his creation for their very lives.

Stewarding God's created world is a biblical mandate. Think of the parable of the talents, in which a master returns "after a long time" to settle accounts with his servants. The master's question to each servant is, effectively, "What did you do with what I gave you?" When a servant gives evidence of faithfulness, the master responds with praise and commendation; the opposite response is true for the servant who fails to demonstrate his faithfulness with what he was given (see Matthew 25). Any worthwhile conversation about creation degradation and stewardship must go beyond the debate about climate change and consider what Jesus said were the great commandments: loving God and loving others. We must admit that our love for God is deficient when we degrade his creation, and our love for our neighbors — both those who live near us and those who live across the ocean — is deficient when we hinder their ability to survive, whether by our negative action or our neutral inaction.

By any account, we humans are less than perfect stewards of God's creation. Have you heard about the North Pacific Gyre? It is an area of ocean larger than the state of Texas — more than 268,000 square miles — clogged with floating trash. Massive underwater currents swirl clockwise, creating a region where tons of debris spin and swirl in what has been called "the world's largest garbage dump." Most of the refuse is plastic — which

takes a long time to break down. This plastic is proving harmful not only to sea life, but also to human beings as it slowly breaks down into smaller and smaller pieces and eventually enters the food chain.[4]

In a recent survey of biochemists, botanists, entomologists, geneticists, neuroscientists, physiologists, conservation biologists, marine biologists, molecular biologists, and other generally smart people, seventy percent said they believe that within thirty years as many as one-fifth of all the species on earth will be extinct. More than thirty percent said roughly half the species on earth would become extinct within this time.[5] This is in addition to the hundreds of species that are already extinct because of human activity.[6] Eradicating something is a poor way to express thankfulness to the Creator. Is this really what it looks like for human beings to be good stewards of God's earth?

Consider once more the impact on our neighbors around the world. Think about the large companies (which you and I support, perhaps unknowingly, with our purchasing habits) whose factories and plants leech chemicals into local water sources, causing sickness and death in surrounding villages. Or how the unsustainable, profit-driven clear-cutting of some forests in developing countries force children to spend hours every day searching for enough firewood to cook their families' meals. (Not to mention the effects on all of us, especially when what is being cut is rain forest, thus destroying some of the most ecologically important land in our world). Or the 600,000 annual asthma attacks that are caused in part by soot from the power plants in the United States. It is estimated that this airborne soot kills around 64,000 Americans each year.[7] Does that sound like "loving your neighbor as yourself"?

> How could I say that I was being a good steward when I was causing so much damage to God's creation?
> **Matthew Sleeth**

Does a floating area of trash larger than the state of Texas really seem like a shining example of good stewardship? Does reckless expansion that renders hundreds of species of God's creation extinct really bring him praise? Does he smile at that?

Imagine a friend of yours is a talented artist. She is going on a long trip and needs a place to store several of her paintings. You say that you'd be happy to keep them for her. Would you throw one of her paintings on the ground and use it as a doormat? Would you hang one on your wall and use it as a dart board? Would you shred another and use it for landscaping mulch? That's what we have done with the Creator's world — we have used it for our own purposes. We have trampled on it, neglected it, and begun to destroy it. I believe it pains God to watch this happen.

One Christian biologist said it well. He notes — as we did at the beginning of this Briefing — that God describes his creation with admiration and pleasure, calling it "good" (Gen. 1:31). So, in his words, "dare we diminish the joy God finds with his handiwork?"[8] Maybe you're thinking, "That's all well and good, but how does it connect with real life? I don't control a huge corporation that is degrading God's creation. I don't poach endangered animals." True, but have you considered how your life — your spending habits, living habits, trash habits, travel habits — might be complicit in the destruction of God's creation? I have been learning just how guilty I really am because of how I've lived. While my previous ignorance doesn't excuse my guilt, knowledge allows me to begin taking restorative steps.

Beyond exploring how we might be supporting practices that degrade creation on a large scale, we should also think about the simple, day-to-day things we can do, like recycling. Each small step we take to care for God's planet and our neighbors is important because we, too, are changed in the process. A single glass jar or tin can on its own is a small thing, but when we are faithful in the small things, we can be faithful in the big things too. The world's oceans are made of single raindrops, creeks, and streams flowing into a larger whole. If you recycle a small box of tins and jars and plastics every week, over the course of your life that's a lot of material that might otherwise end up sitting in a landfill or swirling in the North Pacific Gyre. Or consider how you might begin to "pre-cycle"; that is, before you purchase an item, consider how it is packaged. If we reduce our consumption, buy in bulk, and buy items with less packaging, that would be a huge step toward minimizing our trash output. As one of our friends put it after he'd been recycling for several years, "Otherwise I'm really just sweeping my trash under the carpet of God's beautiful world."

As we learn to be attentive to the small things in life, we will discover that the links between *loving our neighbor*, *caring for the poor*, and *stewarding the earth* are significant. When we care for our world, we fulfill the two greatest commandments. We love God by loving his handiwork, and we love others by reducing the harm our lifestyles might cause them.

The inverse is also true. When we are wasteful, when we carelessly consume more than we need — we're abandoning the two great commandments. We fail to love God because we're degrading his handiwork, and we fail to love our neighbors because our lifestyles are causing them harm.

The world is God's creation and he is the Lord of it. And our neighbors, both near and far, are co-inhabitors of the good earth that God gave. By caring for the earth, we love not only those who are here now, but also those who will inhabit this planet after we are gone. Most of all, we love the God who made it all and called it good.

Among the Holy

Wendell Berry

If we read the Bible, keeping in mind the desirability of those two survivals — of Christianity and the Creation — we are apt to discover several things about which modern Christian organizations have kept remarkably quiet or to which they have paid little attention.

We will discover that we humans do not own the world or any part of it: "The earth is the Lord's, and the fullness thereof: the world and they that dwell therein." There is in our human law, undeniably, the concept and right of "land ownership." But this, I think, is merely an expedient to safeguard the mutual belonging of people and places without which there can be no lasting and conserving human communities. This right of human ownership is limited by mortality and by natural constraints on human attention and responsibility; it quickly becomes abusive when used to justify large accumulations of "real estate," and perhaps for that reason such large accumulations are forbidden in the twenty-fifth chapter of Leviticus. In biblical terms, the "landowner" is the guest and steward of God: "The land is mine; for ye are strangers and sojourners with me."

We will discover that God found the world, as He made it, to be good, that He made it for His pleasure, and that He continues to love it and to find it worthy, despite its reduction and corruption by us.

We will discover that the Creation is not in any sense independent of the Creator, the result of a primal creative act long over and done with, but is the continuous, constant participation of all creatures in the being of God. Elihu said to Job that if God "gather unto himself his spirit and his breath; all flesh shall perish together." And Psalm 104 says, "Thou sendest forth thy spirit, they are created." Creation is thus God's presence in creatures. As the poet George Herbert put it:

> *Thou art in small things great, not small in any ...*
> *For thou art infinite in one and all.*

We will discover that for these reasons our destruction of nature is not just bad stewardship, or stupid economics, or a betrayal of family responsibility; it is the most horrid blasphemy. It is flinging God's gifts into His face, as if they were of no worth beyond that assigned to them by our destruction of them. We have the right to use the gifts of nature but not to ruin or waste them. We have the right to use what we need but no more.

The Bible leaves no doubt at all about the sanctity of the act of world-making, or of the world that was made, or of creaturely or bodily life in this world. We are holy creatures living among other holy creatures in a world that is holy. Some people know this, and some do not. Nobody, of course, knows it all the time. But what keeps it from being far better known than it is? Why is it apparently unknown to millions of professed students of the Bible? How can modern Christianity have so solemnly folded its hands while so much of the work of God was and is being destroyed?

BIO

Wendell Berry is the author of more than 30 books. He has received numerous literary awards, and currently writes from his farm in Kentucky.

Under the Wings of Christ

Megan Robertson

As we laid our chicken down in the hole for her interment, it was not without tears. Each of us gave her one last pat and my husband read Jesus' words from Matthew 23:37: "O Jerusalem, Jerusalem, you who kill the prophets and stone those sent to you, how often I have longed to gather your children together, as a hen gathers her chicks under her wings, but you were not willing." We picked this passage as it was the only Scripture we could think of that referenced a chicken.

We have kept a flock of seven hens for the last three years in our backyard — until we lost Sir Robin. Now there are six. My husband named her after Sir Robin the not-so-brave of Monty Python fame. The others have equally interesting names bestowed by our three children. We have enjoyed a bounty of fresh eggs, fun times, and silly stories because of these birds. There's Sophie, who will roost on the kitchen counter, given half a chance. Henrietta has been known to be game for a ride down the playset slide, and Pookie is a favorite to hold and pet. Any of them will gladly hop the fence into our garden to destroy the freshly planted lettuce bed and generally wreak havoc. But that's not all. Strangely, they have been the wings and feet of Christ at work in our lives.

We brought chickens into our lives and our backyard after an amazing summer of living and helping out on a farm in Canada. We worked with the A Rocha (Christians in Conservation) Canada project, where we witnessed the love of Christ fleshed out in hospitality, community, and creation care. We wanted to bring a bit of the farm back to our busy suburban lives. We wanted to get our kids in touch with where our food comes from. And we like eggs. But we didn't anticipate all the changes that would follow.

Now we stand in a place of grieving like Jesus did. Not over a lost chicken, but over ourselves — God's lost chicks — as we've begun to see our own unwillingness to be gathered under his wings. We can be so much like the Pharisees he condemned in Matthew 23:23 for neglecting "the important matters of the law — justice, mercy and faithfulness."

I may be a good Christian, raising my kids to love Jesus, but woe to me if I neglect these important matters in my daily life.

Now I'm beginning to see the many ways my thoughtless choices affect others and our earth. Every time I use another plastic shopping bag, I add to the millions already polluting our earth. Whenever I leave the lights on or the water running, I'm wasting precious resources that are sadly lacking in many parts of the world. Each time I cook a meal with our hens' eggs, I save on energy and packaging. Each time I choose not to buy another "thing" I don't really need, I free up that money to share with others. For a long time, I missed the vital connection between my own faith and justice, mercy, and faithfulness. But Christ, in the guise of a hen, has begun to change my family and me.

As a family, we've begun to simplify our lives. We're hanging out our laundry, reducing our consumption, spending conscientiously, and giving more freely from our abundance. We're willing to hear this call because we love our neighbors, ourselves, and God's wonderful world in which we all live. These changes aren't always easy, but they're always good — we're in the process of being found and gathered under the wings of Christ.

BIO

Megan Robertson lives with her husband, Marty, and their three children in Santa Barbara, California. She and her husband, along with several good friends, are actively involved in creating a Santa Barbara A Rocha branch that focuses on conservation, education, and community gardens. She homeschools her kids. Their family enjoys camping, gardening, chickens, and their church family at Santa Barbara Community Church.

Serve God, Save the Planet

Matthew Sleeth, MD

> "What does it profit my brethren if someone says he has faith but does not have works? Can faith save him?. . . . For as the body without the spirit is dead, so faith without works is dead also."
>
> **James 2:14, 26 NKJV**

A decade ago, I would have told you that our family was concerned about the environment. I would have said that we were true "conservatives," working to preserve nature. That was talk. We have progressed from talking a good talk to walking a better walk. How did we go from saying we were concerned to actually making a difference?

When God called me to creation care ministry, I was a physician — chief of staff and head of the emergency department — at one of the nicest hospitals in America. I enjoyed my job, my colleagues, my expensive home, my fast car, and my big paycheck. I have since given up every one of these things.

We now live in a house the exact size of our old garage. We use less than one-third of the fossil fuels and one-quarter of the electricity we once used. We've gone from leaving two barrels of trash by the curb each week to leaving one bag every few weeks. We no longer own a clothes dryer, garbage disposal, dishwasher, or lawn mower. Our "yard" is planted with native wildflowers and a large vegetable garden. Half of our possessions have found new homes. We are a poster family for the "downwardly mobile."

What my family and I have gained in exchange is a life richer in meaning. Because of these changes, we have more time for God. Spiritual concerns have filled the void left by material ones. Owning fewer things has resulted in things no longer owning us. We have put God to the test, and we have found his Word to be true. He has poured blessings and opportunities upon us. When we stopped living a life dedicated to consumerism, our cup began to run over.

Today I am one of a growing number of evangelical Christians whom the Lord is using to witness to people about his love for them and for the natural world. The earth was designed to sustain every generation's *needs*, not to be plundered in an attempt to meet one generation's *wants*.

One area we must change is our dependence on foreign oil. When people's lives become dependent on a substance, we call that addiction. An interesting way to judge the strength of the addiction is to see how willing someone is to go without the substance, or how painful life becomes when it is withdrawn suddenly. If we are addicted to something, we tend to start denying or overlooking things — we fail to question its side effects, or the harm it may cause others. We begin lowering our standards.

Ours is not the first generation to be morally blinded by a lifestyle that depends on energy from foreign shores. Slavery was the importation of cheap energy without regard to its moral implications. States that initially forbade slave energy (Georgia, for example) eventually sanctioned it out of envy for the material wealth of their neighbors.

The Golden Rule reminds us to look for the moral side of every issue, including environmental ones. "Love thy neighbor as thyself" — one cannot claim to be a Christian and ignore the Golden Rule. It isn't a suggestion or a guideline; it is a commandment from God.

What's the connection between the Golden Rule and the environment? You might ask, "Isn't my choice of home, car, and appliances just a matter of lifestyle, and therefore not a moral or spiritual matter?" Does God care whether we drive SUVs, leave the TV on all night, or fly around the world skiing? The Bible doesn't mention any of these things, but then again they didn't exist in biblical times. Yet God is love, and if we fail to love our neighbors, how can the love of God abide in us? Because of the example of God's love, we must question the rightness of our actions, even seemingly "non-moral" ones.

BIO

J. Matthew Sleeth, MD, a former emergency room physician, felt like he was straightening deck chairs on the Titanic saving one patient at a time while the whole ship (earth) was going down. Together with his wife and two teenage children, he began to bring his lifestyle in line with his values, cutting back on their fossil fuel by two thirds and electricity use by 75 percent. Following a new calling, Dr. Sleeth resigned from his position as chief of the medical staff and director of the ER to teach, preach, and write about faith and the environment throughout the country.

Our Father's World

Ed and Susanna Brown

"Wow!" one of us exclaimed, "If we could see angel's wings, I'll bet they'd look like that!" Our whole family was sitting on the back deck, braving the chill of an early December evening in Wisconsin to gaze up at the most spectacular display any of us had ever seen. The night was clear, and the Aurora Borealis (northern lights) stretched across the entire sky, shimmering and shifting and glowing. Right above our own house, the pattern made a peculiar, wing-like shape that lingered even as the lights in the rest of the sky came and went.

Two days later, we had occasion to remember that event, when Ed came home from work early to let the family know the unthinkable had just happened — his job was about to disappear. We had been through this before, and we knew that unemployment — eighteen months of it the last time — was no walk in the park. This time we were older and we had three kids in college, though. If there ever was a time to panic, this seemed to be it.

But the image of the angel's wings kept coming back to both of us. After the immediate shock of Ed's news had worn off — even though we were not happy about being unemployed — we began to feel a deep sense of peace about our future. Inexplicably, we knew things were going to be okay. It wasn't much later that we received an email from a missionary couple in Kenya. "Since you're going to be out of a job anyway," they said, "why don't you think about helping us start a new missions organization?"

Craig and Tracy had been struggling for several years to accomplish a dream. They wanted to connect two important ideas: missions, the act of sharing God's love for people; and creation care, the process of working to heal God's broken and degraded creation. Craig grew up in Kenya as a missionary kid, and he has a degree in forestry. Because of his training, he can see how an environmental crisis has swept across this beautiful land. He is dismayed that decades of missionary "successes" — Kenya is 80 percent Christian — have not helped prevent decades of environmental disaster.

Craig and Tracy's dream was to form an environmental missions organization, one that would "transform people and the land that sustains them." We loved the idea, and being honest, we had to admit that God had been preparing us for just such an opportunity. Ed had spent four years at InterVarsity Christian Fellowship learning the principles of non-profit organizational management. And the job that was now ending was at the Au Sable Institute, a premier evangelical environmental organization. Both experiences gave us the opportunity to learn about Christian environmental stewardship from some of the top leaders in the field. Now Craig and Tracy were offering us the chance to put it all together.

On the other hand, the idea of starting an organization from scratch hardly seemed like a rational thing to do. What about those three kids in college? From a financial point of view, the answer to starting this mission was a resounding no! But God doesn't work from our human perspective. After several months of prayer, research, and consultation with friends, we stepped into it. In April 2005, Care of Creation Inc. was born with two employees and a big dream: we would seek to mobilize the church to "pursue a God-centered response to environmental challenges that brings glory to the Creator, advances the cause of Christ, and leads to a transformation of the people and the land that sustains them."

Now it's three years later and we're still going strong. In Kenya we're implementing a four-pronged approach to mobilizing the church ("Promoting a God-Centered Vision; Planting God's Trees; Harvesting God's Water; and Farming God's Way"), which has affected thousands of people. Now we're getting ready to expand to additional countries in East Africa.

Here in the U.S., we're busy mobilizing the North American church through "Our Father's World" seminars that encourage congregations in the U.S. and Canada to incorporate creation care throughout their church programs. Whether it's worship, youth programs, building and grounds, outreach, or the angel's wings stretched above us in the Aurora Borealis — it's all our Father's world!

BIO

Rev. Edward R. Brown is the founding director of Care of Creation Inc. and one of the leaders of the growing evangelical creation care movement. Before creating Care of Creation Inc., Ed was Chief Operating Officer for Au Sable Institute of Environmental Studies, and has worked with InterVarsity Christian Fellowship and as a pastor both in the U.S. and overseas. He is the author of the book *Our Father's World*. Ed and his wife, Susanna, live in Madison, Wisconsin; they have four grown children.

Coming Home

Scott Rodin

His quip floored me. I was proudly showing a colleague my new truck: a sleek black Dodge Ram 2500 long bed with a V8 Hemi engine. My kids had named it Darth Vader. Instead of the expected words of admiration, however, my friend retorted, "You are really supporting terrorism with that thing." He said it with a smile, but I heard the seriousness in his tone.

What took me aback was not his comment, but the fact that I had never stopped for a moment during the buying process to consider the ecological impact of my new gas-guzzling beast. What puzzled me further was that I had every reason to be more ecologically sensitive. I've been an active Christian most all of my adult life. I love the outdoors. I've studied Reformed theology and its insistence that *everything* is God's. I have an appreciation for God's good creation. I've even written books on stewardship! Why didn't this background prepare me to make a more creation-friendly choice in a vehicle?

The answer is simple. I had bought into the distorted perspective that somehow God is only interested in the lives of those who inhabit his world and not in the world itself. In other words, I was living as though God cared about me, down to the number of hairs on my head and the horsepower of my new Hemi, while at the same time living as though God wasn't the least bit concerned with the people (made in his image) who were negatively affected by my decision or with the stunning creation he called into existence and declared "good."

If that sounds absurd, well, it is.

But such is the power of the distortion that keeps deeply devout Christians from leading the charge for the care of God's creation. And I was among them. Even today, Christian voices warn us not be "distracted" by creation care, lest we take our eyes off the issues that are "really important" to God. I came to the conclusion that such a view was biblically misinformed and theologically unsound — not to mention environmentally disastrous!

Since that day in 2002 I have been on a pilgrimage. It has not been a journey to a

distant, unknown land; it has been more like a coming home. It started with rereading Scripture — this time with one eye open to God's intent for his beloved creation and our calling as stewards of that creation. It continued by revisiting the great theologians of church history — and my amazement at how clued-in they were to this high and holy calling. The next step for me was personal and familial repentance. Not only had I failed to live as a good steward of God's creation, I had allowed my children to follow my poor example. I had not challenged misguided notions in my extended family, lifted up godly stewardship in my church body, or been a champion of creation care in my community. There was plenty of fodder for repentance!

The last step, and the one that continues today, is changing my lifestyle. I've learned that living as the "new creation in Christ" now includes a passion for creation care. This step moved me from the spiritual and theological to the practical. For Linda and me, it means diligently recycling everything possible, making buying decisions that are "green," earning the designation of a registered Stewardship Property for our land, joining organizations that promote conservation and creation care, supporting our church's community garden, and speaking out in both our extended families and community.

And yes, it meant trading in my gas-guzzler for a vehicle with better than twice the fuel efficiency — and purchasing our first hybrid.

These are small steps, and many others are doing so much more. But for me, it is the journey that matters most. How surprised I was to find that my passion for creation care did not come from a new theology or different biblical understanding than what I was raised to believe. It was there all along. I just needed eyes to see it, ears to hear it, and a heart open to embrace it. That is the work of the Holy Spirit, calling each of us to come home and discover that across the pages of our Bible, deep in our own theology, consistent throughout our church's history, and written on our own hearts is the calling to love the creation as a natural expression of our love for the Creator.

> Discipleship is taking seriously the way of Christ in all our affairs and concerns.
>
> **Lee C. Camp**

BIO

Scott Rodin heads Rodin Consulting, Inc., and is the past president of the Christian Stewardship Association, now the Christian Leadership Alliance. Dr. Rodin has served as fund-raising counsel to over one hundred organizations in the U.S. and Great Britain, and for five years was the President of Eastern Baptist Theological Seminary in Philadelphia. He holds a PhD in theology from the University of Aberdeen, Scotland, and has authored several books including *Stewards in the Kingdom*. He lives with his wife, Linda, in Spokane, Washington.

NOW WHAT?

Wendell Berry wrote in his book, *The Gift of Good Land*, "To live, we must daily break the body and shed the blood of creation. When we do it knowingly, lovingly, skillfully, reverently, it is a sacrament. When we do it ignorantly, greedily, destructively, it is a desecration." God created the earth and its unfathomably complex ecosystems to support the existence of every living creature. God calls us to be good stewards of his creation and warns us against the desecration — whether intentional or not — of his world.

Reflect

1. *Describe God's heart for creation.* How would you describe God's heart for creation? Obviously it's impossible to see the world exactly from God's perspective, but it can be a helpful exercise to try. If you are at a loss here, read the first three chapters of Genesis with this question in mind. Why does God care about his creation? What within creation does he care about? Conversely, what do you think pains God about the current state of his creation? Spend some time journaling your thoughts. Try to picture God's point of view — if you had created an incomparable work of art, and people disrespected or damaged it, how would you feel? What would your response be?

2. *Consider the challenges.* What do you think is the most difficult part of caring for creation? Is it the theological aspect? The practical? The financial? Once you've identified your biggest hang-ups with stewarding creation, try to determine where those thoughts come from. Is there a deeper reason beyond what appears on the surface? What preconceived notions are you dealing with? What are some ways you can begin working through these difficulties?

3. *What do you think?* How has this section been for you? Frustrating? Confusing? Enlightening? Fill in your own description here, then explore why you've had this response. Take some time to write a bit about your experience reading this section. Be sure to include the thoughts and emotions and questions that it evoked. Has your theological perspective about creation been affected by one of the entries? If so, write

or talk with a friend about whatever it was that influenced your perspective. Has your perception of the created order and your role within it changed at all? Can you think of a time when a part of creation spoke to you about God? What would it be like to lose that place?

4. *Change.* Are there areas of your life that need to change? What are some areas of growth that relate to how you can steward God's creation? Perhaps it's an unnecessary habit you need to eliminate — or a step you need to incorporate into your daily life, like taking a reusable mug to the coffee shop or investing in reusable grocery bags. Maybe you'll want to start drying your clothes outside instead of using the dryer. Spend some time praying and writing your thoughts about what creation care looks like for *you*.

Respond

1. *Examine your rhythms.* What are some patterns you need to reconsider after reading this section? What are some habits you might want to add to your life? Think of the things we all need — clothes, food, transportation — and get creative about how to make some tweaks in these areas. This can be anything from buying second-hand clothing (a form of recycling) instead of always buying new clothes, to eating lower down the food chain (more grains, veggies, and fruits and less processed foods and meat). Or perhaps you can walk or bike to work when the weather permits, instead of driving every day. Or, if you have to drive, find someone to carpool with — you'll cut gas money and pollution in half.

2. *Cultivate thankfulness.* Practice being thankful for the gift of creation all around you — from the crispness of a fall morning to the first snowfall of winter. For clean air, budding flowers, the limitless variety of animals. Remember that it is *all* God's creation, and that he pronounced it "good."

3. *Take a hike.* Appreciation is often the first step to conservation. If you haven't spent much time outside enjoying God's creation, plan a hike — or at least a long walk — sometime in the next week. Depending on where you live, this might mean researching nearby parks, preserves, or other undeveloped areas. But whether you live at the edge of a national park or in the middle of a large city, there are probably green spaces to be found somewhere close by. Breathe in deeply. Look at the sky. Stop and marvel at the beauty of a flower or the intricacy of a pine needle. Make a mental note

of all the different animals, birds, and insects you encounter. Spend time praying and asking the Lord to reveal his heart to you about creation.

4. *Eat locally.* Becoming more aware of where your food comes from is a great step. Gardening, farmer's markets, and Community Supported Agriculture (CSA) are easy, rewarding ways to care for the environment. Buying food locally or even growing it yourself not only supports local growers, but also avoids the pollution and additional expense associated with transporting foods over long distances. Even if you live in a city, some varieties of tomatoes grow well in pots, as do many kinds of spices and herbs. Eating food that's in-season not only tastes better; it cultivates virtues like patience and gratitude. Most major cities have farmers markets where you can buy local, seasonal food — check out *www.localharvest.org* for more information.

5. *Start recycling.* Recycling is a great way to reduce the amount of trash that you and your family create. It's surprising how much can be recycled these days. Contact your local officials to find out whether there's a recycling center in your area and what they accept. If not, get together with some friends and help start one. Or find the nearest recycling center and make occasional trips there with your stockpile of recyclable products. It's a simple thing to recycle, and when you recycle instead of tossing it out, the item is reused instead of clogging a landfill. When you think about it, recycling makes sense.

> To me, practicing mindfulness in the act of consuming is the basic act of social justice.
>
> **Thich Nhat Hanh**

6. *Rethink personal transportation.* If you're like me, it's easy to depend on a car to get around town just because it's, well, so *easy*. But consider how much energy goes into driving a single mile in your car: oil had to be drilled, refined, and transported to the gas station where you purchased it (all requiring vast amounts of energy and thus creating pollution), before you even put it in your car and started driving it. In my city, considering traffic, stop lights, and parking, I've learned that I can get most places just as quickly by riding a bike as I can by driving. Try it for a week. In doing so you won't use any fossil fuels, and you'll even get some exercise and fresh air. If riding a bike or walking isn't an option, consider carpooling or using public transport as a means of using less energy and generating less pollution.

Spread the Word

It can be daunting to confront the global degradation of creation on our own. But tremendous change happens when we work together. Would you consider spreading the word about creation care, the people whose lives are affected, and the organizations that are doing something to make a difference? Now that you've read this chapter, it isn't someone else's responsibility — it's yours. Change begins with individuals deciding that they are going to live differently. What role can you play? Maybe it's inviting some friends to coffee, starting an action group at your church, or getting your youth group to hold a rally. Help change lives. Spread the word. To help you spread the word about the degradation of creation, and any other issue discussed in this book, we've designed a simple, effective tool: *www.zealouslove.org/spread*.

Share Your Ideas

Have a great idea about something other people can do to engage the issue of creation degradation? Do you want to connect with others who are getting involved? Join the conversation at *www.zealouslove.org/share*.

Additional Resources

www.compostthis.co.uk

www.coopamerica.org

www.ecobags.com

www.edenprojects.org

www.localharvest.org

www.recyclethis.co.uk

www.thegreenspot.org

Visit *www.zealouslove.org/ creation* for more information and organizations.

Discover More

In the Field Notes you've heard from several contributors about the devastating reality of creation degradation. You've also heard some about the incredible work that's being done to address the issue, both on a personal and corporate scale. Remember, there is no one-size-fits-all solution. If you want to get involved in this area, check out the following organizations or visit *www.zealouslove.org/creation*.

A Rocha

Vision: A Rocha is an international Christian nature conservation organization.

Method: A Rocha is now a family of projects working in Europe, the Middle East, Africa, North and South America, Asia, and Australasia. A Rocha projects are frequently cross-cultural in character, and share a community emphasis, with a focus on science and research, practical conservation, and environmental education.

Contact:
Barbara Mearns
International Administrator
A Rocha
3 Hooper St
Cambridge CB1 2NZ
United Kingdom
Phone: 0208-574-5935
www.arocha.org

Care of Creation

Vision: Care of Creation was formed to bring together two important themes: love for God's people, and love for God's world. We're evangelical and we're environmental, and yes, we think we can be both.

Method: Care of Creation is a Christian environmental organization seeking to awaken and mobilize the church to care for God's creation in the face of an environmental crisis that is devastating vast areas of the world and hurting our brothers and sisters in the faith. It is also a missions organization because we believe that environmental problems are sin problems, and we are convinced that the church of Jesus Christ is the world's best hope for dealing with this crisis.

Contact:
Care of Creation, Inc.
PO Box 44582
Madison, WI 53744
Phone: (608) 233-7048
www.careofcreation.org

Slow Food USA

Vision: Slow Food USA envisions a future food system that is based on the principles of high quality and taste, environmental sustainability, and social justice — in essence, a food system that is good, clean, and fair.

Method: We seek to catalyze a broad cultural shift away from the destructive effects of an industrial food system and fast life; toward the regenerative cultural, social, and economic benefits of a sustainable food system, regional food traditions, the pleasures of the table, and a slower and more harmonious rhythm of life.

Contact:
Slow Food USA National Office
20 Jay Street, Suite M04
Brooklyn, NY 11201
Phone: (877) SlowFoo(d)
www.slowfoodusa.org

Evangelical Environmental Network

Vision: The Evangelical Environmental Network (EEN) is a non-profit organization that seeks to educate, inspire, and mobilize Christians in their effort to care for God's creation, to be faithful stewards of God's provision, and to advocate for actions and policies that honor God and protect the environment.

Method: EEN's work is grounded in the Bible's teaching on the responsibility of God's people to "tend the garden" and in a desire to be faithful to Jesus Christ and to follow Him. EEN publishes materials to equip and inspire individuals, families, and churches; and seeks to educate and mobilize people to make a difference in their churches and communities, and to speak out on national and international policies that effect our ability to preach the Gospel, protect life, and care for God's creation.

Contact:
Evangelical Environmental Network
4485 Tench Road
Suite 850
Suwanee, GA 30024
Phone: (678) 541-0747
www.creationcare.org

Evangelicals for Social Action

Vision: Evangelicals for Social Action (ESA) is a community of Christians committed to living out their walk with Christ holistically — that is, with the whole of their lives.

Method: Evangelicals for Social Action seeks to promote Christian engagement, analysis, and understanding of major social, cultural, and public policy issues. ESA's board of directors includes many prominent leaders of moderate and progressive evangelicalism. ESA emphasizes both the transformation of human lives through personal faith and also the importance of a commitment to social and economic justice as an outgrowth of Christian faith.

Contact:

The Sider Center on Ministry and Public Policy
6 E. Lancaster Ave.
Wynnewood, PA 19096-3420
Phone: (484) 384-2990
www.esa-online.org

HIV
AND AIDS

Religion that God our Father accepts as pure and faultless
    is this:
to look after orphans and widows in their distress
and to keep oneself from being polluted by the world.

James 1:27

What's your definition of *religion*? When I hear the word I normally think of dry, endless rituals that have no affect on daily life. The biblical definition — presumably a good one since God accepts it as "pure and faultless" — involves being in relationship with people. It involves service. It involves caring for those who are in need. This religion is active in the midst of other people's distress.

Do the words of James challenge your understanding of true religion?

BRIEFING

A couple months ago, Mike and I were living in a tent in a rural community in Eastern Africa. During the weeks we camped out with the Luo people, we shared many meals with our hosts. Before the meal, everyone washed their hands. Someone (usually a woman) would come with a pitcher of water and a bucket to catch the dirty water. Only on rare occasions were we offered soap to wash with as we prepared to use "the natural utensil" (our right hand) to eat. Oddly, several times we were offered soap to wash with *after* we'd finished our meal.

This happened several times during our stay, so I asked a woman who works as a hygiene educator about it. She told me that our hosts didn't want us to leave smelling like food, and since soap is a costly luxury, they'd prefer to use it after the meal. This made no sense at all to me — we'd walked on dusty paths for hours, used the bathroom, and greeted many people with firm handshakes. I didn't care if I smelled like beans when I was done — I'd much rather eat my food with clean hands, especially when my utensils were my own fingers! The hygiene educator agreed, but she said the people simply had never been trained and so they didn't know the importance of washing with soap before eating.

I remember how as a young child, I was taught to wash my hands with soap as soon as I could stand on the stool and reach the sink. Before that, I was lifted up to get the job done. Soap and warm, clean water were always involved. There were times I was annoyed that I had to wash my hands, but I never doubted it was a necessary thing to do. It never occurred to me that some people have never been taught to wash their hands with soap, or, perhaps, to wash their hands at all.

This cultural difference offers us westerners a good way to begin thinking about the AIDS crisis. In a similar, but more costly way, a lack of adequate training and education about HIV is having drastic consequences in many developing countries. In some places, basic understanding about how HIV is transferred simply doesn't exist. Without this knowledge, myths abound about the disease, those affected by it, how it is contracted, and how it can be avoided. People who have the virus are often shunned and stigmatized, which only discourages others from getting tested. Many people do not know there may be antiretroviral drugs (ARVs) available at little or no cost through government- and NGO-sponsored programs. Fear of a lack of treatment options and being ostracized by their community cause many to never find out if they are HIV-positive.

An example of widespread misinformation about HIV and AIDS made headlines in 2006. The then-vice president of South Africa, Jacob Zuma, was accused of raping a thirty-one-year-old HIV-positive woman. During his defense against the purported rape, he testified that it was unlikely he would contract the virus because he was healthy and had taken a shower after having sex with the woman.[1] Activists were furious that someone with so much influence in a country with such a high HIV prevalence (above 15 percent) would propagate such utter falsehoods.[2] In a horrible twist, Mr. Zuma is the former head of South Africa's AIDS council. Recently, he was also elected president of the country.

Friends of ours in South Africa told us that despite an increased international focus on HIV and AIDS and some strong educational gains, the disease is still highly stigmatized — so much so that if a person finds out they are HIV-positive, they may not even tell their spouse. In Zambia and other countries, there is a common belief that having sex with a virgin will cure HIV. This myth is spread by traditional healers — medicine men and women. As a result, instances of child rape have increased significantly in Zambia.[3]

In recent years, HIV and AIDS have received greater media attention. Thankfully, many gains have been made because of increased awareness, education, behavioral change, advances in and greater access to antiretroviral medication, and

> God can always turn evil into good, though perhaps not always in a sense that would be understood by the preachers of sunshine and uplift.
>
> **Thomas Merton**

more funding from wealthy countries. In 2008, the U.S. Congress passed a bill that provides $48 billion for the global fight against AIDS over five subsequent years.[4] Despite such progress, AIDS remains the world's fourth leading cause of death in low and middle income countries, and since the first known report in 1981, over twenty-five million people have died from AIDS.[5] In 2005, AIDS killed approximately 2.2 million people, and in 2007 another 2 million people died.[6] This means that every hour, nearly 230 people die because of AIDS.

When HIV is left untreated, particularly in developing countries where clean water, sanitation, and good nutrition are scarce, the result is almost always an early death for people who would otherwise be in the prime of their lives. This means that communities lose some of their most important members — the very people who normally grow the crops, raise families, send their children to school, and contribute to the local and regional economies. Communities and whole nations have lost significant portions of their populations. In regions like sub-Saharan Africa, AIDS has been particularly devastating. More than two-thirds of all the adults and 90 percent of all the children who have the HIV virus live in this area, and three-quarters of the deaths in 2007 occurred here.[7] Economically and culturally, these countries are in danger of collapse.

So far we have taken a broad view. What happens to a young child when one or both parents die because of AIDS and the orphan must become the head of his or her household? What about the impact on a family who has lost two children to AIDS already, while their third grows sicker every day? As for those who have access to antiretroviral medication, they must now decide how to live with the virus. Will they marry? What if they pass the virus to their children? How will they endure possible stigma and prejudice?

And what does it mean to love those who have been affected by AIDS? I think that part of the answer can be found in the words of Bono, U2 lead singer and prominent human rights activist: "God is in the slums, in the cardboard boxes where the poor play house. God is in the silence of a mother who has infected her child with a virus that will end both their lives. God is in the cries heard under the rubble of war. God is in the debris of wasted opportunity and lives, and God is with us if we are with them."[8]

Many people talk about God being on their side, often invoking his blessing to validate their actions. Sometimes the result is one more verse in a deplorable litany of crimes done in God's name. What *is* clear in Scripture is that God is on the side of the poor, the desperate, and the sick. And, as Bono put it, God is with us if we are with those who are dying from disease, those who are the forgotten consequence of a global injustice.

Those of us living in developed countries have knowledge and resources to help those in great need. Particularly in impoverished countries where information about and access to health care are limited, the wealth and knowledge of the developed world can be effective.

Antiretroviral medication cost around $10,000 per patient per year only a few years ago. Today, it costs as little as $140 per patient per year.[9] To those of us in the developed world, this may seem like a tiny price to pay for life-saving medicine, but to many in sub-Saharan Africa, that sum is a staggering impossibility.

According to UNAIDS, a majority of the nearly 5500 people who die every day from AIDS do so because of "inadequate access to HIV prevention and treatment services."[10]

Those who do have access to treatment — often provided with the help of western donors — live many years beyond those with inadequate access to treatment.

However, money is only part of the story. Many organizations are involved in holistic support and care for the approximately 33 million people currently living with HIV.[11] There are many ways to help those suffering from HIV and AIDS. Perhaps you know someone in your community who has HIV; how might you reach out to them? Some friends of ours adopted a baby from another country who is HIV positive, and now they simply love their new daughter. A couple we know just gave a large portion of their savings to an organization supporting those affected by AIDS. Recently, I met a girl in her twenties who was living in Africa and who, as a single, white woman, adopted the son of an African woman who was dying from AIDS. It's tempting to say these things are not what everyone is called to do, but perhaps that

absolves us of responsibility a little too quickly. True religion, after all, looks after widows and orphans in their distress.

Former UN Secretary-General Kofi Annan has called AIDS "a threat to an entire generation — a threat to an entire civilization."[12] From the halls of government to the chambers of our own hearts, more can and should be done to address this threat. Apathy is not an option, especially not for those who claim to follow Christ. We mustn't ignore the disease or the people it wounds and kills. On the following pages, you will read personal accounts from people who are responding to HIV and AIDS in a variety of ways. Allow yourself to be present with them in these stories. Open yourself to respond in whatever ways God may call you.

A Saint Named Margaret

Scott Todd

In my travels with Compassion International, I've met thousands of families affected by AIDS. I've encountered children whose bodies are destroyed by this terrible disease, and parents who stay up all night, dropping water into the parched mouths of feverish children, trying to coax life where there is only death.

I thought I had seen it all. But then I met Margaret. Her story is one of unrelenting love. Agape, in fact. Perfect love that casts out fear.

I first met Margaret when I was traveling in Uganda with Compassion. I had spent the day visiting families helped by our AIDS Initiative, and Margaret's house was one of our last stops. My guide led me down a dusty path to Margaret's home, a one-room hut made of mud and straw. Margaret and I sat together in that sweltering room, our knees almost touching in the cramped space as she told me her story.

Margaret pointed to a spot a few hundred yards from her house. "That's where I found her," she said. Five years earlier, Margaret had been watering her goats when she heard a baby's cry. She followed the cries and found a basket mired in thick, black mud. As she looked at the crying infant, she had just one thought. *I can't leave her.* This aging grandmother gave no thought to her own poverty, hunger, and desperation. She could only think of the baby at her feet.

African mothers rarely abandon their children. Most will sacrifice everything for their families. But the child Margaret found wasn't just abandoned. Finger-shaped bruises discolored her neck. Dried blood was caked on her body. Margaret knew that only one thing would drive a mother to try to kill her own baby. She had seen mothers in her village driven insane by the guilt of passing AIDS on to their children. I've seen the same thing through my work with Compassion. A mother assumes that if she is HIV-positive, her child will inherit the disease and die. The guilt and shame are overwhelming. Watching her child die a slow death from AIDS is a punishment beyond what she can bear.

I'll never forget Margaret telling me about the choice she faced. I knew that, like most people in her village, Margaret often went to bed with her belly aching from hunger. She was unemployed and elderly. How could she provide the food and medicine this child needed? What had driven Margaret to bring that sickly child into her home, knowing her only reward would be watching a baby die a slow death?

As I sat in Margaret's scorching hut staring at her deeply lined face, she answered my unspoken question humbly. "Someone had already abandoned her," Margaret said softly. "I couldn't do it again."

Margaret's journey was a difficult one. The child, whom she named Doreen, was constantly ill. As Doreen's health worsened, Margaret's frustration grew. Some days, when Doreen lay weak and crying, Margaret regretted her decision to walk toward the cries she had heard in that

desolate field. At one point, Margaret told me she even tried to find another home for Doreen — but when she witnessed the family's abuse of Doreen, Margaret immediately brought her back home. In those moments of desperation, Margaret felt empathy for Doreen's birth mother. That poor woman had tried to end her child's suffering. Now Margaret embraced that suffering every day.

When Doreen was around a year old, Margaret heard about a local church that was partnering with Compassion's Child Survival Program (CSP). This program was created for the 26,000 children under age five who die each day, mostly from preventable or treatable diseases.[13] It is geared for mothers who lack the resources to provide for the physical needs of their children. Nobody fit the mission of the Child Survival Program more than Margaret and Doreen.

As one of the first children registered in Uganda's Child Survival Program, Doreen received immediate and consistent medical care and nutritional supplements. Now she is a different child. Once too weak to sit up, she is now an active five-year-old who runs and plays with her friends. Now Margaret watches her child live instead of dreading her death.

When I look at Doreen and Margaret and the thousands of other families in our programs, I see the face of real love. Without Margaret's powerful love for her daughter, Doreen would have never made it to the Child Survival Program. I see God's love in action as Margaret takes Doreen to the clinic and coaxes her to take the medicine that strengthens her immune system. I see Doreen's sponsor, her health specialists, and her doctors and nurses all standing in the gap for one of God's precious children.

BIO

Scott Todd is Director of Compassion International's Special Operations, which includes the AIDS Initiative and more than a dozen other programs encompassing $30 million in field operations, ranging from disaster relief to Bible distribution. He received his doctorate in immunology from the University of California in 1996. Following his doctorate, Dr. Todd accepted a fellowship in oncology at Stanford University Medical Center, where he was the National Lymphoma Foundation Scholar. In 2003, he left academic research to join Compassion International. Todd is an expert on pediatric AIDS in developing countries.

Beware of TIME Magazine

Dennis and Susan Wadley

One afternoon several years ago I sat down in my favorite chair with the February 2001 issue of TIME magazine, not knowing it would change the course of our family's life. I began to read the lead article which focused on the worldwide AIDS pandemic. As I read the stories of the suffering, stigma, rejection, and death of millions on the other side of the planet, as I stared at the photos of orphans left to fend for themselves, I knew I couldn't just toss the magazine aside and go on with my life. After reading the articles, our family knew that we had to take some sort of action. Through a lot of prayerful seeking, we felt the Lord leading us to South Africa, the country where more people live with HIV than any other place on earth.

Our first "research visit" was to a 100,000-member urban slum outside Cape Town called Philippi. Philippi is an "informal settlement" of outhouses, stolen electricity, and paralyzing gang violence. Soon after our arrival, we realized that those affected by HIV and AIDS are not merely statistics. They are people, just like you and me, people made in God's image. People he deeply and dearly loves. Many are innocent victims, often contracting HIV as a result of rape, through an unfaithful spouse, in a blood transfusion, or even through birth. Gut wrenching stories of pain, fear, loss, and rejection convinced us that we needed to respond with the kind of love we hoped others would show us if we were in similar circumstances.

We returned home and began working, trying to discern the best way to help. A year after those first unforgettable conversations in Philippi, Bridges of Hope International was formed. After another year, we moved our family to South Africa, fully throwing ourselves in, trusting the Lord to lead us.

We plunged into life and work in Philippi, partnering with a local pastor and his wife. We started making connections, building relationships, discovering ways we could help.

Then, six months after we arrived, the world flipped upside down. South Africa is a rough place. In fact, every day more than three hundred murders or violent attacks occur.[14]

C. S. Lewis once wrote "You never know how much you really believe anything until its truth or falsehood becomes a matter of life and death. It is easy to say you believe a rope to be strong as long as you are merely using it to cord a box. But suppose you had to hang by that rope over a precipice. Wouldn't you then first discover how much you really trusted it?"[15]

One afternoon we would have the chance to discover if we really trusted our Lord. Unexpectedly our vehicle was surrounded and we were robbed of all our belongings at gunpoint. It went against every human and parental instinct to stay in the country, rather than calling it quits, and returning home. But even amidst our shock and tears, we felt the Lord leading us to stay. We felt strongly that he had something he wanted us to do there. Our responsibility was to search our hearts and ask ourselves if we were literally willing to surrender our lives to follow his lead.

We kept working, building rapport in the community, trying to help where we could. As time passed we discovered that the reality in Philippi was far more complicated than we had imagined or feared. HIV and AIDS is not a stand-alone problem; it is inextricably linked with poverty, unemployment, violent crime, and a deep lack of hope — the lingering ef-

fects of the apartheid regime that gripped South Africa for more than forty years. It became clear that a myopic approach to HIV and AIDS that ignored these inherent complexities simply wouldn't work. We had to approach people holistically: identifying the wide array of needs and trying to address them one at a time. Again and again we were told that what we were attempting was impossible. It couldn't be done by a couple of volunteers working in a place as tough as Philippi.

The people of Philippi have silenced many of the skeptics. Our South African staff knows how to do their work with or without us, and they've done an incredible job. They rose to the challenge of Philippi and became leaders among leaders, organizing volunteers to care for their neighbors spiritually, physically, emotionally, socially, and mentally. They have created programs to meet the needs of those suffering with HIV and AIDS. They have launched effective programs in their local schools to stem the tide of the disease and to give children hope for the future. They have also provided care to many children who have been orphaned by this pandemic. They have even reached out to gang members, helping more than fifty to reform. Now some of these ex-gang members are sharing their stories in schools, churches, and prisons. Their work has been so effective that other gang members plead with them to teach them how to do the same.

As we got to know some of those in the very center of the HIV and AIDS pandemic storm, we realized that they weren't merely statistics. They were amazing people who have endured unimaginable suffering with great dignity.

More than five years later, the South African staff at Bridges of Hope continues working in Philippi as well as in three surrounding communities. Work has just begun in the neighboring country of Swaziland. It hasn't been easy. There have been many precipices over which we've had to hang. And yet God has held us. Every time. More than that, I have seen the impossible take place. In a place as tough as Philippi, I have seen God bring about change and rekindle hope even where it had been lost.

BIO

Dennis graduated from Biola University in 1984 with a degree in biblical studies. While serving as a pastor in Santa Barbara, California, he completed his master's degree in theology at Talbot Theological Seminary. Susan graduated from U.C. Santa Barbara in 1986 with a degree in English. Susan and Dennis married in 1990. They now have three children: Tasha Grace, Adilyn Rose, and Elijah Lucas. They made their first scouting trip to South Africa in 2001 and co-founded Bridges of Hope International (BHI) in 2002. They moved to South Africa in 2003 to direct the organization and carry out the vision of holistic community development. They returned to the U.S. at the end of 2007 and continue to manage BHI from Santa Barbara.

Gypsy Baby

Martin and Kristi French

Walking out of the run-down Romanian hospital holding a gypsy baby wrapped in filthy rags — my new son — I experienced a moment of transformation and calling, although at the time I didn't realize just how much my life would change. Yes, Kristi and I had made the decision to begin our family by adopting a needy child out of the developing world — a response of sorts to the intersection of our own personal struggles with the hurts of the global community. I was to learn within the next few months, and much more deeply over the ensuing seventeen years, how our Lord desires for us to engage in a life far beyond what we believe we are capable of. Our desire to heal some of the hurts of world poverty in our home, as sincere as it was, lacked a sense of realism. We had no idea what we were walking into.

Less than one month later, after returning home to the USA with our new son, we were just beginning to feel a sense of normalcy in our lives when we received a phone call from the Romanian doctor. The doctor's news was as terrifying as it was brief: my son was HIV-positive. My new one-year-old son — whom we had traveled around the world to find in order to bring into our home to raise as our own — had now been given only two years to live.

AIDS was one of those issues that had swirled around the periphery of my life. I figured I was relatively well educated regarding the disease and its impact on the world, but I never expected to deal with it personally. We knew Romania was ravaged by the disease, and we had made certain that the child we were adopting was not infected. Tests were taken and the necessary questions were asked and re-asked. Looking back, I realize that I was as small-minded and prejudiced as anyone could possibly be against those who carried this burden. I had made a societal caste system of my very own.

That night, a solution did come. I heard God's voice, telling me simply to have courage. The word carried no answers with it. No vision of how the journey would end, and no guarantees against pain and sorrow. He simply said to have courage and walk — this was indeed my son whom I was given as a gift by the merciful hand of almighty God.

Being the parent of an infected child (who has outlived his diagnosis and is now seventeen) gave us an achingly clear view into the heart struggle of those who carry the burden of this disease. Globally, we face the reality of a generation of young people — children, teens, and young adults — infected with and affected by AIDS. More and more of these young people are outliving their prognosis and now face the extreme complexities of relationships, sex, careers, health insurance, and discrimination. One of the most poignant questions they ask is, "How far are we allowed to dream?"

Recently, my son shared his feelings of dirtiness and isolation. He said that there are times when walking through the halls of his high school it feels like the letters H-I-V are painted across his forehead. He wondered if he could really think about marriage and sex and ever being truly accepted. He expressed his own struggle to fully engage in his peer group. He often feels the need to pull away and "take care of himself." He expressed fears about being "dangerous" — even deadly to a girl that he may find himself in love with one day. This brought tears to both of our eyes.

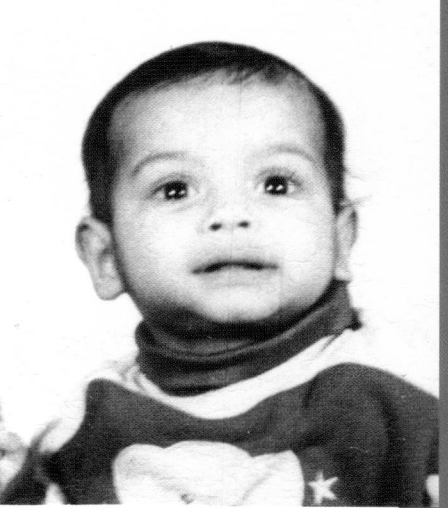

Jesus came to offer life in all of its fullness, for all people — and no less for those afflicted with what Dr. Tony Campolo calls "the modern day equivalent to the leprosy of Jesus' day." Perhaps God in his mercy and ineffable wisdom has offered us, as his bride the church, an opportunity to express his glory and power by reaching out to ostracized men and women — to come alongside those who are living out questions like the one my son asked. Perhaps God is calling us to lead them to a place of peace, clarity, and hope in Jesus Christ.

God has not left us with a map describing all the dangers along the way. He has simply invited us to journey with him into uncharted territory and discover what love is by giving and receiving it without hesitation or fear. My family has experienced the exhaustion and the glories of this journey. We have found healing, and peace, and life in all its fullness. My fear of sixteen years ago — that my child would be HIV-positive — not only happened; indeed it became a great gift of my life. Therein I have experienced the love of Abba Father most deeply.

BIO

Martin and Kristi French embarked on the adventure of their lives in 1990 when they traveled to a Gypsy village in Romania to adopt their son. Their journey continued in 1993 when they traveled to Guatemala to adopt their daughter. Adopting two "throw-away" children was the French's personal vision for what family life should be. Since those early days, they have returned to the homelands of their two children, allowing them to experience the rich Gypsy and Mayan cultures with which they are forever connected, and are seeking to engage as a family in working against the devastation of poverty in the Third World. Martin is currently Pastor of the Arts at Imago Dei Community Church and Chair of Illustration at the Pacific Northwest College of Art. Kristi is a high school educator and the best full-time mom in the world. Their two children, Jacob and Danielle, are high school students, artists, dreamers, and all-around amazing kids.

One Blade of Grass

Susan Slonaker

Today, I weep again for brown-eyed, eighteen-year-old Thomas and remember feeling his thin arms wrapped around me as I lay in his hospital bed, my head against his chest, waiting with him for his final breath to come and go. His thin, wasted body was difficult to hug, like hugging a small child. I wanted to hug him tightly, to hold him here on this earth, but I hugged him gently, aware of his fragility. Admit it or not, we all like to think we're invincible. AIDS has an awful ability to strip that invincibility down to the bare bone. Yet, by allowing Christ to enter into the suffering that AIDS creates, astonishing healing can occur even as the human body surrenders to the disease.

On my morning run recently, I paused, bent down, and marveled at the blades of grass under my feet. I remembered the words of Walt Whitman, "We won't see clearly until we look humbly: Bring all the art and science of the world, and baffle and humble it with one spear of grass." It really *is* amazing — the resilience, and strength of so small a thing. I couldn't help but wonder, "How much more should I marvel at a child?" Even Jesus, when he pointed to a child, the most vulnerable of all people, said, "Whoever humbles himself like this child is the greatest in the kingdom of heaven" (Matt. 18:4).

Usually, children grow like grass. Usually they are not cut down quickly, but today, as I write this, yet another grief-stricken mother has called to inform me that her son has died of AIDS, and the grief of Thomas' death comes flooding back to me. Thomas was a child in our ministry, REACH. Despite the chilling effects of AIDS, we work hard to offer love and hope through relationship, mentoring, education, and other services to those living in the turbulence of the worst pandemic in history. AIDS is a global tragedy, and we're working hard to love those affected here in the United States.

Back in 1999, I was approached by Children's Hospital and Regional Medical Center of Seattle to help love and serve the pediatric HIV-infected population in our communities. Over a long road with many unexpected twists and turns, God has worked in and through more than 250 volunteers and an incredible staff to encourage and support nearly 350 children and family members across the country. AIDS causes not only horrendous physical suffering but brings with it painful social and emotional consequences: isolation, loneliness, demeaning censure, and harsh public opinion. Through programs, resources, and an annual summer camp, REACH provides a safe place, free from stigma and judgment, where families and suffering kids are learning to live life to the full.

Thomas, the beautiful child who had danced with me once, held onto me as he lay dying. His was a valiant fight ultimately suffused with peace and wrapped in sustaining love. "REACH has been a blessing," his mother said, quietly turning to me after he was gone. "A safe place of refuge shared with those of you who came alongside with fun and respect and mostly, with love."

Death beat Thomas' body, but not his spirit. Like him, we each await transition from this life to the next. The love of Christ attends and encourages our journey, and this gift of love can banish fear and teach us to pause. And it is when we pause to marvel and take time to love that we become bearers of hope to others.

BIO

Susan Slonaker is the executive director of REACH Ministries, a not-for-profit organization that focuses on serving families of children infected and affected by AIDS. REACH Ministries is dedicated to the "*least of these*," children living within the worst pandemic in history. Susan serves on community-based committees and boards while actively collaborating in the secular and faith-based community.

Prescription for Hope

Sheri Warren

Just after the tsunami in 2004, I volunteered with an organization working in southeast India and Sri Lanka. During this trip, my eyes were opened to the devastating effects of the AIDS pandemic, and my life was changed. At the time I was single, in my late twenties, and using my vacation time for the trip. I was relatively unaware of the global AIDS crisis until four women in India shared their stories with me, and it made a huge impact.

I met one woman in particular whose story brought me to tears. Her marriage had been arranged according to Indian tradition. Shortly after the wedding, however, she discovered her husband was HIV-positive. He passed the virus to her, and she infected their son. By the age of twenty-six, this young woman was already a widow, and the illness was consuming her body. Her greatest concern was for her son's future. Her family would not take him because of the stigma associated with HIV. She did not know what would become of him once she died. Who would protect him? How would he survive? Would he die of hunger? Would he have a home? This was the moment that AIDS came to life for me. There are 2.4 million people living with HIV in India.[16] For the first time, though, the disease was more than a statistic to me. It was a young mother and her son, standing right in front of me.

At the end of our conversation, I knew I had to do something. I didn't know what, but I knew I would never be the same. I spent the next few years educating myself about the disease and its effects on lives and communities. I read every book I could get my hands on, did extensive research online, and searched journal articles at a university library.

After volunteering for over eighteen years, I began working for Samaritan's Purse in 2007. I chose to join this organization because of its commitment to help those who suffer with the purpose of sharing God's love. I wanted to be a part of both helping hurting people and offering eternal hope and lasting change.

There is currently no cure for HIV and AIDS. There are life-saving treatments, but many of those suffering from HIV and AIDS around the world do not have access to medical care, so some think there is no hope in such circumstances. Our ministry is called Prescription for Hope because we believe Jesus offers hope even in the most desperate situations. Our work offers practical assistance to those infected with HIV, those wondering about their HIV status, those who want to change their lifestyle, and those already clearly affected by the disease.

Several years ago, we held a Prescription for Hope workshop in Cambodia to mobilize the church to respond to the disease in their communities. We quickly realized that the church was not ready for this responsibility. In Cambodia there were 14,000 AIDS-related deaths in 2007.[17] A legacy of genocide, famine, and poverty makes the country especially vulnerable to the deadly disease. In the past, a weak health system has led to misinformation and inadequate care for the infected. Many of the pastors we worked with laughed at the thought of caring for the sick.

Some Cambodian HIV patients are further isolated by traditional religious beliefs and stigma. In Chea's case, for example, his wife took their three children and left him. His neighbors stopped speaking to him. He was desperate and alone, until God used one person to change his life. Chea's pastor in Cambodia received training on how to compassionately care for HIV patients at a Prescription for Hope workshop. Since that time, the pastor has paid frequent visits to Chea and many others — feeding them, holding their hands, and sharing the gospel. The pastor showed Chea the unconditional love of Jesus, even bringing lotion to massage his cracked skin. Chea remarked that the lotion soothed his body, but knowing that someone wasn't afraid to touch him comforted his heart.

When Chea finally accepted the gift of salvation, his self-pity disappeared. His wife visited him and was touched by his repentant heart and newfound peace. Shortly after, she returned home with their children. The pastor taught her how to care for Chea, and she asked him questions about the Jesus who had so profoundly changed her husband.

Chea lay dying on a thin mat, his emaciated body finally succumbing to the ravages of AIDS. Yet, as he made the painful journey toward death, there was peace in his eyes and a broad smile on his face. His wife was at his side when the Lord called Chea home.

Many of Chea's neighbors attended his funeral. One of the village elders asked the pastor, "Why did you visit this man who was doomed to die?" Chea's wife responded, "This man cared for us because he follows Jesus Christ." She then told them of Chea's overwhelming peace on his deathbed. The elder looked at the villagers gathered for the funeral and asked, "Why don't we follow this Jesus?"

It is a privilege to see this kind of transformation in individuals, churches, and communities. After all, while we must do all that we can to stop the spread of HIV and care for those who are already infected, only Jesus Christ offers genuine, death-defying hope for those who will die because of AIDS.

BIO

Now the Prescription for Hope (PFH) Team Leader, Sheri Warren joined Samaritan's Purse staff in 2007. She has a Master's Degree in Public Administration with an emphasis in nonprofit management. Prior to joining the PFH team she was working on completing her PhD in public administration with a research interest in nonprofit/government partnerships to help vulnerable populations. She came to Samaritan's Purse with seventeen years of international humanitarian experience, much of it as a lay leader in other faith-based ministries. Sheri's role with the team is to provide guidance in programming, assure alignment with the mission of the department and organization, and act as a liaison with donor agencies.

NOW WHAT?

With 33 million people infected worldwide, AIDS is poised to surpass the Black Plague as the most severe pandemic in human history, as far as sheer numbers go. In terms of global impact, though, AIDS is already considered by many the worst pandemic in history. It robs people of life, children of parents, and moms and dads of sons and daughters. It devastates economies and hinders countries' ability to build healthy, thriving communities. Yet advances in modern medicine make it possible for those with the virus to live longer and healthier lives than ever before. Stronger education programs with culturally sensitive ways of addressing the spread of HIV are developing. This pandemic *is* being attacked, but it will be a long time before the virus and its aftermath are fully defeated.

Reflect

1. *What do you think?* How has this section been for you to read? Frustrating? Confusing? Enlightening? All of the above? Why do you think this section has evoked the feelings and response that it has? Take some time to journal about your experience reading this section. Be sure to include the thoughts and emotions that it called up, as well as anything new you may have learned, and don't be afraid to ask yourself some hard questions.

2. *Put yourself in another's shoes.* Imagine that you live in sub-Saharan Africa, one of the hardest-hit areas in the world when it comes to AIDS. What if you or someone in your immediate family was infected? How would your life change? What would you spend your days doing? What would your faith look like in this context? Don't rush this answer — spend the necessary time to imagine yourself into someone else's life.

3. *Practice explaining it.* Pretend you are at coffee with a friend who thinks those with HIV should just deal with it themselves or even that it's their own fault that they have the virus. Though this response might evoke some frustration, how might you convince them otherwise? How might you (lovingly) help them understand the need that exists and the reasons why we ought to be helping those who are affected no matter where they live or why they have HIV?

4. *Take a look at yourself.* We all have hidden prejudices and tendencies to categorize people without knowing much about them. Take some time to consider your own thoughts and feelings toward people with HIV. Do you stereotype before getting to know them? Do you subtly avoid such people because you don't know how to interact with them? Perhaps it isn't even direct or intentional. Imagine that a close friend or a family member was HIV-positive. What would you do? How would you bring it up? Would the way you interact change? Take some time here and delve into some of the attitudes, judgments, or stereotypes that might be in your heart, perhaps without your knowledge. Be honest. Open yourself to introspection.

Respond

1. *Be an advocate.* Politics have impact in the world, and politicians listen to their constituents. Write your elected officials and ask them to pass legislation to provide funds for the campaign against AIDS — or thank them if they have already made it a priority. You may need to spend some time researching online, but it can be well worth it. Go to *www.congress.org* (U.S.), *www.parliament.uk* (UK), or *www.parl.gc.ca* (Canada) for powerful tools that enable you to contact your elected representatives. Politics is often a numbers game, so get as many people as you can to join you, and make change happen.

2. *Fund antiretroviral treatment.* Medical treatment that can extend a patient's life costs around $140 per year. That's less than $12 per month — not a huge sacrifice for most of us in developed countries. But for most living in developing nations, it's an impossible sum. Consider giving the forty cents per day it takes to provide someone life-giving medicine through one of the organizations below.

> To try to make others comfortable is the only way to get right comfortable ourselves, and that comes partly of not being able to think so much about ourselves when we are helping other people. For our Selves will always do pretty well if we don't pay them too much attention.
>
> **George MacDonald**

3. *Volunteer.* Mother Teresa spent most of her life caring for the sick and dying, including those affected by HIV and AIDS. While you might not be Mother Teresa, the opportunity for you to spend your days serving in a hands-on way is very real. Perhaps it will be a

weeklong trip or a decade-long season. Begin by praying and researching opportunities online. See where you are led.

4. *Sponsor a child.* There are many organizations that offer child sponsorship, many of which focus on the needs of children and families devastated by AIDS. Whether or not a child gets sponsored can literally mean the difference between death and life.

Spread the Word

Individually, it feels daunting to confront the global AIDS pandemic. But tremendous change happens when we work together. Would you consider spreading the word about AIDS, the people whose lives are affected, and the organizations that are doing something to make a difference? Now that you've read this chapter, it isn't someone else's responsibility — it's yours. Change begins with individuals deciding that they are going to live differently. What role can you play? Maybe it's inviting some friends to coffee, starting an action group at your church, or getting your youth group to hold a rally. Help change lives. Spread the word. To help you spread the word about AIDS, and any other issue discussed in this book, we've designed a simple, effective tool: *www.zealouslove.org/spread*.

Share Your Ideas

Have a great idea about something others can do to engage and help with HIV and AIDS? Do you want to connect with others who are getting involved? Join the conversation at *www.zealouslove.org/share*.

Additional Resources

www.one.org

www.unaids.org

www.worldaidsday.org

www.wr.org

Visit *www.zealouslove.org/aids* for more information and organizations.

Discover More

In the Field Notes you've heard from several contributors about the harsh reality of the global AIDS pandemic. You've also heard about the incredible work that's being done to address the issue, both on a personal and corporate scale. Remember, there is no one-size-fits-all solution. If you want to get involved in this area, check out the following organizations or visit *www.zealouslove.org/aids*.

Compassion International — AIDS Initiative

Vision: Compassion International exists as a Christian child advocacy ministry that releases children from spiritual, economic, social, and physical poverty and enables them to become responsible, fulfilled Christian adults.

Method: Compassion's HIV and AIDS Initiative offers comprehensive and holistic services that allow us to proactively fight this widespread disease one child at a time. Compassion's treatment program is administered through the local church in each community. When the local church monitors health, provides treatment options, and offers prevention education, families willingly begin to work against the devastating effects of HIV and AIDS.

Contact:

Compassion International
Colorado Springs, CO 80997
Phone: (800) 336-7676
www.compassion.com

Samaritan's Purse — Prescription for Hope

Vision: Despite the devastating impact of the HIV/AIDS pandemic, there is hope. Samaritan's Purse's Prescription for Hope program is designed to strengthen the international Christian response to HIV/AIDS; mobilize private, church, corporate, and government resources; and develop a unified plan to defeat this disease.

Method: To more effectively fight HIV/AIDS, Prescription for Hope™ offers a multi-faceted approach to education, training, and behavior change. Our programs are designed to reach out to a variety of people with differing experiences and worldviews.

Programs include: abstinence and behavior change programs for youth, workshops for church leaders, support for mission hospitals, partnership with grassroots organizations, and integrated HIV response through field organizations.

Contact:

Samaritan's Purse
c/o Prescription for Hope
PO Box 3000
Boone, NC 28607-3000.
Phone: (800) 528-1980
www.samaritanspurse.org

Bridges of Hope International

Vision: Bridges of Hope believes that it is possible for individuals who live in extremely dire conditions to find hope — to dream about and actually *change* their future.

Method: Bridges of Hope seeks to build bridges into suffering communities in order to create long-term, self-sustaining solutions to the deep problems of our world, and to motivate Christians and others to share from their abundance of gifts, skills, and resources and to sacrificially invest their lives in taking down the giants of our world that keep people in bondage and despair, using both proven and innovative means.

Contact:
Bridges of Hope
PO Box 6947
Santa Barbara, CA 93160-6947
www.bridges-of-hope.org

REACH Ministries

Vision: REACH Ministries is a Christian organization whose focus is on ministering to the children and families in the United States of America suffering from HIV and AIDS.

Method: REACH serves children and families affected by HIV and AIDS through several programs including: A) REACH Mentoring Program, B) REACH Camps and Psychosocial Progressive Units, C) REACH High School Program, D) REACH Global Initiative, and E) ABC+G Sex Education curriculum.

Contact:
REACH Ministries
309 South G Street
Suite 3
Tacoma, WA 98405
Phone: (253) 383-7616
www.reachministries.org

World Vision — Hope Initiative

Vision: World Vision is a Christian humanitarian organization dedicated to working with children, families, and their communities worldwide to reach their full potential by tackling the causes of poverty and injustice.

Method: The Hope Initiative is World Vision's commitment to do its part in addressing the unprecedented AIDS crisis. World Vision's Hope Initiative is focused on three areas: prevention of the disease, with education particularly aimed at children 5 to 15; care for people infected and affected by AIDS, especially orphans and vulnerable children; and advocacy on behalf of those affected by AIDS. Through the Hope Initiative, special emphasis is given to creating partnerships with governments, churches, and other faith communities, peer agencies, local communities, families, and children. Everyone's efforts will be required to turn the tide on AIDS.

Contact:

World Vision
PO Box 9716, Dept. W
Federal Way, WA 98063-9716
Phone: (888) 511-6548
www.worldvision.org

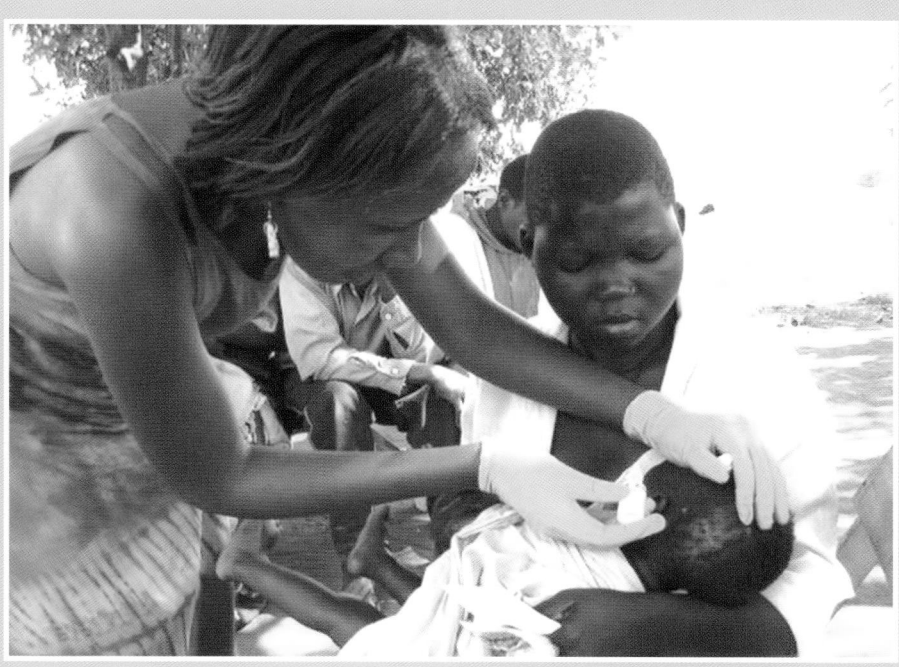

ECONOMIC INEQUALITY

No one can serve two masters.
Either he will hate the one and
  love the other,
or he will be devoted to the one
  and despise the other.
You cannot serve both God
  and Money.

Matthew 6:24

If you live in a developed country, you're among the richest human beings who have ever lived. Most of us would never admit that we "serve money." After all, riches are God's blessing (as the cliché goes). Right?

But would our assertion that we don't serve money withstand deeper examination? What tale do our checkbooks and credit card statements tell? Is our economic story one of self-indulgence or sacrificial generosity?

Consumerism is the driving economic paradigm in most developed world economies, and all too often, followers of Christ buy into this mentality wholeheartedly. Who are you serving? Who do you worship? Spend some time reflecting on this and asking the Lord to open your eyes as you read the following section.

BRIEFING

Last week Danae and I were writing at a local coffee shop. It was a warm afternoon, and a steady stream of people entered the shop looking for refreshment. What astonished me was the number of people who purchased one of those really big, really expensive blended drinks. While I didn't buy one that day, I've definitely had them before and — I can't lie — they're delicious. But have you ever stopped to think about the fact that one luxurious drink (plus a tip) costs around *five* dollars?

Think about that for a moment. Five dollars. Let's just say I decided to splurge this summer and buy two of these tasty drinks every week. Figure three months of summer, four weeks per month … twelve weeks times ten dollars each week … 120 dollars.

You might not think that's all that much, and maybe it isn't compared to what you earn each week. But consider that 2.6 billion people (40 percent of the population) on our planet *live* on less than $2 per day.[1] It's not just that they spend $2 per day; rather, they must make do on an income of less than $2 per day.

To put that in perspective, consider this: $120 is the same amount one of those 2.6 billion people earns working seven days per week for two whole months! Never mind money for food, never mind school fees, and never mind the essential medicine the family needs. My coffee splurge would cost the equivalent of eight weeks of nonstop work for one of the world's 2.6 billion poorest people. (To be honest, the reality is actually worse than what this example suggests, considering that the less than two dollars a day figure does not factor in weekends off — which most of us get. Nor does this example take into account that many people earn way less than two dollars a day. In fact, over a billion people survive on less than a dollar a day.[2])

But (you might argue) a dollar buys a lot more in poor countries than it does in ours. This reasoning can ease our guilt, since it makes our excesses look less excessive and the poverty of billions seem less tragic. But look at some economic indicators, and you'll see that global economic comparisons are a lot more proportionate than we'd like to believe.

Purchasing power parity (PPP) is an economic tool for comparing purchasing power between different currencies. The Economist magazine used this tool to create "The Big Mac Index," a handy way of comparing what a Big Mac costs in different parts of the world. Big Macs are useful for making an overall economic representation because of the many different things which go into them — beef, wheat, vegetables, labor, operations, marketing, and so on. According to the most recent Big Mac Index, a Big Mac costs $3.22 in the United States, $3.90 in Britain, and $1.41 in China.[3] At first glance it seems that a Big Mac in China costs approximately half as much as in the United States or Britain.

This is misleading, however, because we're only looking at part of the picture. To get a more accurate idea of what it *feels like* for the average person to buy a Big Mac in each of these countries, we have to consider the difference between the *ratio* of the cost of a Big Mac to the average citizen's income. We do this by looking at per capita GDP (gross domestic product) for each of these countries.

Per capita GDP in the United States is $45,800, while in Britain it's $35,100. In China, by contrast, it is only $5,300[4]. Now, when you divide the cost of a Big Mac by the per capita GDP, you see what percentage of annual income a person must spend to buy one. The average person in the United States spends only .007 percent of their yearly income when buying a Big Mac, while the average person in Britain spends .01 percent of their annual income. In China, however, the average person will spend nearly .03 percent of their annual income on a Big Mac. This means that a Big Mac is really *four times* more expensive in China than in the United States, even though it costs less than half as much ($1.41 instead of $3.22).

Obviously looking at the cost of a Big Mac isn't a true picture of more necessary things in life like energy, food staples, medicine, and so on. But what's clear is that people face dramatically different economic situations *simply because of where they live*. For most of the people in the world (including you and me), how we're doing economically has less to do with how hard we work and more to do with the opportunities given to us because of our place of birth. I don't know about you, but I have a tendency to pat myself on the back when I consider the quality of my life. The whole "you reap what you sow" thing is pretty ingrained in my psyche. I've studied hard, worked hard; I deserve what I have, and should enjoy it to the full, right?

The major flaw in this way of thinking is that I deserve no credit whatsoever for being born and raised in a developed country. What if I hadn't been born in the United States,

> There's no greater bondage than living only for what I don't yet have and for the evasive approval of people who, frankly, I don't really know or care about and who will always have just a little more than I.
>
> **David Goetz**

one of the richest countries in the world? What if I was one of the 2.6 billion people trying to eek out an existence on the equivalent of less than $2 per day? What if unlimited hard work and perseverance earned me a daily income insufficient to buy my family and me enough food to eat? What if a Big Mac didn't just cost me four times as much as it would someone in the United States? What if it required a week's worth of hard physical labor?

The distribution of wealth around our globe paints a clear picture. The richest regions of the world are where you would think: Western Europe, North America (United States and Canada), Australia, and Japan. The poorest are sub-Saharan Africa, India, and South East Asia[5]. The richest 2 percent of adults own more than 50 percent of all global wealth — the richest 1 percent control about 40 percent of global assets. The poorest 50 percent of the world's adults, by contrast, own less than 1 percent of all global wealth. Members of the top 10 percent are almost 400 times richer than those in the bottom 50 percent. Here's the shocking part: you need only about $2,140 to your name (assets minus debts) to be counted among the *wealthiest 50 percent of the world.*[6]

> And justice, as we have seen, means things like the Jubilee and the sabbatical remission of debts. It means economic structures that check the emergence of extremes of wealth and poverty. It means massive economic sharing among the people of God.
>
> **Ron Sider**

How are we to think about global economic inequality in light of the good news of a God who laid down his riches (2 Cor. 8:9) in heaven to come and be with us? Check out what Paul writes: "Your abundance at the present time should supply their need, so that their abundance may supply your need, that there may be fairness" (2 Cor. 8:14 ESV).

Paul doesn't leave any room for hoarding — it's antithetical in the coming kingdom of the One who sacrificed himself for us. A selfless ebb and flow — holding with open hands everything entrusted to us by God — is what Paul exhorted the Corinthians to display. The paradigm of the follower of Christ is this: if you have more than enough, you should use your excess to help those who are wanting. When they have more than enough, they in turn will help meet your need. This biblical idea of fairness flies in the face of western culture's ubiquitous "what's mine is mine" way of thinking. Maybe it makes you a bit uncomfortable: "Isn't that communism?" Or maybe you flat-out disagree: "You're saying I should give my stuff to some poor person in India?"

Communism failed miserably as a governmental structure because of human sin, but that doesn't absolve Christians from God's command to share our blessings with others. God makes it abundantly clear that hoarding our wealth while others are in need brings only dire consequences. Recall Abraham's response to the rich man in one of Jesus' parables: "Remember that you in your lifetime received your good things, and Lazarus in like manner bad things; but now he is comforted here, and you are in anguish" (Luke 16:25 ESV). The rich man turned a blind eye to Lazarus, who every day had sat at the gated entrance to his house. Perhaps we don't *literally* have starving, sick, forgotten people sitting at the gates of our mansions, but if we make more than $2 per day, we are the rich man in the parable.

Dallas Willard writes that Christians must learn "how to live simply, even frugally, though controlling great wealth and power."[7] His point is that by living simply and frugally, we might use our wealth for others — for selfless rather than selfish purposes. Willard is agreeing with what the apostle Paul wrote: "Each of you should look not only to your own interests, but also to the interests of others" (Phil. 2:4). Instead of my only concern being a luxurious retirement, a bigger house, faster car, or nicer clothes, or that incredible vacation next summer, I should also consider the needs of others. One way to do this is to consume less and use the difference to fund organizations helping those in need. Changing our lifestyles and spending habits can have a dramatic effect over the long term. Simply redirecting $1.50 a day equals more than $25,000 over a lifetime.[8] Or maybe you're willing to consider even bigger changes. Should we really be "upwardly mobile" in terms of cars, houses, clothes, vacations? Why not establish a simple lifestyle and then — despite pay raises and promotions — maintain our standard of living so that more can be given to those in need?

The reality of global economic inequality can seem overwhelming. At the same time, however, each of us is responsible for our own decisions, not the millions of others who live in our country or world. Small choices — from being thankful to being more mindful about our everyday purchases — can go a long way.

Consider these real-world examples of people and churches who have decided to radically change in order to better reflect God's heart concerning inequality. A pastor friend of ours in southern California sold his 2000-square-foot house and moved into a 1200-square-foot house, reducing his mortgage and freeing monthly funds to support

overseas development work. The late musician Rich Mullins voluntarily limited his salary and gave the rest away. He could have been very wealthy but chose to keep far less so that more could be given to those in need. The church we used to attend in Santa Barbara goes to great lengths to be able to give away more than 50 percent of its annual budget. These decisions are by no means easy, particularly in a culture that screams, "Enjoy all you can while you can!"

Jesus said that we simply can't serve two lords. More to the point, he never said faithfulness would be easy. Think of the difference between a single-track mountain trail and a multi-lane freeway. The latter is built for volume, the former only for those who choose to walk it. There's a reason Christ described the life of his followers as a small gate and a narrow road (Matt. 7:14).

How far should we take this? How much money is it okay to have? How much is every Christian called to give? I can't tell you that, and I would be foolish if I tried. That's between you and the King who entrusted you with what you have — the same King who will one day ask you to account for your decisions about money and possessions. One thing I can point to is Jesus' words to those who asked, "What shall we do?" His response is hard to hear — because it means acknowledging that our lives aren't about us. "Whoever has two tunics is to share with him who has none, and whoever has food is to do likewise" (Luke 3:11 ESV).

Jesus goes to great lengths to sober us concerning the responsibility of being wealthy in a world that largely isn't. In one passage that we rich often choose to imagine concerns spiritual or intellectual wealth, he says, "From everyone who has been given much, much will be demanded" (Luke 12:48). How will we answer him when he demands an account from us? How have we used what he has given us? Only for ourselves, or for others as well?

The following pages contain powerful examples of people who are addressing economic inequality from a biblical perspective. There is no "one-size-fits-all" answer. But let their stories and reflections challenge your assumptions and paradigms. If you aren't prepared to examine your use of money, perhaps that fact in itself should trouble you. After all, it is a much better option for us to examine our lives now under the tutelage of the Holy Spirit and guidance of the Scriptures while we still have opportunity to change — better, say, than to discover too late that we've irrevocably missed our chance to love our brothers and sisters around the world.

Advent Conspiracy

Jeanne McKinley

I'm not an expert on economic justice.

Only in the last few years have I thought about it deeply. Of course I've seen the injustice in our world and had my heart broken by stories of starvation and slavery. But the problems always felt so big to me — too big for me to make a difference. After all, my life was focused on raising our four children on a limited budget — how could I save the rest of the world? I often felt paralyzed.

Two years ago, all that changed as our family and our church started celebrating Christmas differently. It started when my husband — also the pastor — was talking with a few fellow pastors. They were sharing about the frustration of leading their churches at Christmastime in the midst of our consumer culture. They lamented the near impossibility of pointing their congregations toward the pinnacle moment of the incarnation of Emmanuel, God with us, in the midst of holiday stress, materialism, and busyness.

Americans spend around $450 billion at Christmas.[9] The worldwide water crisis could be solved with 10 to 15 billion dollars a year.[10] How can the wonder of God becoming a baby enter such a world?

The pastors began to talk about what it would look like to lead their churches in a different kind of Christmas celebration, and a movement called Advent Conspiracy was born.

That Christmas they introduced the four pillars of Advent Conspiracy: Worship More, Spend Less, Give More, and Love All. We shared it with our churches at the end of November. By January over $500,000 had been redistributed to the "least of these" locally and globally.

People who chose to worship Jesus by spending less on the usual "Christmas presents" were responsible for all of this money. We learned to give differently, in more relational ways. A new baseball bat and time with Dad at the batting cages. A pound of coffee and hours of conversation with a grandmother. Creative ideas that didn't cost much but meant something to both the giver and the recipient.

Then we gave the money we saved to fund clean water projects around the world, as well as local projects in our communities. It resulted in twelve clean water wells being built in Nicaragua and Liberia and beautiful relationships built with people in need through local schools and homeless ministries.

My experience that year was the most peaceful, beautiful Christmas season that I'd ever had as an adult. Worship filtered through our home for the whole month, not just for an hour on Sunday. While we were baking cookies, decorating the tree, and making Christmas presents, we talked with our kids about why we were doing Christmas differently. We explained why there wouldn't be so many presents under the tree, helping them be aware of the needs in the world and how much we have to be thankful for. At first we were afraid that they would hate the idea of getting less. Instead they seemed to grasp the idea better than we did. It was truly an all-encompassing worship experience.

A year ago my husband and his friends wondered what would happen if we invited other churches to join Advent Conspiracy. So they began talking about the project everywhere they went. As a result, in 2007, more than seven hundred churches signed up to be a part of it. Millions of dollars were redistributed to every imaginable organization ministering to God's children all over the world. Because people chose to worship more, spend less, give more, and love all, others around the world experienced the reality that God is with us.

The most beautiful change that is coming out of the Advent Conspiracy is the long-term affect it is having on our lives. We're not just thinking about spending differently at Christmas; we're inviting Christ into our finances as a whole, rethinking all of our spending and gift-giving. We're hearing stories like the one about a six-year-old who, while planning her birthday party, asked her friends not to give her gifts but to bring money for the kids who don't have clean water. I just received a simple yet beautiful wedding invitation from a couple in our church who are asking people to donate to clean water projects in their name instead of buying them wedding gifts.

Christ is using his story to change us from the inside out. The ancient miracle of "God with us" is still true today, and I know the world will never be the same because of it.

BIO

Jeanne McKinley has spent part of her time as the director for the Advent Conspiracy since 2007. She is thrilled to watch people worship more, spend less, give more, and love all at Christmas and throughout the year, and to see lives forever changed by the gift of clean water around the world. Jeanne can also be seen all over Portland, Oregon, driving her four amazing children to their various activities and supporting her husband, Rick, Lead Pastor of Imago Dei Community.

Consenting to Consciousness

Marilyn McEntyre

In many years of teaching I've come to understand at least one basic thing about learning: it can be scary. Knowing something we didn't know before can be disorienting, threatening, unsettling. It may require that we rearrange what we thought we knew, to become less comfortable and more accountable, and to act on what we have learned. All real learning entails these consequences, but this is especially true of learning about the systems we inhabit and the processes we rely on for goods, services, food, security, and peace of mind.

When we begin to read about how we get our food, for instance, it doesn't take long to encounter the sobering truth that the people who plant and harvest much of the food we obtain through vast networks of chain stores are often underpaid for long hours of backbreaking labor. Usually they have no health benefits either. Nor does it take long to find out which companies are subjecting laborers in poor countries to substandard working conditions — including squalid housing, no job security, or even direct abuse — in order to provide inexpensive clothing for North American consumers and large profits for stockholders.

Learning for the first time about injustices we hadn't been aware of can be a little like throwing a new chip in a kaleidoscope: one new color changes the whole design. One new fact can sometimes change our understanding of our entire way of life, or of what's "normal" or "harmless," or what it means to be a person of faith. In all likelihood, we will find that some of our most basic assumptions may need to be reevaluated.

I have come to believe that saying yes to Christ means saying yes to seeking truth — truth that will set us and others free, and consenting to act on that truth when we find it. For me, this has meant that even though I haven't given away all my possessions or abandoned my car, I have begun to cultivate new habits of awareness and action — to ask about economic and agricultural and political processes, to consider what I'm supporting when I vote, buy, or travel. It has meant evaluating my moral choices not only in terms of whether I personally lie, cheat, steal, or play fair, but also how the systems that I inhabit function, for whose benefit, and at whose cost.

Like most North Americans, I benefit from the labor of many who are poorer and more vulnerable than I am. I have to live with the disturbing truth that I get more than I have earned from the fruits of others' labors, and they often receive far less than they deserve. I do not believe it's my job to "save the world," but it is my job to be a good steward of the resources entrusted to me — the time, money, and power over which I have any control. There is nothing to be gained by overwhelming myself or others with fruitless guilt, but there is something to be gained by the spiritual discipline of taking participatory responsibility and living generously and justly as a "rich Christian in an age of hunger."[11]

In America's consumer culture, few of us have much opportunity to witness the whole process of production. It's too easy not to know who planted or harvested what we eat, or even what part of the world it comes from. Most of us don't understand the process of designing and building a computer or TV, or of disposing of toxic techno-waste — though we depend heavily on our electronic technologies. We don't know who made the clothes we're wearing, and we don't have to see how little those workers eat or how tired they are at the end of a sixteen-hour day.

To seek truth is to have the courage and will to ask how things came about, to concern ourselves with justice and wisdom and good stewardship in the ways we intervene in the processes of nature. Only to see the surfaces of things, only to concern ourselves with the immediacies of our daily tasks, and only to rely comfortably on products and conveniences without counting the human costs involved in making and maintaining them is a shameful irresponsibility — what the church used to call culpable ignorance. This ignorance — the will not to know for the sake of protecting our own comfort — comes from fear. And fear is a taproot of sin.

So what are the practices that can sharpen our learning edge, help us to push through the fear of guilt or change, and open our hearts wide enough to see and love those whose lives we affect deeply? There are simple practices; the learning curve need not be impossibly steep, and God is gracious. There are small steps you can take toward new habits of fidelity. I would suggest four practices that might be taken on as simple spiritual disciplines: 1) asking the hard questions, 2) acting on what we find out, having asked them, 3) sharing that knowledge and allowing it to lead us into a new relationship with each other and the earth, and 4) allowing our widened awareness to reshape our practices of worship and the focus of our prayers.

In this Internet generation, it is both easier and harder to find out what we might need to know to make more responsible choices and be faithful participants in public process — easier because there is so much information available, harder because there is so much misinformation available too. Still, we may begin anywhere we find elders and authorities we trust and work outward from there, doing the homework required to make our choices more caring. We can do so by raising questions like these:

What are the processes involved in making and delivering what I buy? (It's good to be specific here — this pair of jeans, this pound of coffee, this diamond ring.)

What are the real costs of its manufacture and marketing?

Who is paying those costs?

Who is bearing the risks?

Whose lives are enhanced and whose diminished in the process?

What habits of consumption have I normalized?

Where does my notion of "normal" come from? (Is it normal, for instance, to have fifteen pairs of shoes? Or to produce sixty pounds of trash a week? Or to drive thirty miles to see a movie?)

Is my way of life sustainable? If not, how can I help the coming generation of children prepare for a world in which their economic options are likely to be very different from ours? (How, for instance, might I get involved in educating children about particular processes, teaching them what comes into a house and what goes out of it, and where it goes? Or teaching them how children live in Baghdad or Hong Kong or Manila?)

What do I have to take into account if I widen my sense of personal responsibility to include the policies and practices of corporations and of our government? (What letters might I write, what meetings might I show up at that might make a difference?)

What particular burden of responsibility does my Americaness or my western-wealthiness impose upon me as a Christian?

Such questions are the beginning steps one takes toward making responsible choices. More specific questions to pursue might include these:

What legal protections are in place for the laborers who work as harvesters on mega-farms or as garment makers in the largely outsourced clothing industry?

What are the consequences of exposure to FDA-approved pesticides — for consumers and for those who work in fields that are sprayed?

How has the fast food and the whole convenience food industry changed my eating habits? What particular effects have they had on me and others?

By protecting my high-consumption "way of life," how might I be contributing to others' poverty?

In what specific ways have I become oil-dependent along with so many others, and how does this affect political, corporate, and military decisions? Who is directly affected by oil drilling and the competition for that particular resource?

Who owns the media and what controls do they exercise on what we get to know?

What is happening to the world's soil, water, animal species, air, and ecological balance? What short- and long-term effects are we having on humans and the rest of the natural world that we were given to care for?

What are the consequences of thinking about morality in a purely individualistic manner?

What tensions define for me the relationship between "Christian" and "American" (or "Canadian" or "British") right now?

What, as a Western Christian, might I need to re-examine, resist, or renounce? What might I need to support and commit to?

Along with wide-reaching questions like these, it's helpful to raise some personal "test questions" like these when shopping:

Is this item really something I need? How will owning it and using it serve my deeper purposes?

Can I choose to buy it from a socially and ecologically responsible company?

Can I choose to support local or independent producers rather than those that concentrate disproportionate money and power in a few hands?

How can I make my purchases part of a pattern of choices that help me practice love and justice?

Do I want this enough to relinquish or forego something else?

Honestly asking ourselves questions like these leads to practical choices. Those choices can lead us into new patterns of conversation and community life. Though they may involve some relinquishment and some sobering reassessment, they can be undertaken in a gracious, life-affirming way, keeping the accent on joyful obedience, generous caring, and compassionate curiosity about how others experience the world. When we find our way to others who share these concerns, especially in the context of a community of believers, they can inform our worship and our prayer lives, widening and enlivening in amazing ways our understanding of what it means to be a part of the body of Christ, what it means to be stewards of creation and to love one another, what it means to do justice and love mercy, and what it means to be fully human in this world as we help prepare for its transformation.

Our God is a God of amazing grace. Though we are deeply complicit in unjust systems, I believe God can and does enlarge and transform every effort we make toward living justly, and God hears every prayer we offer on behalf of the vulnerable and the victimized. If we consent to be conscious, we will be blessed with the courage it takes. If we live in solidarity with the poor who are always with us, we will find ourselves less attached to the false security of wealth, and gradually discover the benefits of holding our "treasures on earth" with a more open hand. If we come together in these efforts, we may find ourselves in a more enlivening conversation than we could have imagined, among people who can teach us as we go what it means to heed the great command to "choose life."

BIO

Marilyn McEntyre has been a college professor for nearly three decades. She has written frequently for *Weavings*, a magazine of Christian Spirituality, and edited or authored several academic books and four volumes of poetry. Two upcoming books are collections of personal essays. It is her deep hope that Christians of this generation might find new energies and means to address the cries of the poor, to examine and help re-frame public policies that perpetuate injustice, and to care for the great gifts of language and the natural world that were put into our common keeping. Marilyn and her husband, John, a Presbyterian pastor, live in northern California and enjoy frequent visits from their six adult children and five small grandsons.

Sustainable Investments

Carter Crockett

The free market economy, as we call it, has a powerful capacity to enthrone certain market participants and overlook others. Those enthroned are those most capable of creating wealth. The process builds on itself, like a wave just before it crests: those that have achieved success are the most appropriate recipients of added investment, while those at the bottom seem justifiably overlooked. Altruism, unfortunately, has no place in today's free market economy. Philanthropy is often seen as an inefficient waste of limited resources.

What have appeared to be the immutable laws of business are, thankfully, changing. A profound shift occurs when a seemingly new concept is applied to the marketplace: grace.

Micro-finance, micro-credit, and micro-enterprise development are different terms used to describe the phenomenon where credit is given to those the market has deemed unworthy. Rather than investing in those that have already succeeded, micro-finance attempts to invest in those who haven't had the chance yet. Rather than imposing "proven" Western business plans on those in developing countries, micro-finance attempts to invest in the dreams of local entrepreneurs. Rather than funneling large amounts of financial aid in paternalistic ways that seem like mere drops in a very leaky bucket, micro-finance provides small loans with the intent of helping communities transform themselves and make sustainable changes.

It is an investment model that works best in places where there are grave economic injustices: where governments steal aid from the people who need it most, where the working poor (especially women) are ignored or marginalized, where financial markets remain underdeveloped, and where hard-working, ambitious people lack basic access to resources. Amazingly, this model thrives by relying on those deemed to have no value, no experience, and no hope.

My curiosity about micro-finance drew me to see it firsthand in rural China. I traveled

with the committed and compassionate people of HOPE International, a Christian organization that has been doing micro-enterprise development for more than seven years
in a country often hostile to those who believe in God. HOPE serves those largely overlooked by the amazing economic transformation currently underway in China — people
like Wang Xiao Ying.

When HOPE's loan officer first met Wang Xiao Ying in the ten-square-foot stall that
served as her retail store, he found a guitar shop that was unique but struggled among
the other vendors in the market. Shortly after Wang Xiao Ying received her first loan from
HOPE International, her small business began to flourish like never before. With the added
investment, she soon expanded to a sixty-square-foot area offering ten different types
of musical instruments — and music lessons as well. Today, after receiving her thirteenth

loan, she owns her own store building and can avoid the high rents she once paid in the market. Her profits allow her to support her grandmother, grandfather, and mother-in-law, and recently decreased the potentially overwhelming stress when her husband was hospitalized.

Wang Xiao Ying also credits her loan officer with helping to bring her to faith in Jesus Christ. "We became good friends, we communicated about family and faith, and my loan officer was a great help to me in my spiritual walk," she says. Wang is now an active member of a local church. She hopes one day to expand her store and establish a conservatory that will bring beautiful music to the people of her city.

In the eyes of HOPE clients like Wang Xiao Ying, I've seen dreams ignited and nurtured. I've seen tiny investments offered with sacrificial love that can transform lives and communities. In the darkness of economic injustice, such rays of light bring healing illumination. Grace bears fruit, and it is contagious, wherever it is unleashed — even in the free market economy.

BIO

Carter Crockett is a leader in social entrepreneurship, and has worked as a marketer/entrepreneur in Seattle, Washington, and as a scholar/professor at Westmont College in Santa Barbara, California. Carter is the co-founder of Karisimbi Partners, an organization that picks up where microfinance leaves off by helping to develop emerging economies, establishing industry clusters, strengthening communities, and empowering visionary business people. Carter lives with his wife, Kerry, and their two children in Kigali, Rwanda.

Merely Gifts

Marva Dawn

My own personal wake-up call shook me to the core in the summer after my junior year in college, when I sang in a college choir traveling around the world to strengthen churches. During ten days in India I was overwhelmed by the thousands of beggars. I saw countless numbers of dead bodies in the streets, and I watched the workers who scooped them into large wheelbarrows and hauled them to the city dump to be burned. My naïve life turned upside down there; I knew as a Christian that I could not ever ignore the poverty and injustice I had seen. I felt called by God always to work to counteract world hunger and deprivation.

Since then I have become increasingly troubled by the state of wealthy U.S. churches. Why do we not pay more attention to God's commands to feed the hungry and clothe the naked? We seem to ignore the real situation of the unfairly divided globe. What kind of wake-up call would be effective?

While our relatively small part of the world eases its pain by means of the production of more commodities and the consumption of them, the rest of the world suffers an opposite kind of hopelessness — when persons are not able to secure what is necessary to live. *No one* should die from hunger or suffer from malnutrition when you and I and many others have so much!

We cannot really solve the problem of our world's injustices by merely giving a little more of our surplus to fight hunger. More deeply, we need to be freed from our reliance on material consumption to find happiness, especially because wealthy countries consume at a rate unsustainable by the earth.

Why do some people in the world need to expend the earth's resources to such a degree that the rest of the globe is deprived of its share and the earth is endangered? How did hope become so fettered that such behavior seems to be the only way to keep despair at bay? I believe that hope in the Triune God is so strong that it breaks the shackles that fetter us. Consequently, we can face squarely the nature of our fettering.

Christ has decisively conquered the powers and thereby sets Christians free in life and mission to value the powers and their gifts, to be grateful for the genius God gave to human beings to develop them and yet also to restrict the powers to their true place and resist their overwhelmings. It is the same with all principalities and possessions; they are merely gifts. Similarly, we hold our own talents, skills, character, ministries as gifts toward which we manifest a proper humility that restricts them to their rightful limitations. This Christian understanding of ourselves and the powers gives us immensely profound — and practical! — guidance in our search for ways to end the fetterings. And that will deepen our hope, even as the genuine hope of Christianity enables us to face the fetters in the first place and to work for true justice with all of our gifts.

(Excerpted from the Introduction to Unfettered Hope, *xvii-xxi)*

BIO

Dr. Marva J. Dawn is a scholar with four masters degrees and a Ph.D. in Christian Ethics and the Scriptures from the University of Notre Dame. An internationally renowned theologian, author, and educator Dr. Dawn serves as Teaching Fellow in Spiritual Theology at Regent College in Vancouver, BC, Canada. Under Christians Equipped for Ministry (CEM), she has preached and taught at seminaries, clergy conferences, churches, assemblies, and universities throughout the United States and internationally. Dr. Dawn is also a popular preacher and speaker for people of all ages. She is the author of numerous articles and over twenty books. Marva and her husband, Myron, a retired elementary school teacher, live in southwestern Washington State.

The Workers Are Groaning

Shane Claiborne

Israel's desire for a king led them down a path of destruction. Becoming "like the other nations" would make Israel a chaotic society, full of violence, cheating, and harm (1 Samuel 8 ff).

When we are talking about a baptized empire, one that has dazzled the church into conformity, we are not just talking about the violent militarism of Rome or the United States or Iran or North Korea. We are also talking about a much more prevalent, subtle, and powerful empire that seeps into every home — our daily global lifestyle.

In the last hundred years, the average person's life has become dizzyingly complicated. Even the seemingly simple act of drinking a cup of coffee involves an intricate international system of bean pickers, international shipping (fueled by oil from who knows where), packaging (in what?), roasting (by energy from who knows where), domestic shipping, driving to get it (using car parts and gas from around the world), and so on. It's like a cup of coffee has been dragged halfway across the earth, leaving trench-like marks along the way.

Another, possibly the greatest, unholy aspect of our economy is its exploitation of people. While our economy floats on cheap oil, it too is carried on the backs of cheap laborers. If we ask, Why do so many of our products come from China? we can certainly say this is aided by cheap oil for shipping, but it's essentially founded on easily exploited labor.

The hundreds of thousands of jobs that have been lost in the United States testify to "job creation" in foreign countries. Left in the wake are our neighborhoods, blighted with hundreds of abandoned factories and hundreds more abandoned homes. Christians have no problem helping the poor. But question whether our "blessings" are borne on the backs of the poor and things get messy. The call to "Make poverty history" needs a partner: "Make affluence history."

Years ago, some folks from our communities attended a rally against overseas sweatshops. They had not invited the typical rally speakers — lawyers, activists, and academics.

Instead, they brought the kids themselves from the sweatshops to speak. We listened as a child from Indonesia pointed to the giant scar on his face. "I got this scar when my master lashed me for not working hard enough. When it began to bleed, he did not want me to stop working or to ruin the cloth in front of me, so he took a lighter and burned it shut. I got this making stuff for you." We were suddenly consumed by the overwhelming reality of the suffering body of Christ. Jesus now bore not just marks from the nails and scars from the thorns, but a gash down his face, for when we have done it to the "least of these," we have done it to Christ himself. How could we possibly follow Jesus and buy anything from that master? The statistics had a face. Poverty became personal. And that messes with you.

Into the economics of the world, the letter of James speaks a word of rebuke: "The wages you failed to pay the workers who mowed your fields are crying out against you. The cries of the harvesters have reached the ears of the Lord Almighty" (5:4). This isn't simply about fairly paying the immigrants who mow our lawns; it's about the way our world's economy siphons wealth from the poor up to the rich. And we are all part of it.

But the God of mammon calls out, "How could we buy cheap shirts without the sweatshops of Honduras? How could we get cheap fast food without the migrant tomato farmers in Florida?" God hears the workers' groaning.

BIO

Shane Claiborne is an author, activist, and recovering sinner — a Tennessee hillbilly with a love for bluegrass music. He is a founder of The Simple Way and a long time member in the Potter Street Community, an intentional community in Kensington, Philadelphia. Shane is a board member of the Christian Community Development Association and has helped birth and connect radical faith communities and intentional hospitality houses (*newmonasticism.org*).

NOW WHAT?

Most of the issues in *Zealous Love* are somewhat removed from our lives. Most of us don't know people who drink dirty water and have to walk to fetch it; most of us are not, have never been, and probably never will be refugees; and pretty much all of us have had the chance to go to school. But economic inequality is directly connected to our lives. With determined effort, we can live justly in this area, or, like many others, we can keep the issue at arm's length and live in what Marilyn McEntyre calls "culpable ignorance." Are you willing to engage this issue and live for justice in your daily life?

Reflect

1. *What do you think?* How has this section been for you to read? Frustrating? Confusing? Enlightening? All of the above? Why do you think this section has evoked the feelings and response that it has? Take some time to write about or talk through your experience reading this section. Be sure to include the thoughts and emotions that it called up, and don't be afraid to ask yourself some hard questions.

2. *Change.* Are there areas of your life that you might need to change? Perhaps it's a superfluous habit that, once curtailed, will enable you to direct a greater portion of your resources (time, money, education, connections) to selfless rather than selfish pursuits. Perhaps it means reexamining your preconceived notions about what is "normal" for you. Just because something is standard for other people doesn't mean it is what you are called to. Spend some time praying and writing down some thoughts about what this might mean for your own life.

3. *Examine your rhythms.* What are some patterns in your life that you might need to reconsider? It can be anything from choosing to not buy on the Sabbath to choosing fair trade clothing items or setting an income ceiling for yourself or your household. Perhaps you don't need to buy a five-dollar coffee drink on the way to work; instead, maybe you can support an organization doing development somewhere in the world. Spend some time examining your lifestyle.

4. *Go frugal.* When you hear words like *simplicity* and *frugality*, what comes to mind? Do you have negative or positive associations with these words? In light of the reality that almost half of the world lives on less than $2 a day, what should these words mean for you? What might simplicity and frugality look like in your life? Get specific. Brainstorm. Don't dwell on things that are far-removed from your life; focus on things that touch you on a daily basis.

5. *Keep the conversation going.* Imagine that right now, this very moment, a person from a developing country is sitting in the chair beside you. Never mind language barriers. What would you talk about? What do you think would surprise him or her about your life? How would that person respond to your lifestyle, as well as the culture in which you live? Be imaginative. Allow yourself to go deeper. Consider the paradox that your world is different in almost every way from that person's, yet the reality is that you inhabit the same planet. Wrestle with this truth and what it means for you as you pursue an active love for your brothers and sisters around the globe.

Respond

1. *Cultivate thankfulness.* Like the other global issues we've explored in *Zealous Love*, economic inequality may feel far too big and complicated for you to do anything about. "What can we — normal, everyday people — do about global GDPs?" I asked skeptically when first looking at this issue. Perhaps being thankful for what we have instead of always wanting more is a good way to start. Practice being thankful for the things you have in your life — the major things (house, car, family, health, education, job, etc.) as well as the minor things (laundry detergent, peanut butter, bread, milk, etc.).

2. *Fast from luxury.* Try for a week to limit your personal or family spending. Remember, more than a third of the world's population — 40 percent — survives on less than $2 per day. Try limiting yourself to $5 – $10 per day for a week. Food, transportation, entertainment, clothing, and so on. Consider it a fast from luxury. Doubtless, you'll be frustrated by how limited your options are. But allow yourself to pray for those who have no choice but to live on far less every day.

3. *Buy fair trade.* We are consumers. And consumers often oppress the poor and defenseless, whether deliberately or not. Buying fair trade items — everything from chocolate to furniture to shoes — helps to ensure that those who work to provide the

products we consume are fairly compensated for their labor. Commit to purchasing fair trade items whenever possible, or take a first step and discover more about the many options that are available. Check out *www.tenthousandvillages.com*, *www.fairtradefederation.org*, and *www.fairtrade.net* for great ideas and additional information.

4. ***Downsize.*** This idea is a bit more intense. What might it look like for you to downsize your life? How could "downward mobility" replace our culture's sinful insistence on upward mobility? Maybe God is asking you to sell a cherished vehicle and buy one that's less flashy and more fuel-efficient. Maybe, like our pastor friend in Southern California, you're being asked to sell your house and move into a smaller one — or to sell any clothing you haven't worn in the last year. Culling our lives can be painful, but the process helps us center our life on what is important, rather than on what we own. Ultimately, our freedom and growth depend on our willingness to prune branches that are not bearing fruit.

5. ***Calling all business owners!*** If you own a business, you have a unique opportunity to work for economic justice. Let this motivation shape your business practices. Consider how your company impacts the lives of not only your customers but your employees as well. If you're a manufacturer, consider everything from design to production to the end user. Hold yourself to a higher standard than the one demanded by the Better Business Bureau. Brainstorm with some of your friends and advisors about particular methods and standards you can employ to make your business more economically just. Consider employing people who might otherwise have difficulty finding a job.

Spread the Word

Individually, it feels overwhelming to try to transform global economic inequality. But tremendous change happens when we work together. Consider spreading the word about economic inequality, the lives that are affected by it, and the organizations doing something about it. Now that you've read this chapter, it isn't someone else's responsibility — it's yours. Change begins with individuals deciding that they are going to live differently. What role can you play? Maybe it's inviting some friends to coffee, starting an action group at your church, or getting your youth group to hold a rally. Help change lives. Spread the word. To help you spread the word about economic inequality, and any other issue discussed in this book, we've designed a simple, effective tool: *www.zealouslove.org/spread*.

Share Your Ideas

Have a great idea about something other people can do to engage the issue of economic inequality? Do you want to connect with others who are getting involved? Join the conversation at *www.zealouslove.org/share*.

Discover More

In the Field Notes you've heard from several contributors about the harsh reality of global economic inequality. You've also read about the incredible work being done to address the issue, both on a personal and corporate scale. Remember, there is no one-size-fits-all solution. If you want to get involved in this area, check out the following organizations or visit *www.zealouslove.org/economics*.

Hope International

Vision: HOPE is a global, faith-based, non-profit organization focused on poverty alleviation through micro-enterprise development.

Method: HOPE serves people living in Afghanistan, China, the Dominican Republic, the Democratic Republic of Congo, Haiti, India, Moldova, Philippines, Romania, Russia, Rwanda, South Asia, and Ukraine. HOPE's vision is to enable sustainable economic development that results in significant and lasting change, temporal and eternal, in the lives of many people living in poverty.

Contact:

HOPE International
227 Granite Run Drive
Suite 102
Lancaster, PA 17601
Phone: (717) 464-3220
www.hopeinternational.org

The Simple Way

Vision: To Love God. To Love people. To Follow Jesus.

Method: The Simple Way is an intentional faith community. Each of us is created for community and in the image of community, and yet everything in the world tries to rob us of this divine gift. The life of the simple way is the story of that struggle to love and to be loved. The most radical thing we do is choose to love each other, again and again. If you are a seeker of the Way, may our story feed you hope, or at least keep you from making all the same mistakes.

Contact:

www.thesimpleway.org

Advent Conspiracy

Vision: Advent Conspiracy is an international movement seeking to correct the scandal Christmas has become by worshiping Jesus through compassion, not consumption.

Method: Members of Advent Conspiracy worship fully, spend less, give more, and love all.

Contact:

www.adventconspiracy.org

Opportunity International

Vision: Opportunity International is a non-profit organization dedicated to helping the working poor.

Method: We provide small loans that allow poor entrepreneurs to start or expand a business, develop a steady income, provide for their families, and create jobs for their neighbors. We also offer savings, microinsurance, business training, and many more services to 1.1 million working poor in twenty-eight developing nations.

Contact:

Opportunity International — USA
2122 York Road, Suite 150
Oak Brook, Illinois 60523
Phone: (800) 793-9455
www.opportunity.org

Evangelicals for Social Action

Vision: Evangelicals for Social Action (ESA) is an association of Christians seeking to promote Christian engagement, analysis, and understanding of major social, cultural, and public policy issues.

Method: ESA emphasizes both the transformation of human lives through personal faith and also the importance of a commitment to social and economic justice as an outgrowth of Christian faith.

Contact:

The Sider Center on Ministry and Public Policy
6 E. Lancaster Ave.
Wynnewood, PA 19096-3420
Phone: (484) 384-2990
www.esa-online.org

Additional Resources

www.afjn.org

www.cauzal.com

www.jubileeusa.org

www.simpleliving.org

www.tomsshoes.com

Visit *www.zealouslove.org/ economics* for more information and organizations.

The End
of the Beginning

Thank you for reading *Zealous Love*. We hope that you've found it to be not only inspirational and educational, but also encouraging. As you've been reminded, our world is in desperate need. Human trafficking, unclean water, refugees, hunger, lack of education, creation degradation, HIV and AIDS, and economic inequality collectively threaten the lives and livelihoods of billions of men, women, and children all made in God's image. We hope the Field Notes, the personal accounts of everyday people taking steps to fight injustice, have moved you toward informed action in your own life.

Let us offer one small piece of advice. Because there is so much need in our world, it would be foolish to try to make a difference everywhere. There's a reason you and I must sleep at night, a reason we can't carry the world's weight on our shoulders: we weren't designed to solve all the world's problems by ourselves. When we try, we become overwhelmed very quickly. Christ himself said: "The poor you will always have with you" (Mark 14:7). This statement is by no means an excuse to do nothing, but it ought to frame our attitude toward social justice. We were not meant to obsess over *solving* the problems in our world. Rather, we are to be mindful and focused on sacrificial *serving* where and how God calls us.

Our challenge to you is to spend time prayerfully considering how God is calling you to get involved. Perhaps you have several ideas you're already beginning to pursue. If so, keep on. However, if you're feeling a bit overwhelmed, let us suggest that you choose one area of focus. Remember the old cliché, "jack of all trades, master of none"? It's true. Don't try to be an expert on

> God saw all that he had made, and it was very good.
> **Genesis 1:31**

every injustice we've discussed in *Zealous Love*. Certainly they're all important, and each is affecting millions or perhaps billions of people. By reading *Zealous Love*, you've been generally informed about many issues; now is the time to become passionate about one. Focus your efforts, your energy, and your time on the area to which you feel most called.

How can you make the greatest impact? What gifts, connections, and passions has the Lord given to you so that you might use them for his glory?

Notice what Paul wrote to the church at Ephesus: "For we are God's workmanship, created in Christ Jesus to do good works, which God prepared in advance for us to do" (2:10). What are the "good works" which God prepared in advance for *you* to do? How will you know if you don't ask him? How will you hear him if you aren't listening? Some of us are called to give up every comfort and material blessing and dedicate ourselves to service in places of extreme darkness. Consider Richard Angoma in Uganda working on his family's rural farm to aid war refugees, or Sean Litton of IJM living in Thailand with his family, identifying and prosecuting human traffickers.

Others are called to use our resources to support the work of those on the front lines. Consider Francis Chan serving on the board of Children's Hunger Fund, or Marilyn McEntyre challenging students to think about how they live and to question the ways they contribute to the pain and injustices done to others.

Many of us need to reconsider our lifestyles in order to better "love others as we would want to be loved." Think of Scott Rodin examining the purchase of his new gas guzzler or Megan Robertson hanging up her family's clothes instead of using the dryer. Perhaps while reading *Zealous Love* you've felt compelled to consume less so that you can give more. Act on that — don't let yourself become comfortable and insulated.

If we truly heed Jesus' call to abandon ourselves and follow hard after him, something other than the need for self preservation will begin to take root and flourish in our hearts. But the resultant rhythms of selflessness and love for our neighbors will take on different forms for all of us because we are all uniquely created and have been given different responsibilities in our world.

What does that look like for you? We've tried to provide a few opportunities and ideas to get you started. At *www.ZealousLove.org*, you can discover more ideas and resources, as well as encounter thoughts shared by others. Do you have a great idea about how people can get involved? Post it online and inspire someone else! This book is not the final word on any of these issues. Our hope and prayer is that it would serve as a springboard for serving the most desperate of our brothers and sisters.

One of the best ways to begin moving forward is connecting with others who are passionate about the same issue as you. Remember, "two are better than one" (Ecc. 4:9). We need each other. Get together with some of your friends, family members, colleagues, or fellow students. Start the conversation. Encourage one another. Discover together. Dig in, do the research, ask the hard questions, examine your life, and surrender yourself to the leading of our good and gracious God.

Finally, brothers and sisters, don't give up. This is a marathon, not a sprint.

Keep on, and enjoy the journey.

Suggested Reading

If reading *Zealous Love* has sparked your interest, you may want to read some or all of the books listed below. Keep on learning and growing!

Better Off by David Brende

The Cost of Discipleship by Dietrich Bonhoeffer

Death by Suburb by David Goetz

Diet for a Small Planet by Frances Moore Lappe

Disposable People by Kevin Bales

Early Christians in Their Own Words by Eberhard Arnold

God's Politics by Jim Wallis

Good News About Injustice by Gary Haugen

Hope in the Dark by Jena Lee and Jeremy Cowart

Irresistible Revolution by Shane Claiborne

Jesus for President by Shane Claiborne

Living More with Less by Doris Janzen Longacre

Living on Less and Liking It More by Maxine Hancock

Mere Discipleship by Lee Camp

Nickel and Dimed by Barbara Ehrenreich

No Moment Too Small by Norvene Vest

Not for Sale by David Batstone

Pilgrim at Tinker Creek by Annie Dillard

The poetry of Gerard Manley Hopkins

Thanks

We've both been thrilled and honored to work on *Zealous Love*. The truth of any book project, though, is that it simply wouldn't exist without the collective efforts of many people who may or may not receive the credit they are due. Though we have doubtless forgotten some of you, know that we are immensely thankful to all of you who played a part in helping to create this project.

Specifically, though, we would like to thank the following:

You, the Reader — Thank you for taking the time to read *Zealous Love* and delve into these issues of social injustice. We've been thinking about and praying for you quite a bit as we've worked on this project — praying that the Lord would use *Zealous Love* to draw you closer to himself and to lead you one step further on the path that he has for you.

Our Contributors — Immense thanks to all of you who contributed to *Zealous Love* amidst world-changing work and hectic schedules. It's been inspiring to work with you on this project and learn a bit about the tremendous tasks the Lord has assigned to you. Thank you for seeking to love others, for desiring justice, for loving mercy, for living in the way we're all called to.

Zondervan — Thanks for believing in this project enough to agree to publish it! It's been incredible working with all the various teams, and we're thankful to be in your house.

Angela and Becky — Thank you for your many hours of editing, thoughtful critiques, and wise insights. It's been awesome working with you on *Zealous Love*, and we look forward to whatever comes next! And thanks, Beth, for laying it out in such a creative, compelling way!

DC Jacobson and Associates — It's been tremendous working with you, and we're really excited to continue the relationship that we've cultivated through this project. Thanks for letting us partner with you!

Critiquing Readers — Thank you for the time that you spent helping us strengthen the manuscript when it was raw, unedited, unfinished, and in need of lots of love. Your encouragement and suggestions were vital in helping *Zealous Love* become what it needed to be.

Our Friends and Family — We're both indebted to you for your love, encouragement, and support as we worked on this project. Thank you for believing in it and for encouraging us in the process when the going was difficult. We love you all very much.

Notes

Zealous Love: An Introduction

1. ILO website, *www.ilo.org/global/About_the_ILO/Media_and_public_information/Press_releases/lang--en/WCMS_005162/index.htm*.

2. United Nations Development Programme, *Beyond Scarcity: Power, poverty and the global water crisis*, Human Development Report 2006, pp. 2, 23, *http://hdr.undp.org/en/reports/global/hdr2006/*.

3. This number is deduced from UNICEF sources, which estimate that 53 percent of the annual 10 million child deaths in our world are caused by hunger. UNICEF, *Progress for Children: A Report Card on Maternal Mortality*, no. 7, September, 2008, p. 1, *www.unicef.org/publications/files/Progress_for_Children-No._7_Lo-Res_082008.pdf*. And UNICEF Biovision Forum 2007 Fact Sheet. Available from: *www.unicef.org/voy/takeaction/takeaction_3712.html*.

4. UNESCO Institute for Statistics, July 2002 Illiteracy Statistical Spreadsheet, "Regional adult illiteracy rate and population by gender," *www.uis.unesco.org/en/stats/statistics/literacy2000.htm*.

5. UNAIDS, *2008 Report on the global AIDS epidemic*, p. 32, *www.unaids.org/en/KnowledgeCentre/HIVData/GlobalReport/2008/2008_Global_report.asp*.

6. United Nations Development Programme, Human Development Report 2007 / 2008, p. 25, *http://hdr.undp.org/en/reports/global/hdr2007-2008/*.

Part 1: Human Trafficking

1. U.S. Department of State 2008 Trafficking in Persons Report, p. 7. Available from: *www.state.gov/g/tip/rls/tiprpt/2008/*.

2. Ibid.

3. UNICEF website, *www.unicef.org/protection/index_exploitation.html*.

4. ILO website, *www.ilo.org/global/Themes/Forced_Labour/lang--en/index.htm*; IJM website, *www.ijm.org/ourwork/injusticetoday*; UN News Centre, "UN and Partners Launch Initiative to End 'Modern Slavery' of Human Trafficking," March 26, 2007, *www.un.org/apps/news/story.asp?NewsID=22009&Cr=slave&Cr1*.

5. Paul E. Lovejoy, *Transformations in Slavery: A History of Slavery in Africa* (Cambridge: Cambridge University Press, 2007), 19.

6. UN News Centre, "UN and Partners Launch Initiative to End 'Modern Slavery' of Human Trafficking," March 26, 2007, *www.un.org/apps/news/story.asp?NewsID=22009&Cr=slave&Cr1*.

7. CIA World Factbook, Country Comparisons – GDP Chart, *www.cia.gov/library/publications/the-world-factbook/rankorder/2001rank.html*.

8. Polaris Project website, *www.polarisproject.org*.

9. U.S. Department of State 2008 Trafficking in Persons Report, pp. 18 – 28.

10. Polaris Project website, *www.polarisproject.org*.

11. Ibid.

12. ILO website, *www.ilo.org/global/Themes/Forced_Labour/lang--en/index.htm*; JM website, *www.ijm.org/ourwork/injusticetoday*; N News Centre, "UN and Partners Launch Initiative to End 'Modern Slavery' of Human Trafficking," March 26, 2007, *www.un.org/apps/news/story.asp?NewsID=22009&Cr=slave&Cr1*.

Part 2: Unclean Water

1. United Nations Development Programme, *Beyond Scarcity: Power, poverty and the global water crisis*, Human Development Report 2006, p. 2, *http://hdr.undp.org/en/reports/global/hdr2006/*.

2. Ibid.

3. Ibid., 6.

4. WHO website, "Water, sanitation and hygiene links to health," updated November, 2004, *www.who.int/water_sanitation_health/publications/facts2004/en/index.html*.

5. United Nations Development Programme, *Beyond Scarcity: Power, poverty and the global water crisis*, Human Development Report 2006, p. 4, *http://hdr.undp.org/en/reports/global/hdr2006/*.

6. Ibid., 3.

7. United Nations Development Programme, *Beyond Scarcity: Power, poverty and the global water crisis,* Human Development Report 2006, p. 6, *http://hdr.undp.org/en/reports/global/hdr2006/*.

8. BibleGateway website, NIV keyword search, *www.biblegateway.com/quicksearch/?quicksearch=water&qs_version=31*.

9. United Nations Department of Economic and Social Affairs, *World Population to 2300*, 2004, p. 13. *www.un.org/esa/population/publications/longrange2/WorldPop2300final.pdf*.

10. Anna Borzello, "Ridding the Karamojong of Guns," *BBC News*, January 22, 2001, *http://news.bbc.co.uk/2/hi/world/africa/1130704.stm*.

11. Fredrick Buechner, *The Magnificent Defeat* (New York: HarperOne, 1985), 105.

12. United Nations Development Programme, *Beyond Scarcity: Power, poverty and the global water crisis*, Human Development Report 2006, p. 34, *http://hdr.undp.org/en/reports/global/hdr2006/*.

Part 3: Refugees

1. Human Rights Watch website, *http://hrw.org/doc/?t=refugees&document_limit=0,2*.

2. UNHCR *Convention and Protocol Relating to the Status of Refugees*. Available from: *www.unhcr.org/protect/PROTECTION/3b66c2aa10.pdf*.

3. Human Rights Watch, "Italy/Libya: Gaddafi Visit Celebrates Dirty Deal," *www.hrw.org/en/news/2009/06/09/italylibya-gaddafi-visit-celebrates-dirty-deal*. June 9, 2009.

4. UNHCR *Convention and Protocol Relating to the Status of Refugees, Article 33*. Available from: *www.unhcr.org/protect/PROTECTION/3b66c2aa10.pdf*.

5. "Refugees survey says 500,000 Iraqis fled fighting in 2007," *USA Today*. 6/19/2008. *www.usatoday.com/news/world/2008-06-19-refugeesurvey_N.htm*.

6. World Refugee Survey 2007, Key Statistics, table 1 *www.refugees.org*.

7. UNHCR Publication, "Measuring Protection by Numbers," Nov. 2004, p. 4.

8. Church World Service Website. *www.churchworldservice.org/site/PageServer?pagename=action_what_assist_main*.

9. Per capita GDP (gross domestic product) is a useful tool for comparing the economic output of different countries. It is the per-person average for goods and services produced by a nation during a given year.

10. U.S. Committee for Refugees and Immigrants, World Refugee Survey 2007, "Ratio of Refugees to Host Country Populations and Distribution by Host Income," tables 12 – 13, *www.refugees.org/uploadedFiles/Investigate/Publications_&_Archives/WRS_Archives/2007/table%20112-13.pdf*.

11. U.S. Committee for Refugees and Immigrants, World Refugee Survey 2007, "Principal Sources and Hosts of Refugees," tables 7 – 8, *www.refugees.org/uploadedFiles/Investigate/Publications_&_Archives/WRS_Archives/2007/table7-8.pdf*.

12. BBC, "Should it be Burma or Myanmar?" *BBC News*, September 26, 2007, *http://news.bbc.co.uk/2/hi/uk_news/magazine/7013943.stm*.

13. Nobel Peace Prize 1991, "Aung San Suu Kyi Biography," *http://nobelprize.org/nobel_prizes/peace/laureates/1991/kyi-bio.html*.

14. BBC, "Q&A: Uganda's northern war," *BBC News*, August 29, 2006, *http://news.bbc.co.uk/2/hi/africa/3514473.stm*.

Part 4: Hunger

1. Food and Agriculture Organization of the UN, *Briefing Paper: Hunger on the Rise*, September 17, 2008, *www.fao.org/newsroom/common/ecg/1000923/en/hungerfigs.pdf*.

2. World Food Programme, 2006 Annual Report, p. 33, *www.wfp.org/content/wfp-annual -report-2006*.

3. United Nations Development Programme, *Fighting Climate Change: Human solidarity in a divided world*, Human Development Report 2007/2008, p. 25, *http://hdr.undp.org/en/reports/global/ hdr2007-2008/*.

4. World Food Programme leaflet, *Hunger and Health*, World Hunger Series 2007, p. 1, *www.wfp .org/sites/default/files/WHS_leaflet_English_2007.pdf*.

5. World Food Programme website, *www.wfp.org/hunger/stats*.

6. World Food Programme leaflet, *Hunger and Health*, World Hunger Series 2007, p. 1, *www.wfp .org/sites/default/files/WHS_leaflet_English_2007.pdf*.

7. Bread for the World website, "Hunger Facts: International," *www.bread.org/learn/hunger-basics/ hunger-facts-international.html*.

8. CDC website, "Heart Disease Facts and Statistics," *www.cdc.gov/heartDisease/statistics.htm*.

9. WHO website, "Cardiovascular disease: prevention and control," *www.who.int/dietphysicalactivity/ publications/facts/cvd/en*.

10. T. Colin Campbell and Thomas M. Campbell, *The China Study* (Dallas: BenBella Books, 2006), 117.

11. Rosamond W., Flegal K., Friday G., et al. Heart disease and stroke statistics — 2007 update: a report from the American Heart Association Statistics Committee and Stroke Statistics Subcommittee. Circulation 2006; 113:e69 – 171, *http://circ.ahajournals.org/cgi/reprint/113/6/e85*.

12. World Food Programme website, "Contributions to WFP 2006," *http://one.wfp.org/appeals/ wfp_donors/Contributions_WFP.pdf*.

13. "Little Accord in a Round Table of Diet Experts," *New York Times*, February 25, 2000, *www.nytimes. com/2000/02/25/us/little-accord-in-a-round-table-of-diet-experts.html?scp=1&sq=February%20 25,%202000,%20diet%20experts&st=cse*.

14. This number is deduced from UNICEF sources, which estimate that 53 percent of the annual 10 million child deaths in our world are caused by hunger. UNICEF, *Progress for Children: A Report Card on Maternal Mortality*, no. 7, September, 2008, p. 1, *www.unicef.org/publications/files/ Progress_for_Children-No._7_Lo-Res_082008.pdf*. And UNICEF Biovision Forum 2007 Fact Sheet. Available from: *www.unicef.org/voy/takeaction/takeaction_3712.html*.

15. UNICEF, *Progress for Children: A World Fit for Children Statistical Review*, no. 6, December 2007, p. 1, *www.unicef.org/publications/files/Progress_for_Children_No_6_revised.pdf*.

16. UNICEF, "Key Facts," Biovision Children's Forum, March 2007, *www.unicef.org/voy/media/ Biovision_Fact_Sheet_Agriculture_Eliminating_Hunger_final.pdf*.

17. USDA, *Household Food Security in the United States, 2005*, USDA Economic Research Service, November 2006, p. 16, *www.ers.usda.gov/Publications/ERR29/ERR29.pdf*.

18. Ibid.

19. Either Ghandi or Charles Dickens, though sources vary on this point.

Part 5: Lack of Education

1. World Bank website, "Education and Development," *http://web.worldbank.org/WBSITE/ EXTERNAL/TOPICS/EXTEDUCATION/0,,contentMDK:20591648~isCURL:Y~menuPK:282393~pagePK:2 10058~piPK:210062~theSitePK:282386,00.html.*

2. UNESCO, *The Quality Imperative*, Education for All Global Monitoring Report 2005, p. 45, *http:// portal.unesco.org/education/en/ev.php-URL_ID=35939&URL_DO=DO_TOPIC&URL_SECTION=201 .html.*

3. Ibid., 16.

4. Ibid., 17.

5. UNESCO, *The Quality Imperative*, Education for All Global Monitoring Report 2005, p. 17, *http:// unesdoc.unesco.org/images/0013/001373/137333e.pdf.*

6. Ibid., 21.

7. UNESCO, *The Quality Imperative*, Education for All Global Monitoring Report 2005, p. 45, *http:// portal.unesco.org/education/en/ev.php-URL_ID=35874andURL_DO=DO_TOPICandURL_SEC- TION=201.html.*

8. Adele Ramos, "355 teachers take PSE – the results are controversial," *Amandala Online*, February 3, 2007, *www.amandala.com.bz/index.php?id=5460.*

9. M. Seastrom, L. Hoffman, C. Chapman, and R. Stillwell, *The Averaged Freshman Graduation Rate for Public High Schools From the Common Core of Data: School Years 2002-03 and 2003-04*, National Center for Education Statistics, p.5, *http://nces.ed.gov/pubsearch/pubsinfo.asp?pubid=2006606rev.*

10. United States Department of Justice, Bureau of Justice Statistics website, "Education and Cor- rectional Populations," *www.ojp.gov/bjs/abstract/ecp.htm.* (Accessed on 5/21/2008.)

11. Kevin Watson, The Oxfam Education Report, Oxfam. 2000, p. 30.

12. BBC, "Illiteracy 'hinders world's poor'," *BBC News*, November 9, 2005, *http://news.bbc.co.uk/go/pr/ fr/-/2/hi/uk_news/education/4420772.stm.*

13. UNICEF, *Progress for Children: A World Fit for Children Statistical Review*, no. 6, December 2007, p. 12, *www.unicef.org/publications/files/Progress_for_Children_No_6_revised.pdf.*

Part 6: Creation Degradation

1. United Nations Development Programme, *Fighting Climate Change: Human solidarity in a divided world*, Human Development Report 2007/2008 Summary, p. 11, *http://hdr.undp.org/en.*

2. Ibid., 16.

3. Intergovernmental Panel on Climate Change, *Climate Change 2007: Synthesis Report*, p. 37, *www .ipcc.ch/ipccreports/ar4-syr.htm.*

4. Greenpeace website, "Trashing Our Oceans," *www.greenpeace.org/usa/campaigns/oceans/ follow-the-journey/trashing-our-oceans*.

5. Ed Ayres, "Worldwatch Report: Fastest mass extinction in Earth history," *ENN*, September 16, 1998, *http://web.archive.org/web/20011222210519/www.enn.com/enn-features-archive/1998/09/091698/ fea0916_23526.asp*.

6. Reuters, "Humans spur worst extinctions since dinosaurs," *ABC News Online*, March 21, 2006, *www.abc.net.au/news/newsitems/200603/s1596740.htm*.

7. Matthew Sleeth, *Serve God, Save the Planet* (Grand Rapids: Zondervan, 2007), 66 – 7.

8. Grinning Planet website, "Biblical Perspectives on Species Protection, excerpted testimony of Joseph K. Sheldon before the House Committee on Resources, 28 Apr 2004," *www.grinning planet.com/2004/07-13-2x/christian-stewardship-environmental-article.htm*.

Part 7: HIV and AIDS

1. Michael Wines, "South Africa Acquits Zuma in Rape Trial," *New York Times*, May 8, 2006, *www .nytimes.com/2006/05/08/world/africa/08cnd-africa.html?_r=1andoref=slogin*.

2. UNAIDS, *2008 Report on the global AIDS epidemic*, p. 39, *http://data.unaids.org/pub/ GlobalReport/2008/jc1510_2008_global_report_pp29_62_en.pdf*.

3. Delphine Zulu, "Will Sex with a Virgin Cure HIV/AIDS?" *The WIP*, July 6, 2007, *www.thewip.net/ contributors/2007/07/will_sex_with_a_virgin_cure_hi.html*.

4. U.S. Congress H.R. 5501-49 Title IV Sec.401(a). Available from: *www.pepfar.gov/documents/ organization/108294.pdf*.

5. UNAIDS, *2008 Report on the Global AIDS Epidemic*, p. 15, *http://data.unaids.org/pub/ GlobalReport/2008/JC1510_2008GlobalReport_en.zip*.

6. Ibid.

7. Ibid., pp. 39, 33, 39.

8. American Rhetoric website, *Bono: Keynote Address at the 54th National Prayer Breakfast*, February 2, 2006, *www.americanrhetoric.com/speeches/bononationalprayerbreakfast.htm*.

9. One website, "HIV/AIDS, Tuberculosis, and Malaria," *www.one.org/aids_poverty*.

10. UNAIDS, *2007 Aids Epidemic Update*, p. 4, *http://data.unaids.org/pub/EPISlides/2007/2007 _epiupdate_en.pdf*.

11. UNAIDS, *2008 Report on the Global AIDS Epidemic*, p. 16, *http://data.unaids.org/pub/ GlobalReport/2008/jc1510_2008_global_report_pp11_28_en.pdf*.

12. UN Special Session on HIV/AIDS, "General Announcement to NGOs and Civil Society," June 25-27, 2001, *www.un.org/ga/aids/announcement.htm*.

13. UNICEF, *The State of the World's Children 2008: Child Survival*, p. 1, *www.unicef.org/publications/ files/The_State_of_the_Worlds_Children_2008.pdf*.

14. John Simpson, "South Africa faces crime challenge," *BBC News* February 9, 2007, *http://news.bbc.co.uk/2/hi/africa/6347717.stm*.

15. C. S. Lewis, *A Grief Observed* (New York: HarperOne, 2001), 34–5.

16. UNAIDS, *2008 Report on the Global Aids Epidemic*, p. 219, *http://data.unaids.org/pub/GlobalReport/2008/jc1510_2008_global_report_pp211_234_en.pdf*.

17. UNAIDS, *2008 Report on the Global AIDS Epidemic*, p. 222, *http://data.unaids.org/pub/GlobalReport/2008/JC1510_2008GlobalReport_en.zip*.

Part 8: Economic Inequality

1. United Nations Development Programme, *Fighting Climate Change: Human solidarity in a divided world*, Human Development Report 2007/2008, p. 25, *http://hdr.undp.org/en/media/HDR_20072008_EN_Complete.pdf*.

2. Ibid.

3. *The Economist*, Big Mac Index, February 4, 2009, *www.economist.com/markets/bigmac*.

4. CIA, "Country Comparisons – GDP – per capita (PPP)," World Factbook, *www.cia.gov/library/publications/the-world-factbook/rankorder/2004rank.html*.

5. James B. Davies, Susanna Sandström, Anthony Shorrocks, and Edward N. Wolff. *The World Distribution of Household Wealth*, United Nations University — World Institute for Development Economics Research, February 2008, p. 11, *www.wider.unu.edu/publications/working-papers/discussion-papers/2008/en_GB/dp2008-03*.

6. Ibid, 7.

7. Dallas Willard, *The Spirit of the Disciplines* (New York: HarperOne, 1990), 215.

8. Here's the math: $1.50 x 365 = $547.50 x 50 = $27,375.

9. National Retail Federation, "NRF Sees Subdued Holiday Gains in 2006," September 19, 2006, *www.nrf.com/modules.php?name=News&op=viewlive&sp_id=150*.

10. United Nations Development Programme, *Beyond Scarcity: Power, poverty, and the global water crisis*, Human Development Report 2006, p. 8, *http://hdr.undp.org/en/media/HDR06-complete.pdf*.

11. Ron Sider, *Rich Christians in an Age of Hunger* (Nashville: Thomas Nelson, 2005).

For speaking inquiries,
please visit *www.zealouslove.org/speaking*.

SERIES: *Start*

Becoming a Good Samaritan Leader's Pack

Six Sessions

Michael R. Seaton

Becoming a Good Samaritan is the first widely distributed Christian curriculum explaining Christian social responsibility and justice, a topic that has been building a great deal of buzz within the ranks of Church leadership, but has not yet ignited — as an action based movement — the people who matter the most … the millions of potential Good Samaritans sitting in the pews. The time is NOW. These six dynamic sessions cover issues like poverty, AIDS, racism, genocide, child slavery, the disenfranchised (widows, orphans, the disabled), caring for the environment, and the dynamic impact a single Samaritan can make. Hosting each of the six sessions will be John Ortberg. This curriculum will also feature global leaders like Gary Haugen, Shane Claiborne, Brenda Salter-McNeil, Bishop John Rucyahana (Rwanda), Bishop Desmond Tutu, Chuck Colson, Zach Hunter, and many others. These presenters and other participants, both known and unknown, will be woven into each session, creating a fabric composed of topical experts, theologians, front-line workers, victims, encouragers, first-timers — so that those viewing can get a complete picture of the challenges and an understanding of how they can get involved — right where they live.

6 Sessions, pack: 978-0-310-32590-1

Pick up a copy today at your favorite bookstore!

Share Your Thoughts

With the Author: Your comments will be forwarded to the author when you send them to *zauthor@zondervan.com*.

With Zondervan: Submit your review of this book by writing to *zreview@zondervan.com*.

Free Online Resources at
www.zondervan.com

Zondervan AuthorTracker: Be notified whenever your favorite authors publish new books, go on tour, or post an update about what's happening in their lives.

Daily Bible Verses and Devotions: Enrich your life with daily Bible verses or devotions that help you start every morning focused on God.

Free Email Publications: Sign up for newsletters on fiction, Christian living, church ministry, parenting, and more.

Zondervan Bible Search: Find and compare Bible passages in a variety of translations at www.zondervanbiblesearch.com.

Other Benefits: Register yourself to receive online benefits like coupons and special offers, or to participate in research.